Scene of the
Last Grand Adventure

Scale 0   100   200 Miles

The
Last
Grand
Adventure

THE LAST GRAND

ADVENTURE

WILLIAM
BRONSON

With
RICHARD REINHARDT

MC GRAW-HILL
BOOK COMPANY
NEW YORK ST. LOUIS SAN FRANCISCO
DÜSSELDORF LONDON
MEXICO SYDNEY TORONTO

On behalf of our father we dedicate this book to our mother,
Marilyn Bronson, whose love he cherished above all other things
in the world.

Knox, Meg, Nate, and Ben

Book design by John Beyer

Library of Congress Cataloging in Publication Data

Bronson, William. 1926–1976.
The last grand adventure.

Includes index.
1. Klondike gold fields.   I. Reinhardt, Richard,
joint author.   II. Title.
F931.B85   971.9′1   77-2616
ISBN 0-07-008014-3

PHOTO CREDITS

Alaska State Historical Library: 205 bottom left. Bancroft Library, University of California: Half-title; title; 12 (2); 13 (2); 15 (4); 16 (3); 17 top left and top center; 18 (3); 19 top right and bottom (3); 25 bottom; 37 bottom; 49 bottom; 50 (2); 51 bottom; 64 (2); 65 top; 68 (2); 74–75 top; 77 top; 78 bottom; 81 top left; 84–85 top; 87 top; 89 top; 91 (2); 100–101; 104 bottom; 105 top; 114 bottom; 120 top; 121 top; 122–123 top; 124 bottom; 129 bottom; 130 top (2); 132 bottom; 136 top; 140–141 top; 150 left (2); 152 center and bottom; 156–157 top; 158 top; 167 bottom; 168 (2); 169 bottom; 183 center; 184 bottom; 185 bottom right; 187 top; 188 (2); 190 top left (2); 191 bottom; 193 top and bottom right; 195 (2); 196 bottom; 197 (3); 198 (4); 199 (4); 200 (4); 201 top; 203 center; 206–207 top; 208 top right, bottom left and right; 209 top; 210 (2); 211 (3); 213 top; 215 bottom; 216 top; 218; 219 (2); 220 bottom; 221 (2); 222 bottom; 223 bottom; 224 (3); 225 top; 227 bottom; 228 top center and bottom; 229 (2). James Blower: 66–67 top; 72. Marilyn Bronson: Acknowledgments page portrait; 109 bottom right. California State Library: 33 top. Robert De Armond: 22 top (Edward de Groff photo); 22 bottom; 88 center; 99 bottom; 102 bottom; 107 top; 110–111 (2); 112 top; 115 top and bottom right; 116 (3); 117 bottom; 118 (2); 119 (3); 120; 149; 157 bottom; 161 top left; 163 bottom; 170 top. William W. Jorgenson: 24 (3); 25 top (2); 42 top; 43 top; 44 top; 76 bottom; 86 center and bottom; 120 bottom; 169 top; 183 top and bottom; 185 top and bottom left. Library of Congress: Opposite page 1, bottom; 1; 86 top; 88 bottom (2); 89 bottom right; 96 bottom; 99 top; 102 top. Ralph E. Mackay: 4 top; 6; 7 top. McBride Museum, Whitehorse, Y.T.: 172 left. Carrie McLain: 190 top right. Murdock's Gem Shop, Whitehorse, Y.T.: 178 bottom. Museum of the City of New York: Opposite page 1, top; 2 top left and right and bottom right. National Museums of Canada: 51 top left; 108 top; 132 top left; 144 bottom; 160 bottom; 164 bottom; 175 bottom left; 177 top; 179 center. Oakland Public Library, California Room: 133 center. Provincial Archives of Alberta: 17 top right; 62–63 (3); 66–67 bottom; 70 (2); 71 (3); 73 (2). Provincial Archives of British Columbia: 131 bottom right; 165 top; 178 top. Public Archives of Canada: 165 top; 173 (2); 174 (3). Seattle Historical Society: 4 bottom; 5 top; 8 bottom; 9 top and bottom; 11 top; 155 bottom. University of Alaska Archives: 14 bottom right; 17 bottom; 19 top left; 20–21; 23 top; 26 bottom; 27 (2); 45 center and bottom; 47 top; 69 (3); 94 bottom; 106 bottom; 107 bottom; 123 bottom; 125 top; 138 top; 139 (2); 150–151 bottom; 154 top; 160 top; 170 bottom; 172 right; 175 top left and bottom right; 177 center and bottom. University of Washington: 3 bottom; 7 bottom; 8 top right; 9 center; 10 bottom; 11 bottom; 14 top; 26 top; 30 top; 32; 33 bottom; 34; 37 top; 38 top; 39 (2); 43 bottom; 45 top; 46 top and bottom; 47 bottom; 49 top; 51 top right; 52; 53; 54 bottom; 55 (2); 56 (2); 57 (2); 58 (3); 59 top; 60; 61 top; 65 bottom; 74–75 bottom; 76 top; 77 bottom; 78 top; 79 bottom; 80 (3); 85 bottom; 87 bottom; 88 top; 89 bottom left; 90 (2); 92 (3); 93 (2); 94 top; 95 (3); 96 top; 97 (2); 98 (2); 102 center; 103; 104 top; 105 bottom; 106 top; 108–109 bottom center; 109 top right; 114 top and center; 117 top; 121 bottom right; 124 top; 125 bottom; 126 (3); 127 (3); 128 center and bottom; 129 top; 130 bottom (2); 131 center left; 132 top right; 133 top; 135 bottom; 136 bottom; 137 (3); 138 center ahd bottom; 141 bottom; 142 (2); 143; 144 top; 147; 148; 150 top right; 151 top; 152 top left; 153 (2); 155 top; 161 top and bottom right; 163 top; 164 top and center; 166–167 top; 171 (2); 175 top right; 176 center left and bottom; 179 top and bottom; 180–181 (2); 182 (3); 184 top and center; 186 (2); 187 bottom; 189 (2); 190 bottom; 191 top; 192 (2); 201 bottom; 202 (3); 203 top and bottom; 204 (2); 205 top and bottom right; 207 bottom; 209 bottom right; 213 bottom; 214 (2); 215 top (3); 216 center and bottom; 217 (2); 220 top; 222 top; 226 bottom; 227 top and center; 228 top left. Russ Waggoner: 208 top left; 209 bottom left; 223 top; 225 bottom. Washington State Historical Society: 10 top; 29 bottom; 35 top; 38 bottom; 40–41; 44 bottom; 46 center; 54 top; 79 top and bottom right; 80 bottom right; 81 top right; 114 center; 121 bottom left; 125 right; 128 top; 133 bottom; 135 top; 145; 146; 193 top left. T. H. Watkins: 14 bottom left. White Pass & Yukon Railroad: 226 top.

Pictures not otherwise credited are from the William K. Bronson Collection.

ACKNOWLEDGMENTS

Anyone who has scanned the front matter of any of William Bronson's previous books has had to notice the precision with which he acknowledged his debt to every person who had made a contribution, large or small, toward the creation of the work. He rarely forgot the source of the smallest tid-bit of information, the tiniest gesture, or the encouraging word.

Bill did this not just out of a sense of gratitude, although gratitude indeed he felt. (He loved the quote, "All writing is too hard," and he certainly appreciated any help he got along the arduous way.) He did it also because it gave him great pleasure to get his friends' names into print. He perhaps overestimated the joy it would bring to unwitting participants, but for his part it was a gesture of genuine appreciation. And he did it for all the other good reasons. He just wanted people to know that he had been thinking about them. In his first book he thanked his grandmothers and managed to squeeze quite a few others of his vast family into the credits. The fine humorist Stanton Delaplane once wrote a column in which he lamented the fact that he didn't have the necessary roster of grandmothers, aunts, uncles, and cousins to boost the sales of his own book that was published at about the same time as Bill's best-selling *The Earth Shook, the Sky Burned*.

Following Bill's tradition, I went through his files and compiled a list of as many names as I could find—names of persons to whom I had typed Bill's letters, names of persons I had met along the way, names of persons of whom Bill had spoken so frequently that I knew they had made significant contributions, names of libraries and librarians. (I do hope we have not left out any of the latter, for William had a very, very special feeling for librarians, without whom he really could not have written three of his four books.)

So we have a long list of people who helped, and we thank them for Bill, and for ourselves. But there are others whose names and special kindnesses were carefully stored away in Bill's mind, as well as others whose names I may have overlooked in my search. Please forgive me and, knowing who you are, realize that Bill did not forget you.

Bill would have thanked Lou Ashworth, who served as the first editor of this book; Frank Matonti, who guided the book through its middle stages; Frank's gracious assistant, Erna Helwig, who held the reins on so many complex production problems during the many changes of direction; and Peggy Conroy, whose first task as managing editor at McGraw-Hill Books was the awesome one of collecting the pieces from two coasts *without* the author for consultation and putting these pieces together, with understanding, good humor, and great skill. He most certainly would have thanked McGraw-Hill for that company's patience. Bill signed his contract so long ago that the document has begun to yellow with age, and never once did anyone speak harshly of the delays. And he specifically would have thanked West Coast Editor Frank Goodall, a dear and valued friend, who signed up Bill to write this book.

Among the generous, inexhaustible sources of information and encouragement to which Bill was especially grateful were Robert N. De Armond of the Alaska Historical Library; Robert D. Monroe, head of the special collections department of the University of Washington Library; Carrie McLain, the resident historian of Nome, Alaska; Paul McCarthy, Renee Blahuta, and Janet Tani of the University of Alaska Archives; Anna M. Ibbotson of the Washington State Historical Society; and the entire staff of the Bancroft Library of the University of California at Berkeley, headed by Dr. James Hart and including such dedicated and talented research scholars as James Barr Thompkins, Irene Moran, and Robert Becker. It is from such historic treasures as these that the majority of the photographs in this book were drawn.

Invaluable contributions came, as well, from James Blower of the Provincial Museum and Archives of Alberta; Jane Waller of the Alaska State Museum; William Jorgenson, of Juneau, Alaska; Ralph E. Mackay of Seattle; the staff and Friends of the W. D. McBride Museum; Mrs. K. Desrochers of the National Museums of Canada; Russ Waggoner; T. H. Watkins; Lawton Kennedy; General James H. Doolittle; Alan Ottley of the California State Library; Diane Johnston and W. Brian Speirs of the Yukon Archives, Whitehorse, Y.T.; Jerry Kearns, head of the Print and Photographic Section of the Library of Congress; S. W. Horrall, historian of the Royal Canadian Mounted Police; Frances H. Buxton of the California Room, Oakland Public Library; and Madeline Helling, librarian of Nevada County, California, and her able staff.

I find it hard to believe that Bill did not use any of the marvelous resources of the California Historical Society in the process of writing this book, but I find no record. All the same, I want to acknowledge our grand old friend, Dr. J. S. Holliday, Director of the Society; Virginia Gerhart, past Assistant Director; Maude Swingle, gracious volunteer, whom Bill always so much appreciated; dear Renee Grignard, Director of Public Relations; Marilyn Ziebarth, current Director of Publications; and another grand old friend, Roger Olmsted, past Publications Director. If not specifically for their help on this book, they know why they're being thanked.

Thanks also are due to several persons who graciously consented to allow portions of copyrighted works to be quoted in these pages: Franklin Walker, for permission to quote from his *Jack London and the Klondike;* Allan Starr, for authority to reprint an extensive passage from *My Adventures in the Klondike and Alaska,* by Walter Starr; American West Publishing Company for permission to reprint portions of the articles "Nome" and "Eskimo," by William Bronson, which appeared in different form in *American West Magazine* in July, 1969, and July, 1970, copyright © 1969 and 1970 by the American West Publishing Co., Palo Alto, California; Dorothy Jean Ray, for allowing extended references to her perceptive and unique articles on the Eskimo arts of the

Seward Peninsula; Herbert Heller, for permission to quote several passages from his delightful book *Sourdough Sagas,* copyright ©
1936 by Comstock Editions; Carrie McLain for permission to quote from her pamphlets of Nome history; for permission to quote
from *A Dog Puncher on the Yukon,* by Arthur Treadwell Walden, copyright 1928 by A. T. Walden, copyright © renewed 1956 by
Walden L. Ainsworth, reprinted by permission of Houghton Mifflin Company; and Robert Henning, publisher, and C. H.
Rosenthal, associate publisher, of the Alaska Northwest Publishing Company, Anchorage, Alaska, for numerous courtesies and
valuable advice in the researching of this book.

Thanks, too, for the hospitality and open-hearted welcome for which the people of the Northwest are justly famous. We
remember with gratitude the Rev. Kenneth Snider of Dawson; Mike Miller of Juneau; Rie Muñoz of Juneau; the staff of the Yukon
Territory Department of Travel and Information (Harvey Dryden, Ken Sillak, Major Evans); and the White Pass and Yukon
Railroad (Frank G. Downey, John Gellis, Dave Pepper, Roy Minter).

In a rough draft, Bill also acknowledged his considerable debt to the men who had written of their experiences in the last grand
adventure.

"In editing these works," Bill wrote, "I have taken small liberties by changing spellings, paragraphing, and making other
stylistic corrections to improve readability. In no place have I made changes that affect the writer's literary style or the drift of his
story. I can only hope that my readers will appreciate the lack of use of footnotes and of the word *sic.* I have a strong feeling that
these writers, long since gone, would not have objected to the minor adjustments I've made: Arthur Treadwell Walden, William
Ogilvie, Jeremiah Lynch, Tappan Adney, Rex Beach, Jack London, Joaquin Miller, Walter Starr, "Scotty" Allan, A. E. Ironmonger
Sola, John Sydney Webb, Edward Curtis, Lynn Smith, Nevill A. D. Armstrong, James D. Wickersham, F. D. Whiting, Frank
Buteau, Hamlin Garland, Henry Davis, T. A. Rickard, and Henry Toke Munn."

There are two other persons whom it has become my destiny to write onto this page of appreciation, and because they are so
very important, the words come with difficulty. They did so much, because there was *so much* left to be done at the time of Bill's
death: gathering, planning, picture selection, juggling, cutting, adding, and a considerable amount of writing, including many
captions and all the final chapter of the book. Richard Reinhardt, the writer, and John Beyer, the designer, together managed to do it
all and, in the process, to preserve William Bronson's style and to make sure that his full intent was carried out. (Dick even managed
to write more than half of these acknowledgments, all the while making it appear as though I had done the entire thing by myself.
Would that I had!) They were able to do this not only because they are two of the best talents in this business, but also because they
were Bill's close friends. They understood him so well—the way he thought, the way he worked. And they loved him.

It is ironic, indeed, that this last book by Bill Bronson should have been named, by him, *The Last Grand Adventure,* but
appropriate that these good companions should have shared so much of the adventure with him. Thank you, dear friends, for
everything. You have done a splendid job.

Marilyn M. Bronson
Berkeley, July, 1977

CONTENTS

CHAPTER I

RUNNING AWAY TO FAME AND FORTUNE

"In an incredibly short space of time the inhabitants of the coast cities were beside themselves with excitement . . . A stampede unequalled in history was on . . ."

The last decade of the 19th Century in America has been written into popular history as the Gay Nineties, and gay they were for some. But as always in the telling of man's affairs, the truth and the dream are not necessarily the same. We remember P. T. Barnum, John Philip Sousa, the dime novel, Mark Twain, the Floradora Sextette, and the Chicago Fair, but we have forgotten that the Nineties, in fact, were a nightmare for millions who were caught in the crushing depression that followed the Panic of 1893.

It was in 1892 that 18 men were killed in a battle at the Carnegie steel mill at Homestead, Pennsylvania, between strikers and Pinkerton guards hired by company president Henry Frick. The strike was not a cause but a symptom of the collapse which was soon to follow. Andrew Carnegie, the great philanthropist, while still holding more than half the stock in his steel empire, had retired to his castle in Scotland and was not in direct control of operations. In anguish, he wrote of his feelings on the tragic affair to British Prime Minister William Gladstone, in response to a sympathetic letter, "This is the trial of my life (death's hand excepted). Such a foolish step—contrary to my ideas, repugnant to every feeling of my nature. . . . The pain I suffer increases daily. The Works [the Homestead mill] are not worth one drop of human blood."

The first immediate sign of impending economic disaster was the failure of the Philadelphia and Reading Railroad in January of 1893. When National Cordage, the rope trust, went under in May, the Panic was on. Banks, mortgage companies, corporations fell on every hand. The Erie, Union Pacific, and Northern Pacific railroads went with the rest before the year was out. One hundred thousand unemployed were reported in Chicago; the New York City figure stood at close to 70,000, but an additional homeless and helpless mass which had arrived in desperation compounded the misery. Money was so scarce and credit so overstrained that before the end of 1895 scores of the most powerful businesses in the country went under.

In the wake of the Panic came the calamitous Pullman strike of 1894—one of the classic confrontations between American capital and labor—which led to the conviction and six-month imprisonment of Eugene Debs, the president of the American Railway Union. (In 1920, while he was again in prison, sentenced for his opposition to American entry into World War I, Debs was to poll almost a million votes as a Socialist candidate for the Presidency.)

The extremes of gustatorial life in America at the close of the 19th century are graphically portrayed in the three photos on these pages, extremes that were reflected in every aspect of life. Top left, a banquet in honor of Jim Fiske, a financial buccaneer in a sea teeming with others. None of the gentlemen appear to have been in the least embarrassed by posing for the camera with laurel wreaths on their thinning crowns. Bottom left, thriving street vendors sold their umbrella space for advertising and hot frankfurters for three cents or two for a nickel. Above, a clam seller in the heart of Mulberry Bend, a new-immigration Italian stronghold in Manhattan. All three photos were taken in New York.

In the same year Jacob Coxey, a wealthy Ohio reformer, formed an army which marched on Washington to impress, in his words, ". . . upon Congress the necessity for giving immediate relief to the four million [one-sixth of the work force] of unemployed people and their immediate families, consisting of twelve to fifteen million more." His army, which numbered but 400, was one of almost a score that reached Washington. The demonstrations left a lasting impress on the future of social legislation, although decades would pass before some of the gross inequities they protested were righted.

Following the Panic, production continued to disintegrate. What we call today the Gross National Product dropped by 20 percent. Food consumption dropped drastically. In the absence of sufficient relief provisions, many people lived on the brink of starvation.

In 1896, the foreign drain on gold reserves and the lack of credit brought the country to an economic nadir not known since the depression of the mid-1870s. Populism was on the rise and farmers and working men were roused by the call for free silver—"16 to one" was the cry—and the champion who emerged to lead the movement was the Democratic Presidential candidate, 36-year-old William Jennings Bryan, the "Boy Orator from the Platte," who took on the amiable William McKinley of Ohio in the most critical election in terms of issues—really one issue, bimetalism—since the Civil War. Bryan's words stirred the electorate:

"The great cities rest upon our broad and fertile prairies. Burn down your cities and leave our farms, and your cities will spring up again as if by magic; but destroy our farms, and the grass will grow in the streets of every city in the country."

With one of the most memorable lines ever delivered to a political gathering in the history of the country, he had entranced the delegates to the Democratic convention that year with these undying words: "You shall not press down upon the brow of labor this crown of thorns, you shall not crucify mankind upon a cross of gold."

It was Bryan's finest hour, but he lost the election. Never before had so

Above left, flower vendors at Eastertime on Broadway, with two of New York's finest surveying the scene. Above, a group of breaker boys on their way to lunch after finishing half a shift at a Kingston, Pennsylvania, coal mine. Below, a newsstand at an entrance to the Third Avenue El in New York.

much money been poured into a propaganda campaign as the Republicans did that year, and it was not really for gain as much as it was for principle: the gold standard was a rock on which American—indeed, world—commerce was then built. Fear remained so widespread that much of the nation's gold coinage was hoarded.

No part of the country was hit worse than the West, particularly the Northwest. Along the shores of Puget Sound many were reduced to living on the clams they could dig from the sands of the beaches.

The country was hungry for change, for some glimmer of hope that there might be a way out of the despairing stagnation of the time.

All of this is but a glimpse at the trying social and economic context into which the *Excelsior*, a wooden-hulled steam schooner leased by the Alaska Commercial Company, docked in San Francisco on the 15th of July of 1897.

From the decks a small group of men struggled down the gangway with grips and suitcases, bottles and moosehide pokes bulging with gold. Altogether it was estimated that a ton of the precious yellow stuff was brought ashore that sunny day. The arrival marked the confirmation of reports that had trickled out of the northland that a new bonanza, one that would rival the richest of any known, had been found.

In a day, the word flashed across the country: an unbelievably rich gold strike had been made on the tributaries of the Klondike River, deep in the Canadian Yukon 2500 miles north by sea and land from San Francisco.

Two days later, when the *Portland* steamed into Seattle with more than two tons of gold from the Klondike, the city went wild. Half the streetcar motormen, for instance, left their jobs. Even Mayor W. D. Wood resigned to head for the gold fields.

The entire nation's response was little short of madness. Newspapers carried accounts of the fortunes made by such men as Clarence Berry, who had left work on a fruit ranch near Fresno in 1894 to seek his fortune in the frozen reaches of the Yukon Valley. Berry returned to California in 1895 to marry his sweetheart, and the couple decided to give gold mining one more try. In June of 1896, with his bride, he reached the town of Fortymile, one of several important mining camps downstream from the point the Klondike meets the Yukon. Less than three months later George Carmack and two Indian companions, Skookum Jim and Tagish Charlie, found coarse gold on Rabbit Creek, a stream that flowed into the Klondike, later to be renamed and known around the world as Bonanza Creek.

Berry was working as a bartender when the news arrived, and although he had to think twice about making the effort to go up and stake a claim—false alarms were constantly reported in those years—he decided he

The July 17, 1897, issue of the *Seattle P-I*, perhaps the most exciting peacetime story ever run in the history of the city.

A group of returning Klondike miners in front of the Commercial Hotel (Ed Holland, Prop.), San Francisco, 1897. The man behind the little boy is Jack McQuesten, "Father of the Yukon."

The steam schooner *Excelsior* at dock in San Francisco, the first gold-laden vessel to arrive from the Yukon.

Seattle's Cooper and Levy, one of many merchandisers in coast cities to cash in on the rush. Future miners are sitting on 50-pound sacks of flour, which along with bacon and beans formed the fundamentals of Yukon cuisine.

had little to lose and joined the stampede. He couldn't have dreamed what he was eventually to find.

He was one of the miners who arrived in Seattle aboard the *Portland*. However, he was pestered so badly by swarms of the curious that he and his wife fled to San Francisco, but San Francisco wasn't much better in this respect. It is easy to see from the opening paragraphs of a front-page story carried in the July 21st (1897) edition of the *San Francisco Chronicle* why Klondike madness swept the land. Remember that at the time a good meal could be bought in a restaurant for 25 cents.

" 'Two million dollars taken from the Klondyke region in less than five months, and a hundred times that amount awaiting those who can handle a pick and shovel tells the story of the most marvelous placer digging the world has ever seen.'

"This was the remark made yesterday by Clarence Berry of Fresno, who, with his wife, has just returned from the great frozen North, where gold is found in such quantities as to dazzle the imagination and startle the skeptical. At the Grand Hotel yesterday Mr. Berry was the recipient of many congratulations. Old miners called to see him and also to examine specimens of the wonderful region that yields nuggets as big as hens' eggs.

"In this they were not disappointed, for in room 111 the successful prospector had on exhibition a most glittering array of nuggets, aggregating in value $4000. On the table were to be seen half a dozen small vials and bottles, each containing from $100 to $500 in gold dust. The smallest of these contains just $100, and was the first taken by Mr. Berry from the claim which yielded so handsomely during the five months he worked it. There were two bottles, labeled $500 and $200, which, Mr. Berry said, were the yield from one pan, the third taken from the mine.

"Incidentally it may be mentioned that Mrs. Berry took out during the season over $10,000 in nuggets, ranging in value from $300 to $231. The lady is naturally very proud of her accomplishment, as is also her husband.

"The arrival of Mr. Berry and others has tended to increase the excitement over the Klondyke discovery. Six brawny miners, including Mr. Berry, arrived yesterday, each loaded down with the fruits of untold trials and hardships, the substantial proofs of the most marvelous discovery of the age. All day at the hotels and resorts nothing else was talked about but the remarkable find made by these men. Everybody talked of gold and the money-mad crowd surged around the places where those who had found the precious metal in such quantities were staying.

"Berry is regarded by the miners as one of the luckiest men on earth. He went to the Klondyke as a tenderfoot, but came out a wealthy man and with prospects that may make him many times a millionaire."

Tappan Adney, the *Harper's Weekly* correspondent, summed up the national reaction:

"The Seattle papers, equally alive to the interests of their own city, as

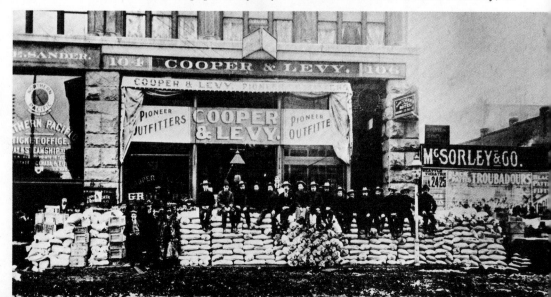

An assorted team of large dogs poses during a trial run before embarking for the north. Few were to prove adaptable to the rigorous demands of the severe sub-zero weather that prevailed more than half the year.

the outfitting-point for Alaska, plunged into the story with sensational fury. If the stories of wonderful fortune needed corroboration, there were nuggets and sacks of shining gold displayed in windows of shops and hotels. One hundred and thirty thousand dollars' worth of gold, brought by one man from the new diggings, was displayed in one window in San Francisco.

"In an incredibly short space of time the inhabitants of the coast cities were beside themselves with excitement. 'Coast Again Gold Crazy,' was the Eastern comment. A stampede unequalled in history was on."

Lynn Smith, a young watchmaker from Indiana, gives a picture of the flavor of the times in his account of his first day in Seattle:

"There were lots of men headed for the same place on the train west and the trip was full of interest. We sat up all night when we went through the Rocky Mountains and finally reached Seattle. It was full of men and women as busy as bees. When we walked through the railroad yards, we saw cars full of a species of animal new to us and upon inquiry found they were reindeer ready for shipment to Alaska from Lapland. These held our attention for some time.

"We then noticed a crowd around a man demonstrating how to save gold with a new panner that whirled around, and we left him after paying for and leaving our order for one. On the next corner on a vacant lot a man was standing, shouting 'Here is what you want, save your money and time, and don't work building a boat after you get north. Let us build it here and ship it knocked down and get ahead of the rest of the bunch. You can be panning gold while they are building their boats.' So we had to buy one so as not to lose any time and we paid for it on the spot. This was pretty good business for one day in Seattle, but it was not over yet.

"We four innocents (two from Anderson and two from Logansport, Indiana,) had to see the sights, so we headed for Billy the Mugs, and then on to the Paris House, otherwise known as the House of All-Nations. This proved to be very interesting, especially the little slant-eyed Japanese girls, who were new to us greeners. When we filed into a room which had no chairs and it was found out that all we wanted was to do a little kidding, we were politely asked to move on. We were told there were about six hundred women of all shades and colors, and about seventy-five different nations represented here.

"Our next move was to a vaudeville and dance house. We didn't dance, so we took a booth upstairs and in a few minutes two dames named the

A British advertisement, typical of the flood that followed the arrival of the Klondike news.

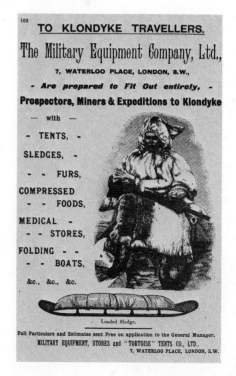

The *Australia,* one of the best ships in coastal trade, ready to embark from San Francisco. While women and children joined the rush, their numbers were small; this voyage was to be a stag party. Note the man at the bow of the ship next to the ensign who, with the wave of his hat, symbolized the optimism of the adventure.

Clark sisters came in. One planted herself on Pickel's knee and said, 'Come on boys, buy a bottle,' and pushed the button. She was playing with his watch charm, and when one of us bright boys, who had secured a $20 bill with the No. 1000 on it on the back, showed his bank roll of ones and twos with the apparent $1000 bill on the outside, the other sister sat down on his knee and wanted to get married right away. However, we were lucky and left after spending only about four dollars, for it was soon noised around the house that the party in No. 8 were pikers and we were not bothered further. We had seen enough thrills and actions for our first day and headed for the hotel, a tired bunch after just getting our eyeteeth cut, seeing the cruel world uncut and as it was in the west in those days. Everybody was money mad.

"As I recall it, we met the next morning and, after holding a post-mortem over the Paris House, turned our attention to finding a boat to take us north. We wanted a boat to take us to Skagway and one that was safe and wouldn't sink, so we began our search which took us several days."

As they were to learn, the job of securing passage on any kind of vessel was not simple. This wire dispatch, which was sent out from Seattle on the 21st of July, indicates the magnitude of the fever:

"The news that the telegraph is bringing the past few days of the wonderful things of Klondike, in the land of the midnight sun, has opened the floodgates, and a stream of humanity is pouring through Seattle and on to the golden Mecca of the north. It is a crowd at once strange, weird, and picturesque. Some say it eclipses anything in the days of '49. The good ship *Portland,* which recently brought a million and a half of treasure to this port, sails for Alaska to-morrow at noon. She will carry every passenger and every pound of cargo that she has the ability to transport. The *Portland* has booked for this passage fifty first-class and ninety-eight second-class passengers. The names of an ex-Governor and a general are in the list. Fifteen hundred passengers are booked for Alaska for the overland passage. Every available steamer is full. The steamers *Queen, Mexico, City of Topeka, Al-Ki,* in rotation, will sail by August 5th, to be followed by the *Willamette, City of Kingston,* and *City of Seattle,* pressed from service elsewhere."

These weren't the only vessels that were rushed into service to the north. Ships left East Coast ports and sailed around Cape Horn, and many left from foreign shores once the impact of the news was felt. So great was the demand and so high the profit potential that every conceivable kind of hull was drawn into service regardless of seaworthiness. Old side-wheel steamers, condemned sailing vessels, barges, coalers, pleasure craft—name it and it probably was represented in the fleet.

Two colorful Californians who joined the herd early in the going, each of whom was among the few thousand who made it all the way to Dawson before the end of the year, were Joaquin Miller and Jack London. Miller had already built a strong literary reputation and was headed for the Klondike mines as correspondent for the Hearst newspapers. London was looking for fortune and adventure. Fortune eluded him, but he was to return home with the experience on which he drew to become one of the leading writers of his time.

Miller, the Poet of the Sierra, left on one of the first departures "with forty pounds on his back and his face to the morning star." His pack was loaded largely with bacon, tea, and hardtack and he declared:

"I am going up to get the information for the poor men who mean to go to the mines next summer. If I find the mines limited either in area or thickness, my first duty will be to let the world know.

"I will not need the usual provisions because, having got right down to

A well-dressed crowd jammed a Portland dock in the wake of the news—some well-wishers and others trying to find some way to buy their way to the great northern bonanza.

Cover of a book written by an Englishman who spent years in the hostile Yukon watershed. His account, published in 1897, dwelt more on homesickness and the day-to-day toils of a sourdough than on the grisly image his publisher implied here.

the bedrock of the cold frozen facts, I shall take the next steamer leaving Dawson and return straight to San Francisco.''

There was to be no steamer from Dawson. Miller, then 57 years old, was trapped by the eight-month Yukon winter without provisions. The threat of starvation grew as the nights lengthened, and he was forced to attempt the 300-mile trek to Fort Yukon over the frozen river with about a thousand others. He and most of those who set out were forced to give up and try to return to Dawson. Although there were several deaths, Miller made it back, but only at great cost: he lost a finger, an ear, part of a toe, and suffered the excruciating pain of snow blindness. But he survived with the help given to him by others and was to return to his Oakland home in the summer of 1898.

Regardless of the hardships that lay ahead and the dire warnings that were issued by men in a position to know the facts, the tens of thousands

The ebullience of the day was charmingly expressed over and over again by the dockside crowds that gathered in the summer of 1897 in San Francisco, Portland, Tacoma, Seattle, Victoria, and Vancouver, all of which competed with intense civic zeal for the trade generated by the rush.

7

Captain Jack Crawford was perhaps the most overlooked eccentric that joined the rush. A frontiersman, promoter, poet, but never a shrinking violet, the old spellbinder played a prominent part of Dawson's early years.

who burned with gold fever wouldn't stop to listen. As Adney observed:

"Men threw up good positions in banks, and under the government; others, with homes and families, mortgaged their property and started; while those who could not command the one to two thousand dollars considered as the very least necessary to success were grub-staked by friends equally affected by the excitement but unable to go in person. The newspapers were filled with advice, information, stories of hardship and of good fortune; but not one in ten, or a hundred, knew what the journey meant nor heeded the voice of warning. 'There are but few sane men,' says one, 'who would deliberately set out to make an Arctic trip in the fall of the year, yet this is exactly what those who now start for the Klondike are doing.' And this:

'TIME TO CALL A HALT
Only a Few Will Be Able to Reach Dawson
This Year'

And another:

'WINTER WILL SOON SET IN THERE
Suffering Seems Inevitable
What Gold-Seekers Must Endure—Their Chief
Food in Winter is Bear-Fat, and a Bath or
a Change of Clothing is Death.'

Many hundreds were destined to die of scurvy, freezing, pneumonia, dysentery, spinal meningitis, typhoid fever, smallpox, murder, avalanche, marine disaster, suicide, influenza, or starvation. It is impossible to exaggerate the struggle and suffering that lay ahead.

Adney continued:

"One does not fully comprehend the helplessness of average mankind until he meets some of these men on the streets. Scores of men would never have gotten one inch to the northward of the town of Victoria without the help of others. Two men in three virtually are carried along by the odd man. They are without practical experience; it is pitiful to see them groping like the blind, trying to do this thing or that, having no notion of what it is to plan and to have the ends fit like a dovetail. I asked a Frenchman from Detroit how he meant to get over the pass—was he taking a horse? 'Oh no; there would be some way.' And yet he knew that every returning steamer is bringing word like this, which is from a recent private letter from Dyea to a large outfitter: 'For Heaven's sake, if you have any influence to prevent it, do not let any one come here without horses; hundreds of people will be encamped here all winter, unable to get across.'"

Of horses, which Adney knew well, he wrote:

"The horses, alleged to be pack-horses, that are being brought into Victoria for sale amuse every one greatly. There are ambulating boneyards, the infirm and decrepit, those afflicted with spavin and spring-halt, and many with ribs like the sides of a whiskey-cask and hips to hang hats

The *Queen,* another jam-packed coastal steamer ready to depart from Seattle. Pierre Berton, in his book *The Klondike Fever,* described what followed: "The *Queen* broke her steering gear in the Wrangell Narrows and threatened to keel over, causing such a panic that one woman tried to kill the captain with a pistol and had to be handcuffed."

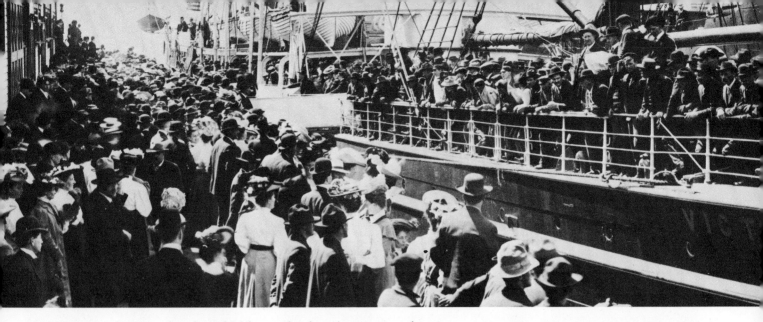

on. With their drooping heads and listless tails, they are pictures of misery. Yet they are being bought to pack over the hardest kind of trail. Why, some of them at the Hudson's Bay Company's wharf look as if a good feed of oats would either break their backs or make them sag beyond remedy, while their legs seem barely able to support their bodies. They are brought in from all quarters of Vancouver Island and the mainland. Till now they have been without value or price. Twenty-five dollars up is the invariable price asked, and it is ludicrous to see some of their owners, who a month ago would have fainted in their tracks at the sight of five dollars, how, when you ask the price, shift about, swallow once or twice, and say, 'Twenty-five dollars.' 'Thirty dollars' means that the owner has a pretty fair horse, probably an old packer; but 'twenty-five dollars' now in Victoria means that much clear profit, and they have plenty of takers. . . .

"It is rare amusement to a tenderfoot, getting together a pack train. A little knowledge of horses helps, but I suppose one should not expect too much. As long as one's pack-train looks positively no worse than one's neighbor's he does not mind. Although he may have a spotted cayuse as big as a sheep alongside a fifteen-hand raw-boned roan mare, no one is expected to do any better with the time and material at command. Victorians believe that next spring there will be a wholly better lot of horses; they do not believe the present supply of wrecks will last any longer. My packers consist of a black with a bone-spavin which causes him to throw his leg crossways when he trots; his mate is a small bay pony, narrow-chested; then there is a white-faced 'pinto,' a large roan mare, and a bully little packer nearly two feet lower than the old roan. Her name is Nelly, the only name I could get of any of my horses. The sixth one is a nondescript—just a thin sorrel horse. They make a brave show with their new pack-saddles and coils of new lashropes."

No one knows how many started out for the gold fields that year and

In scenes that must have swelled the hearts of shipowners, it's obvious that the public could not have cared less about the unconscionable increases in the cost of passage north. In the *laissez-faire* market of the times, shippers were able to get away with it.

the year following, but the best estimates put the figure in the neighborhood of 100,000. Of these, according to a U.S. Department of Labor bulletin published in 1898:

"By actual count, 40,000 men started for and reached the Yukon gold fields during the year beginning with July 15, 1897. It is conservatively estimated that 20,000 more undertook the journey, but were unsuccessful in their efforts to reach the Yukon, a large proportion becoming discouraged and returning home, while many thousands joined the collateral stampedes to various points on the coast or are still struggling on the trails to the Klondike."

Of the remaining 40,000, many lost heart or found when they reached the West Coast that the cost of passage and an outfit was beyond their resources. Shipping companies advertised prices (of course subject to change) that were ridiculously low. When the *Portland* returned to St. Michaels the price of passage tickets, including meals and river-boat passage up the Yukon to Dawson, jumped from $200 to a standard $1000—and there were those who would pay a $500 premium if they could find a ticketholder willing to sell.

In addition to this factor, the North West Mounted Police, guarding all access to the Yukon, established a new rule in 1897: every man and woman entering had to carry with them food supplies sufficient to last a full year. This—along with the need for tools and equipment sufficient for survival—could run, according to Tappan Adney, who knew what he needed, from $1000 to $2000, although promoters claimed that $500 was enough.

There was no way to stem the rushing tide of single-minded humanity, and shipowners took every possible measure to wring the last dollar possible out of the throng.

Overloading was atrocious; every inch of space on deck and below was uniformly crammed with men, women, and a few children, their food and gear, goods, and general cargo. Dogs, horses, and other livestock and their feed were jammed in unmercifully. Comfort and cleanliness went by the board; the food was generally terrible, and safety was of secondary concern. The primary objective was to get there any way you could. One ship, the *Clara Nevada*, illegally carrying passengers with dynamite in the cargo, blew up before it reached Skagway, killing all 65 passengers and

A group of Laplanders, posing for the photographers in Seattle, were hired to convoy a herd of reindeer from the Scandinavian north to New York, thence by rail to Seattle and ship to the Dalton Trail, and finally by barge to Dawson—all in the name of relief of the starving Klondikers. They did their best, but the expedition was a failure, largely because the animals could not subsist on the vegetation of the trail. Below, the *Willamette*, the converted collier which carried correspondent Tappan Adney north in the first wave following the arrival of glittering evidence of the Klondike's riches.

crew members aboard. There were a number of serious wrecks, but by good fortune, considering the circumstances, relatively few other deaths.

The story of a week or so in the life of one of the ships converted for the run to Skagway is a revealing instance of the haste and lack of care that characterized marine travel from West Coast ports in the hectic months following arrival of the treasure ships in July. Adney tells the story:

"The steamer *Bristol*, a large steel collier, was chartered on a few days' notice, and advertised to sail several days before our boat. She was hauled into the outer wharf, and the carpenters went aboard with scantling and converted her entire hold into stalls two feet in width for horses; and there were stalls on deck, and hay on top of them. Rough bunks were put in, filling every available spot on the ship. It was a scene on the dock such as Victoria had never seen before. Scores of men were at work building scows, with which to lighter the freight ashore at Skagway . . . loading the bags containing the miners' supplies, and hoisting one by one the five or six hundred horses aboard. It characterizes the haste with which the crush has had to be met that, after leaving, the ship returned to port to adjust her top load, after a delay of four days beyond the advertised time of sailing, during which time the poor animals were crowded in close rows, with no chance to lie down, and, below, not even chance to breathe. The men were hardly better off than the horses, two of which are of my outfit. . . ."

Of his own departure, he wrote: ". . . we are all aboard the *Islander*. She has left her wharf at Victoria, to the sound of cheer after cheer from dense crowds, which have taken possession of every vantage-ground. The stalwart forms of the mounted police, truly a fine-looking body of men, take the crowd, and cheer after cheer goes up for them. There are no more lusty shouts than those given by thirty-six small boys perched in a row on the ridge-pole of the wharf overlooking the water. 'Three cheers for the mounted police!' and 'Three cheers for Klondike!'

"There are sad faces aboard, and a tear moistens the eye of more than one hardened miner who is leaving wife and family behind. But we are glad because of the cheering crowd, for, as Jim [his young partner] remarks, it would have seemed pretty blue if there had been nobody here.

"As the echoes of the cheers that greet our departure die away and the

Above, a rusty old bucket, the *Cleveland*, known as a bad luck ship in South American trade, departs from Seattle loaded to the high Plimsoll mark. Those who were left at the dock in San Francisco when the *Humboldt*, below, left port may have been sorry they missed the chance to join W. D. Wood, who wired his resignation as mayor of Seattle when the *Excelsior* arrived with its gold-heavy cargo and then chartered the steamer for the trip north. Those who sailed with him regretted it even more. (See Chapter 5.)

city fades from view in the growing darkness, we go, each of us, about his respective affairs. Some, worn out by the work and excitement of getting off, turn in early to bed; others take a look at the horses, which are making a regular hubbub on the lower deck. We find them wedged side by side in a long row along each side of the ship, with heads towards the engines, and no chance to lie down. Frightened by the pounding of the engines, and the blasts of the whistle, they are throwing themselves back on their halters and biting and kicking. Jim McCarron, ex-cavalryman, U.S.A., is now in his element, and I think he wants to show his friends, the mounted police of whom a detachment of 20 was aboard, that he, too, knows a bit about horses. . . .

"Several of our halters are broken, and it looks as if we would have to take alternate watches, but Jim patches up some rope halters. Next day the animals had quieted down, but nearly every horse has a mark from the teeth of his neighbor. Poles should have been put across, separating them."

Almost all ships regularly put in at Juneau, then Alaska's largest city, and many of them also docked at Wrangell, a lawless town at the mouth of the navigable Stikine River. That settlement first flourished during the rush to the Cassiar gold fields in northern British Columbia in the mid-1870s and enjoyed a healthy, lawless revival after the Klondike Rush began. Two stories about Wrangell, each recorded by an eyewitness, convey something of the shoot-em-up, West-of-the-Pecos character of America's last frontier towns: Wrangell, Skagway, Dyea, Nome, and their satellite settlements. In the first year or more they were ungoverned and ungovernable. To the federal government, Alaska was still Seward's Folly, good for the annual salmon pack and fur seals of the Pribilof Islands of the Bering Sea, and little else.

Arthur Treadwell Walden, a dog puncher who was returning to the Yukon with a cargo of merchandise, tells this story of his visit in 1897:

". . . the steamers bound for the Klondike stopped at Fort Wrangel, which was quite a sizable town at this time, being the port of entry for the Stickeen and Teslin Lake route. It was a smaller edition of Skagway, and its chief occupation was fleecing the Cheechakos [an Indian word universally used for greenhorns; old-timers were always called sourdoughs].

"There was a man on board with his sixteen-year-old son. In the few hours that the boat stopped at Fort Wrangel he lost all his money at some bunko game. The son, having more sense than the old man, stayed on board. The father on coming back to the boat was very much cut up about the affair and told his son what had happened.

"Without saying a word to his father, the boy went to one of the passengers and borrowed a six-shooter. He went ashore and walked into the gambling-hall where his father had lost all his money. The old man couldn't have done this because, having lost his money, he was a marked man and would probably have been killed by a 'booster' if he ever could have got near the table where he had been fleeced.

12

Ketchikan was one of the established Alaskan cities that many of the north-bound ships passed or stopped at during passage. The stunning art of the Indians of southeastern Alaska fascinated the transient gold-seekers as surely as it did the photographers who recorded it so beautifully. The magnificent totem pole below stood at the head of Ketchikan's modest wooden pier.

"But the boy walked up to the table, deliberately drew his gun, and pointed it at the dealer. The man was very much astonished, not connecting the situation with the father's loss. Even here a grown-up couldn't have accomplished what the boy did. He informed the gambler that he wanted his father's money back, and the boosters thinking it a good joke on the dealer, and the dealer himself having a sense of humor, the boy received the full amount. The boy then put up his gun, turned, and went out of the saloon, with evidently no thought of the harm that might come to him. I think his courage had as much to do with his safety as anything."

Greenhorn Lynn Smith and his three pals finally booked passage out of Seattle and after they slept in their clothes for the first five days, taking off only shoes and socks "so if we had a wreck we could swim better," their ship tied up in Wrangell.

"We walked ashore and a man came up to us and said, 'Have you boys got a map of the country?' We said we had none and he said, 'I saw a sign up the street that read Bureau of Information. Let's go there and get one.' We went (poor boobs) and stepped inside a large tent and upon entering noticed that a man stepped in front of the flap of the tent, closed it and stood inside with a rifle. We wondered at this and then noticed that there were gambling devices of all kinds. We didn't fall for them because we were short of money, having spent more with those Seattle fakers than we had intended. Upon going outside we noticed a crowd around 'Big Whitie,' who I recognized as having been with the Wallace's Circus in Indiana. He was working his shell game.

"Doc (one of the boys on our boat) tried to guess which shell had the pea under it and a big Swede was also guessing. Doc quit, but the Swede started to double up, ran short of money and went to his belt for more. While he was at it the cappers all rushed around him and while one of them was helping him in front, another shipped out a knife and slit his belt and took his roll. About one hundred of us were watching—all afraid to make a move. At any rate we were glad to get back on the boat again—and we had learned something else. Never bet on another man's game. Boys, remember this and stick to it through your lives, you can't beat a man at his own game."

And so it went on the voyage north to Skagway and Dyea and the trails beyond that led to the headwaters of the Yukon. With all the troubles, it was merely a beginning.

Juneau at the time of the rush was Alaska's biggest city and the last stop-off before Skagway or Dyea, the principal ports of entry to the great Klondike adventure. Juneau was built on the gold found in 1880 which led to the development of the most important hard-rock mines in all of the territory.

Players in a Living Drama

Gold rushes, like great construction projects, natural disasters, and wars, always inspire photographers. Everybody senses, all at once, that he is taking part in an *historical event*—a moment in the featureless flow of time that will endure, imbuing its participants with a sort of immortality. It was with this sense of historic destiny that dozens of photographers joined the stampede to the Klondike, working in the field and in studios, authenticating reality for those who were living it. This collection is a sample of their work, a small reflection of their tastes and interests, and of the color of the time. Left: a lovely belle, perhaps inspired by Calamity Jane, indicates she is not to be trifled with. Below: (left) a veteran Chilcat Indian packer and (right) an old sourdough whose grizzled beard bespeaks his years in the Yukon.

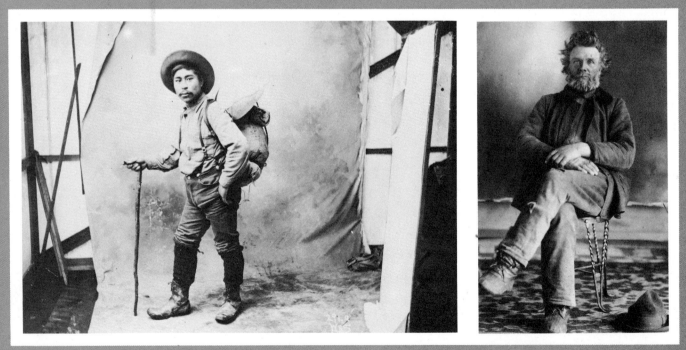

When three Scandinavian prospectors found placer gold in the bleak tundra of Alaska's Seward Peninsula in 1898, they set off a second phase of the stampede to the North, one that brought thousands of white adventurers into the hunting grounds of the Alaskan Eskimo. Nome City, the capital of the new gold rush, was built on the site of an Eskimo fishing camp, and the excitement (and money) generated by this strange new community attracted Eskimos each summer from King Island, Little Diomede Island, and numerous communities on the mainland. Fascinated by the dignity and beauty of these Bering Sea natives and their handmade costumes of seal fur and walrus gut, the studio photographers of Nome created a superb record of a unique culture at the moment of its destruction—for the Eskimos would never return to their old ways after seeing the bright lights of Nome.

15

Some of the studio work done at the turn of the century in Alaska and the Yukon is superior to all but the very finest done today. There is a majesty in the portrait of Chief Ano-Tlosh of the Taku tribe which once flourished near Juneau. The Takus were a subtribe of the Tlingit, one of the principal tribes of Southeast Alaska, all of which were highly developed culturally long before the Russians and Americans arrived. The artwork of these people, as exemplified by the Chilcat blanket the chief is wearing, was, and is today to some degree, among the finest indigenous forms in the world. Their carvings, perhaps most conspicuously their totem poles, are unique and exquisitely fashioned.

There has never been a lack of interest in pictures of young ladies anywhere or anytime in history as far as anyone can determine, and, the wishes of the women's liberation movement notwithstanding, so it will always be (or God save the Republic). The sultry beauty with the snowshoes was named Sla-Gun, a Southeastern native, and the girl with the extraordinary tresses on the far right was an Eskimo from Cape Prince of Wales.

16

Reindeer were first imported to the Seward Peninsula in the early 1890s by the Reverend Sheldon Jackson and Captain Mike Healy of the revenue cutter *Bear*, and in 1894 the first Laplanders were hired to help nurse the fledgling reindeer industry. Two of them pose in native dress, top left. Top center, a portrait of Chief Schwatka, whose name had to have been taken from U.S. Army Lt. Frederick Schwatka, who in 1883 was the first American to travel the length of the Yukon. The chief was, at the time the picture was taken, the oldest guide in Alaska. The dashing gentleman in the upper right, Mr. C. C. Crews, sat for his portrait in Edmonton before setting out on the disastrous "trail" north. The photographer captioned the picture at left, "The Old and the New Klondikers."

More examples of the elaborate decorative art of the Tlingits, left and below. The matron on the far left, Stene-Tu, stands wrapped in a Chilcat blanket with her friend, Kaw-Claa. Below, she poses with her son, who holds a ceremonial representation of their moiety (clan), the Ravens.

William Howard Taft, below left, in the costume of the Arctic Brotherhood, a U.S.–Canadian fraternity that was formed after the Rush. Close examination reveals that Taft's head was carefully snipped from another photo and superimposed on this one. The President did not wear a ring on his left pinky, for one thing, and the first President to visit Alaska was Warren Gamaliel Harding. Harding died in San Francisco's Palace Hotel shortly thereafter, but the events were unrelated.

Herr Iden-Zeller was indeed a globetrotter and, if appearances are revealing, something of an Arctic dandy. Iden-Zeller was the first European to cross the Tschaun Mountains of Siberia on foot.

A man identified only as Smith stood before the camera with his dog Kiyi, who, to judge from his trappings, was the lead dog in his master's team. The photographer's caption reads "Kiyi, who saved Smith's life May 20th, 1899, on Otter Lake."

Four more native girls, identified by the photographers from left to right, "The Chilcat Klootch," "Reverie of a Stikine Maiden," and Mollie Delilak and Annie Buck, "late students of Carlisle University, Penn." The first two are Tlingits and the latter two, Eskimos.

CHAPTER II

FINDERS KEEPERS, LOSERS WEEPERS

*"When the others joined him, the moose meat was
cooked and they had a feed. Then he showed
them the gold in the sand . . ."*

Charter members of the Yukon Order of
Pioneers at Fortymile in the Yukon Territory, 1892. Some of these men had been
in the Yukon basin for almost 20 years
when the picture was taken. Standing,
back row, from left to right: Gordon
Bettles, Pete McDonald, Jim Bender,
Frank Buteau, George Matlock, Al Mayo,
Pete Nelson, Tom Lloyd, Bill Stewart,
unknown. The three standing in the center are also unidentified. Seated: Fred
Hart, Bill McPhee, unknown, Jack
McQuesten, George Harrington, unknown, Hootch Albert. In all, an extraordinary gathering.

The waters of the mighty Yukon rise in the mountains of northern
British Columbia and, in a grand arc, flow 2300 miles through the
Yukon Territory and Alaska. Down the course of the river the landscape
varies from the craggy mountains of its upper reaches to the brooding,
sparsely timbered mountains of its central stretches on to the meandering,
marshy Yukon Flats, abounding in waterfowl. Beyond, the country is less
dramatic as the river flows on to its immense delta on the Bering Sea.

The first Europeans to follow its waters were Russian traders, who
worked upstream to establish their outposts. They sought furs rather than
gold, as did their British and Canadian counterparts of the Hudson's Bay
Company, who came overland through the Mackenzie River basin in the
1840s to build Fort Yukon at the mouth of the Porcupine and Fort Selkirk on
the Pelly. These, like the Stewart, White, Tanana, and Koyukuk Rivers,
were major tributaries of the Yukon.

The fierce Chilcat Indians who guarded the southern gateway to the
Yukon basin, the Chilcoot Pass, burned Fort Selkirk in 1842 and re-
established their trading dominance over the Stick Indians of the interior.
Two years after the United States bought Alaska from the Russians for
$7,200,000 in 1867, the U.S. Army steamed upstream to Fort Yukon, raised
the American flag, and with that the men of Hudson's Bay Company settled
accounts and withdrew.

Although reports of gold had been made earlier, the first prospectors to
arrive in the Valley—Jack McQuesten, Arthur Harper, Al Mayo, and Fred
Hart—came down the Porcupine in 1873.

The Alaska Commercial Company, based in San Francisco, had
obtained exclusive rights to the rich sealing grounds of the Pribilof Islands
from the government when Alaska was acquired from the Russians, and
soon after set up trading posts on the Yukon and took over the abandoned
Fort Yukon post. When the prospectors arrived, they found that the Valley
upstream for more than 850 miles was theirs to share with the natives
alone.

William Ogilvie, chief surveyor for the Canadian government in the
Yukon, tells the story of the genesis of the idea that gold might be found
there:

"The first man who thought of trying the Yukon as a mining field, so
far as we know, was Arthur Harper. Born in the county of Antrim, Ireland,
in 1835, he left it while yet a boy to try his luck in America. He spent some
time on the Atlantic seaboard of the United States, but being of an

Surveyor, later Yukon Commissioner, William Ogilvie's cabin near the Canadian/Alaskan border, 1895. The quarters were palatial—22 feet long and only seven occupants for the winter. The rock stove was three feet high and wide and eight feet long. The mortar was a clay they had found nearby. Primitive and remote as it was, it was home to the crew until spring came. Ogilvie: "I never spent a more comfortable winter in my life than in that house."

The young boys of Sitka, Alaska's capital, in a Fourth of July foot race, 1888. Sitka was the old Russian capital, and it remained so after American purchase in 1867 until Juneau went into ascendancy and was named capital in 1906.

An elegant *al fresco* banquet held by Governor Alfred Swineford near Sitka in the late 1880's. Alaska was remote in the American consciousness, but most of the amenities of life were available in the southeastern Alaskan towns.

adventurous nature he drifted westward to the Pacific slope goldfields, and in the latter years of the sixth decade of the past century was in British Columbia. Fortune did not favour him over-much, and he looked about him for new fields, untried, to renew his quest. He had possessed himself of a copy of Arrowsmith's map of British North America, which gave a pretty thorough representation of the topography of the country covered by the Hudson's Bay Company, from whom Arrowsmith got much of his information. A study of this map led Harper to believe that there was a much more extensive gold-bearing field in the north than any one suspected. He saw the head-waters of the two most important branches of the Mackenzie, the Liard and Peace, flowing from well-defined auriferous areas in British Columbia; he saw the Yukon, through its affluents, rising in the same field, and he convinced himself that if gold were plentiful on the sources of the Mackenzie, it was just as plentiful on the Yukon. Not only did he convince himself, but he convinced four others sufficiently to test the theory with him. . . ."

His party included Fred Hart, a fellow countryman—a man who also would be remembered as one of the Yukon's great pioneers.

McQuesten, who was to become known as the "Father of the Yukon," was born in Maine in 1838 and as a young man had made his way west. When news of the gold fields on the Fraser River of British Columbia arrived in the States he joined the rush in 1858. In 1863 he set out working his way north, prospecting and trading with the natives as he went. His long journey took him through the Slave Lakes and eventually westward to what must be called a fateful meeting with the Harper party on the Sikanni Chief River in British Columbia where the men decided to throw their lots together. One of the men accompanying McQuesten was Al Mayo, and the three of them—Harper, McQuesten, and Mayo—were to dominate trading on the upper Yukon from 1874 to the time of the big strike on the Klondike creeks. They were men of strength and courage and purpose; men who rank in the first file of American pioneers.

As they worked northward to the Mackenzie they prospected fruitlessly. But the journey was not without relief from the exhausting work and boredom, as one can easily draw from the story William Ogilvie recounts in his book, *Early Days on the Yukon:*

"One of the items of Harper's outfit was a five-gallon keg of strong black rum, and at every Hudson's Bay post visited this was tapped and drink passed round. His recollections of some of the results were amusing, and he

A warm cabin, a deck of cards, and some amiable companions constituted gracious society for prospectors and explorers on the upper Yukon in the 1870s. Below: Fred Hart, one of the great Yukon pioneers, who trekked through the northwest with Harper and McQuesten.

used to repeat them in humorous style. At one place a large Highland Scotchman who was handed the keg to take it to the house did not wait for that, but drawing the bung cork put it to his mouth, and before any one could interfere had taken a veritable *drink*, not a glass. The result was somewhat amusing, if not a little brutal.

"In a short time he was wildly intoxicated, and turned berserker, defying all creation to come on and have it out with him. Being a giant in strength, there was a well-manifested inclination shown to let him have it all as he wished, and as no one came near him, he seized a large train dog that was looking on, and taking the front legs in one hand and the hind ones in the other he flung the brute around his neck, the dog howling the while as only those wild wolfish dogs can howl. The human brute seemed to find enjoyment in this, for he marched around the fort square, howling in unison with the dog. No one was anxious to interfere and the performance was kept up till exhaustion and sleep overtook the man, and he slept the sleep of the unrighteous till Harper and his party left. Harper thought this the most unique display he had ever witnessed, and often recalled it with mingled feelings."

Far to the north they ascended the little Rat River and crossed over the divide that separates the Mackenzie and Yukon watersheds. From there they descended the Porcupine to Fort Yukon. Alaska Commercial Company agent Moses Mercier greeted them like long-lost friends and did all he could to assist them. Years later, McQuesten affectionately recalled this of their first meeting: "He let us have fifty pounds of flour. It was all that he could spare. That was quite a treat to us, as that was the first we had had for two years."

An early view of Circle City, hub of commerce for the rich Birch Creek placers. Gold was discovered there in 1893, and Circle City, built by Jack McQuesten, quickly became the most important American settlement in the Yukon Valley. When the news arrived from the Klondike a few years later, Circle City was all but deserted.

Below, the Chilcoot Pass in 1895. Same view a year later, bottom. Most travelers at that time took the Petterson route to the right of the more direct passage straight up to the summit. Right, view from the top of the pass south toward Dyea taken the winter before the big rush.

Soon after they arrived Harper headed upstream to prospect on the White River, more than 400 miles up the Yukon River from Fort Yukon. McQuesten and most of the rest who had come down the Porcupine, in Ogilvie's narrative'' . . . went down about fifty miles and wintered in the vicinity of Goat Mountain. They killed five moose and two bears in the fall, and in the winter set their nets under the ice in a near-by lake and caught all the white fish they could use. In the spring they returned to Fort Yukon by dog-team, having brought four with them from the Mackenzie. On May 10th [of 1874] the ice broke up and ran thickly for three days; on the 20th

Harper and party joined them from up-river, and on June 4th Mercier, McQuesten and party, and Harper and party all started for St. Michael in Mercier's barge, arriving June 20th. François Mercier, Moses's brother, was in charge there, and he took McQuesten, Mayo, and Hart into the employ of the company. Harper and the others got provisions and returned on the steamer to the Tanana River, where they spent the season prospecting. The boat reached Yukon August 20th, and as good reports of furs had come from the region of the then 'Tron Deg' (now the Klondike), McQuesten continued with the boat and established Fort Reliance . . .," which was a mere six miles below what was to become the city of Dawson.

In the fall of 1874, Harper joined McQuesten and Mayo in the employ of the ACC as a trader, a career that was to frustrate his dream of finding a mother lode or coarse gold in abundance. In 1875, the three decided to move out temporarily because of trouble with the local Indians, who were resentful of the foreign intruders. Ogilvie describes their departure and return:

"Before going they concealed ('cached' the local term is), as well as they could, all the supplies in the place, among other things a mixture of arsenic and grease, which they used as rat poison. After they left the Indians looted the post, and finding this compound proceeded to mix it with some flour and make bread. The result was, two old women and one blind girl died. In the fall McQuesten came up with an outfit for the store, and of course had to make terms with the Indians. After a pow-wow it was agreed that the Indians would pay for what they took out of the store if McQuesten would pay for the women poisoned—a very one-sided settlement we would think when we consider the Suffragette movement of the present day.

"After McQuesten had billed them to the limit for the goods appropriated, he asked, almost in terror, we may suppose, how much they thought the women worth. A short calculation at current rates fixed the prices as follows: the two old women were not valued at all, being a nuisance, and for the young one, ten skins, the current terms of the country, about six dollars, was demanded. This amount was cheerfully paid, and some presents given besides, and the prompt payment and kindliness established the very best of feeling."

In 1886 Harper and McQuesten established a post at the Stewart River, where very fine gold had been found in the bars upstream in 1885. No sooner had they made the move than coarse gold, the kind that makes the hearts of men who seek it race, was found on Fortymile River, so named because it was about 40 miles below Fort Reliance. The important town of Fortymile sprang up in 1887, and of course McQuesten and Harper established a new trading center.

All the while, men and a very few women and children had been trickling into the country, principally over the Chilcoot Pass, above the headwaters of the river. The first non-native to make his way past the 3000 Chilcats who guarded the pass was an American by the name of George Holt. This was in 1875, and how he managed to do it will probably remain a

Above, two pictures of early sojourners who breeched the Chilcoot Pass before the Klondike discovery.

Fortymile was on the Canadian side of the border and, until the Birch Creek find and the emergence of Circle City, was the most important settlement on the river. This picture shows what the Yukon could do during the spring breakup. Great chunks of ice were driven up the banks under tremendous pressure from above if the downstream passage wasn't clear.

Circle City's fire department didn't enjoy the most sophisticated equipment available, but at least the town never burned down—which can't be said about most mining camps.

Despite the dominance that Dawson was to establish on the Canadian side of the border, the town of Fortymile went into decline slowly. Today it is a lifeless ghost town.

mystery forever. When he emerged with gold nuggets given him by Indians of the interior, he precipitated a minuscule rush. Twenty men from Sitka, accompanied by a small American gunboat, arrived at what was to become the thriving town of Dyea (pronounced dye-ee), and a few blank shots from the vessel's Gatling gun convinced the natives that it might make more sense to do business with the invaders than to continue the challenge. From 1880 onward, the Chilcats worked as porters over the pass, and when the big rush came in 1897, they were to boost their penny-a-pound rates between Dyea to Lake Lindeman to as much as fifty cents, or whatever the market would bear.

In 1893, diggings were discovered on Birch Creek by prospectors McQuesten had outfitted and directed to the creek. In the same year he founded Circle City, which survives to this day. With the establishment of this town, the Yukon Valley took on an almost cosmopolitan character.

The history of the Yukon abounds in tales of "wonder and curiosity" (as James Hutchings titled his book of California fact and lore in the 1850s), and McQuesten figured in many—not because he was flamboyant, but because he was solid and giving. One of the great stories of the time that has come down to us characterizes the spirit of that extraordinary period before the great rush of 1897–1898 and of Jack McQuesten himself. Ogilvie told it this way:

"McQuesten, though never so actively connected with mining as Harper, was nevertheless in sympathy with it, and aided the craft all he could, by helping them with supplies and material, as much as lay in his power. Many a story is told in the Yukon, and by the old-timers wherever they are, of Jack's goodness of heart, and leniency in collecting accounts, and we cannot let the occasion pass without recalling one at least, typical of all the rest. A miner who had got an outfit on credit, to be paid for at next clean-up, came in to see Jack, intending no doubt to do the 'square thing'; saw him, and after the usual 'howdys' and 'ho's' asked Jack how much he owed. Examination showed the balance against him to be slightly over seven hundred dollars. The information surprised the debtor into the exclamation—

"'Seven hundred! H—l, Jack, I've only got five hundred, how'm I goin' to pay seven hundred with five?'

"'Oh, that's all right, give us your five hundred, and we'll credit you with it and go on as before.'

26

"'But, d—n it, Jack, I haven't had a spree yet.'

"'Well, go and have your spree, come back with what is left, and we'll credit you with it and go on as before.'

"Alas for human frailty, when he came from his spree there was nothing left, and kindly Jack let him have another outfit, increasing the indebtedness to about twelve hundred, to be paid for *next clean-up*, and so *ad infinitum*."

By 1895, there were at least 1000 outsiders in the Valley. Five hundred more were to come in before summer ended in 1896.

Bars and dancehalls flourished, and, while the traditional miner's law was still the single line of control in all matters of dispute, life in general was tranquil, albeit difficult, particularly on the creeks and the trails.

The discovery of gold in the Klondike was strikingly different from the discovery of gold in California half a century earlier. In California, it was by sheer chance that John Marshall spotted flecks of gold in the American River while building a mill race for his employer, John Sutter. In the Yukon Valley, by contrast, the whole economy of perhaps 1500 outsiders long had been based on trapping, trading, and searching for gold. These pioneers already had found gold in handsome amounts on the Stewart River and the Fortymile, and in the region of Birch Creek. The Birch Creek diggings, alone, yielded about $900,000 in 1896.

Jack McQuesten, called by his fellow pioneers, "The Father of the Yukon," stands near the far left, behind the head of the black dog, in front of his headquarters in Circle City. To his left stands Fred Hart. McQuesten spent almost 25 years in the Yukon, married a native woman in 1878, and raised a large family there. (The children were all sent to private schools in California.) But when the big rush came the changes in life were more than he cared to bear, and he went into semi-retirement in Berkeley. At this writing his daughter, Crystal McQuesten Morgan, still lives in the big house he built on Hopkins Street.

Winter supplies at Rampart, a new camp, that sprang up in summer of 1896. It was here that Rex Beach, whose literary career had yet to take form, spent the better part of a year before moving on to Dawson and later Nome.

It was in that year, however, that several persistent prospectors made a find that was to eclipse all previous discoveries. Here is how William Ogilvie recounts the story of the strike on Rabbit Creek, a tributary (later renamed Bonanza) of the Klondike River:

"In August, 1896, the world-startling discovery of the Klondike was made, which for a year or two put a period to all exploration and prospecting except in its immediate vicinity. . . .

"Leading up to the discovery of the Klondike, that all credit may rest where it is due, we have to go back of the date a year or two."

Joe Ladue, a New Yorker of French-Canadian descent, had arrived in the Valley in 1882 and was to be remembered in history as one of the Yukon's extraordinary pioneers. After failing to make a go of it as a prospector, he went to work for Harper and McQuesten. When in 1889 the latter two decided it would be in their mutual interest to end the long-standing partnership, Ladue and Harper joined forces.

As Ogilvie continues, "Joe was for some time in charge of the new trading-post at Ogilvie, where all the incoming miners called on their way down the river, and he never failed to encourage them with tales of wonderful prospects at newly found places.

"Among those who came to the Yukon seeking adventure, before the Klondike discovery, was Robert Henderson, from Big Island, off the north coast of Nova Scotia. He had been a sailor for some years, and in that capacity had been pretty well over the globe. Of an adventurous nature, he took to hunting for gold, not so much to become rich as to find adventure, for those who know him best do not believe he would work the richest claim on earth if he had to stay on it till it was worked out. . . .

"In July, 1894, Henderson and two associates . . . arrived at Ogilvie, where they found the ever-smiling Joe Ladue in charge. He was ready for them with a good story about the prospects on Indian River, which joined the Yukon nearly twenty miles below them. It was comparatively virgin ground, and that was enough for Bob Henderson. . . ."

After spending two years in frustrating hardship on the creeks of the Indian, he crossed over the divide that separates the Klondike from the Indian and descended to a creek which he named Gold Bottom. There he found a two-cent prospect (when prospectors found bare traces of gold they were described as "colors," but when the amount was measurable, even as little as two cents, it was called a prospect), and since he had seen nothing better decided to work the ground. Henderson went out for supplies and on the way back decided to pole up the Klondike rather than the Indian. Ogilvie continued:

"At the mouth of the Klondike he saw George Washington Carmack . . . Henderson, in accordance with the unwritten miners' code, told Carmack of the discovery he had made on Gold Bottom, and invited him to come up and stake. Carmack was then engaged in salmon-fishing with his Indian friends and associates, the male members of whom were Skookum, or 'strong,' Jim, and Tagish Charlie. As Henderson tells the story Carmack promised to take it in, and take his Indian associates with him, but to this Henderson strongly objected, saying he did not want his creek to be staked by a lot of natives, more especially natives from the upper river. Carmack seemed to be offended by the objection, so they parted. I have this story substantially the same from both Henderson and Carmack, the latter, of course, laying a little stress on the objection to the Indians."

Carmack and his companions at that point decided to cut enough logs to float a raft of logs to Fortymile to sell to the sawmill there. The almost straight salmon diet they had been living on had gotten them down and they needed the money to buy some variety.

Arthur Harper, another of the great Yukon pioneers, perhaps second only to McQuesten in importance. He, like Ladue, died of tuberculosis before he could enjoy the fruits of his long years in the north.

Robert Henderson, who first discovered gold in the Klondike River watershed. He missed the big strike on Bonanza Creek, though, and the credit went to George Carmack.

Jim went up Bonanza Creek looking for suitable logs and, having found them, went down to the creek to make certain there was enough depth to float them out. In so doing, he found colors at several places and, spurred on by the thought of making a paying discovery, panned some grass-root dirt, found a number of fair prospects, and returned to his partners.

About 20 days after their encounter with Henderson, the three decided to go up Bonanza and cross over to Gold Bottom to see what that creek might promise. Ogilvie:

"Travelling up the valley through the thick underbrush at that season was tedious and fatiguing, and the mosquito-laden atmosphere added torment to fatigue.

"A short distance below where they afterwards made discovery, both Jim and Charlie told me they, while panning during a rest, found a ten-cent pan. This discovery caused a ripple of excitement . . . and it was decided that if the Gold Bottom trials failed they would devote further attention to this place. The Indians both told me they asked George if they would tell Bob of this find, and that George directed them to say nothing about it till they came back, if they did, and investigated further, then if they found anything good they might tell.

"Travelling was so tiresome and tedious in the valley that, when they came to the confluence with the creek now called Eldorado, they took to the divide between it and Bonanza, and followed the crest of this divide around the head of Bonanza Creek, where, finding the marks made by Henderson, they descended to him. Arrived there they were nearly bare of provisions, and completely out of tobacco, a serious predicament for Jim and Charlie. Henderson, either through shortage himself or dislike of the Indians, or both, would not let them have anything, though Jim and Charlie both assured me they offered to pay well for all they could get. . . .

"As they did not find any prospect approaching in value the ten-cent pan on Bonanza, they remained a very short time at Henderson's camp, and made their way back to the head of the creek which first gave fame to the Klondike—Bonanza. Before they got far down it their provisions were entirely exhausted, and as they prospected on the way down, and Jim was hunting for meat, their progress was slow; and their hunger was becoming acute, with exhaustion and weakness fast following. To shorten the story of Jim and Charlie, for they dwelt long on this part of the narrative, Jim at last, when they were all too tired and weak to do further prospecting, got a moose. . . .

"After killing the moose, Jim says he called on the others, whom he had left some distance away, to come to him. While waiting for them to come he looked in the sand of the creek where he had gone to get a drink, taking with him a bit of the moose. He found gold, he said, in greater quantities than he had ever seen it before. When the others joined him the moose meat was cooked, and they had a feed. Then he showed them the gold in the sand.

"They remained two days at this place panning, and testing the gravel up and down the creek in the vicinity. After satisfying themselves that they had the best spot, and deciding to stake and record there, they got into a dispute as to who should stake discovery claim, Jim claiming it by right of discovery, and Carmack claiming it, Jim says, on the ground that an Indian would not be allowed to record it. Jim says the difficulty was finally settled by agreeing that Carmack was to stake and record discovery claim, and assign half of it, or a half-interest in it, to Jim, so on the morning of August 17th, 1896, Carmack staked discovery claim five hundred feet in length up and down the direction of the creek valley, and No. 1 below discovery of the same length; both the full width of the valley bottom, or from base to base

Skookum Jim (James Mason) found gold on Bonanza Creek, but his companion, George Carmack, convinced him that an Indian would not be allowed to make a claim and filed one himself. Later, Carmack gave Jim half interest that made him wealthy and respected until his death in 1916.

Carmack (below) was married to an Indian woman, preferred Indian ways, and consequently was known along the Yukon as "Siwash," a slightly contemptuous name for the Indians of the north Pacific Coast.

Tagish Charlie was the other man with Carmack and Skookum Jim when the Bonanza discovery was made. He too had a rich claim and enjoyed a full life in Carcross, where he ran a hotel after selling his interests in 1901. In 1906, after a strenuous evening at the bar, he fell off a bridge and drowned.

Adney's drawings of the Klondike creek mining methods. Top, the relationship of the buried ancient creek bed to the existing creek. Center, cross section showing prospect holes, with Number 4 hitting paydirt. Bottom, a typical prospect hole.

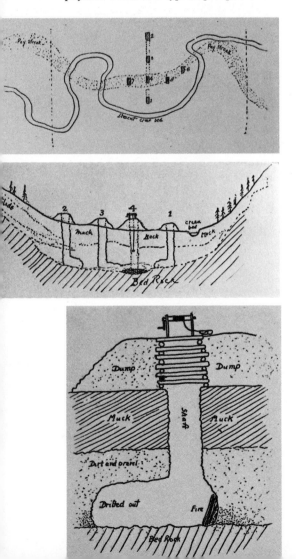

of the hill on either side, as the regulations then read. No. 2 below was staked for Tagish Charlie, and No. 1 above for Skookum Jim.

"The gold they panned out of the surface gravel on discovery was put into a Winchester rifle cartridge shell and the party went to camp at the mouth of the Klondike. There a small raft of saw logs was prepared for the saw-mill at Fortymile. Carmack and Charlie went down on it, and Jim was sent back to the claim to watch it, as the country all around there was alive with men looking for the Henderson discovery. . . .

"Henderson has always bitterly resented Carmack's neglect to send him word of the new discovery as he—Henderson—says Carmack promised he would do, if he found anything better than where they were working on Gold Bottom. The result to Henderson was that he did not learn of the new discovery which was brought about through his own labors and invitation to come to Gold Bottom till after all the ground on both Bonanza and Eldorado was staked . . . Henderson could not, owing to the short season and falling water, lose the time to go to the office at Fortymile, and record his claim on Gold Bottom, until after Andrew Hunker had located on the creek below him, and had gone down to Fortymile, and not only recorded a discovery claim, but had the creek named after him, notwithstanding that Henderson had marked a large tree at the junction of this creek with the Klondike when he left his boat there on his way up in July, 'This creek to be known as Gold Bottom Creek.'

"As the mining regulations then were, only one discovery was allowed in a district, the boundaries of which were fixed by the Government Agent. A discovery was allowed on Bonanza Creek to Carmack, and another on Gold Bottom, or as it was misnamed Hunker, to Hunker, and no more would be allowed in the Klondike district.

"The result was Henderson, after his two years' hard work, and his proclaiming his find and inviting every one he met at all interested in mining, and some he knew were not, to try the new field, had only an ordinary claim in it."

So within a few days of their discovery, Carmack and Tagish Charlie made their way to Fortymile to register their claims. And Skookum Jim remained behind to guard the ground they had staked.

Carmack had adopted native life patterns, and for this simple, if unjustified, reason, he was not respected. Such was the sentiment of the times. His story was largely discounted since old "Siwash George," as he was called, wasn't a miner basically, and lived completely out of the mainstream of settlement life.

In Bill McPhee's saloon he produced the cartridge he had filled with the coarse gold, and experienced miners knew by the very look of the stuff that it had come from a source unknown to them.

One of the first to believe Carmack and to leave Fortymile to stake was Clarence Berry, who was grubstaked by McPhee. McPhee was as open-handed and trusting a man as Jack McQuesten. While Berry wasn't the only celebrated miner of the Klondike, the history of his enterprise and success was to make him a national figure the next year.

Many others also believed Carmack and rushed off to the Klondike creeks, but some of the old-timers were hard to convince. Tappan Adney wrote of some of the conversations among those who hadn't joined the original stampede when the first news came downstream:

"Word came to Fortymile that Louis Rhodes had two men working for him, and was getting good pay. 'That's a lie,' said one man. 'Louis Rhodes! when was *he* able to hire two men?' Next word came down that Ben Wall was getting two-bit dirt. 'Hell!' says Nigger Jim; 'I've known Ben Wall these ten years, and he's the all-firedest liar in the Yukon.' When they heard that Berry was getting $1 to the pan, they laughed. Klondike 'was a bunco—nothing but a bunco.'"

But they were to learn, and learn soon, that it wasn't "bunco."

Arthur Walden was on Bonanza at the time the first stakers had returned to settle in for the winter after registering their claims at Fortymile. Circle City was 220 miles below the mouth of the Klondike and it took months for the news of the strike to arrive there. It was Walden who brought the news:

"Everybody had been so excited and busy trying to get down to bedrock, to find out what he had on his claim, that there had been no communication with the lower river. As a large proportion of men working at the diggings had partners in Circle City, they were very anxious to get letters down to them, and, as I happened to be the first man to go down after the new discoveries, I went back with quite a large mail, each man howling to his partner to throw everything and come up and be rich for life.

"I made the trip back without tent and stove, having sold mine on the creeks. This is the way they used to travel in the early days, and it was called 'siwashing.' When I was about a hundred miles from Circle City, I was overtaken by Hughie Day, the first United States mail carrier with the first official mail ever carried into Circle City. Not daring to take the time to go up the creeks, he had stopped at Dawson only one night, where he met men who had told him about the richness of the country. But he had no letters to verify it, as I had them all.

"He was a wonderful traveler. Being spurred on by starvation, as he had been unable to replenish his food supply at Fortymile, he overtook me, and, as I had enough food to get us both in, we traveled together for some days. When within a day of Circle City he asked me to lend him a couple of my best dogs, and not to hurry that day, as he wanted to get as far ahead of me as possible. He also asked me not to say anything about his having been with me, as he was proud of his reputation as a traveler and was rather ashamed of having loitered along with me. The upshot of it was that he got into town two or three hours ahead of me.

"Here he made the great mistake of telling the news of the wonderful discoveries in the Klondike. But as he had no vouchers for it, nobody believed him, which made Hughie mad. He happened to overhear someone say that 'the cold had got Hughie at last' and this made him furious. This was the state of affairs when I got in: pity on one side, and rage and exasperation on the other.

"On my arrival I went into Harry Ash's saloon, slammed my letters down on the bar, and called for a drink of beef-tea. (Dog-drivers don't drink whiskey in the winter-time.) I well remember Harry Ash, as he disregarded

Winter's labor at the windlass. While others worked below to muck paydirt from the drifts, the men above hauled it to the surface and added it to the growing dumps to await the spring thaw and running water. If the temperature dropped under 50° below, all work ceased.

my order for a drink and ran through a batch of letters until he came to one for himself.

"By this time the men had heard of the arrival of another down-river dog-team, and began to come into the saloon to get the news, or maybe Hughie had mentioned me, and they came in to verify it. Harry Ash finished reading his letter, and then jumped over the bar, exclaiming, 'Boys! Hughie is right! Help yourselves to the whole shooting match. I'm off for the Klondike!'

"Then began the wildest excitement, as man after man got his letter and thought he was rich for life. Harry's invitation was promptly accepted and a wild orgy began. Corks weren't even pulled, and necks were knocked off bottles. I never got my beef-tea, so I went to the cabin of a friend of mine to get something to eat, and had hardly started when the whole rabble was after me. Then for forty-eight hours there was no peace: it was questions, questions, questions.

There was plenty of work for those who had no claims of their own in the early days. The work was hard and the 60-hour week was long, but at $10 a day there were few complaints. If a man was very careful he could build up a small stake for himself, but the monotony of life in the diggings drove most men to town, where they happily parted with their earnings.

"The next morning Harry Ash pulled out, and the big stampede to the Klondike had started. My batch of mail had killed Circle City in less than an hour. Cabins had been selling at a flat rate of five hundred dollars and dogs at from twenty-five to fifty dollars each. I was almost immediately offered three fine cabins for any dog I chose to designate. This either meant that a dog had gone up to fifteen hundred dollars or, what was actually the case, that cabins had dropped to about eight dollars."

When the Circle City men arrived, they found what was to prove almost all of the richest ground already staked, but some of them had enough money to buy out original stakers—almost invariably at prices far below what would eventually be proved the real value.

Perhaps the most extraordinary example of the early miscalculation of the ultimate value of the new find was the experience of Dick Lowe who, like many others, sought a "fraction." A fraction was a section of ground lying between two claims where one or both of the adjacent claims had staked more than the 500 feet of creek bed between them. Lowe found an 86-foot fraction close to where Bonanza and Eldorado (the second creek staked, which proved to be richer than Bonanza) joined, and, after hesitating and looking for something more promising, he staked it.

Lowe, an old prospector and muleskinner who had enjoyed both success and disappointment in the Black Hills Rush of 1875, tried to peddle his fraction for $900, but there were no takers. With nothing better to do he sank one shaft to bedrock and found no trace of a paystreak. The second struck paydirt and in one week he took out more than $45,000. The fraction proved to be the richest patch of gold-bearing land of its size the world has known. It yielded Lowe $400,000, and it was said that as much more was high-graded (stolen by workers) or taken by others from the paydirt dump. This story has every earmark of being a gross exaggeration, but it matters not. Four hundred thousand dollars was equal then to almost ten times that in buying power at 1976 prices.

Poor Dick Lowe got drunk and more or less stayed drunk until he died in San Francisco in 1907. He squandered tens of thousands in the bars and dancehalls and at the gambling tables of Dawson, then married a dancehall girl who helped him spend the remainder.

No sooner had the news of the strike arrived, leaving Fortymile nearly deserted, than the Mounties moved a sizable contingent to Dawson and built their first barracks there. Keeping order in Dawson was never a serious problem from the very beginning.

The first thing the Klondike stampeders did after staking was to build cabins for the long winter which was soon to descend. The boring staple diet—beans, bacon and sourbread—was relieved with dried fruit and tinned meat, and, on occasion, a bottle of something special.

Winter was long and dark, and the miner's cabin, cramped as it may have been, was home—a warm refuge. Most cabins were about 12 by 16 feet with a roof extension in front where supplies could be stored. A stove, a table, rough chairs or benches, narrow bunks, and an ever-present water bucket near the fire made up the typical interior. There were few, if any, amenities.

His story, of course, is only one of hundreds like it, for a number of the original stakers of the rich Klondike creeks either sold out too early and far too cheaply or scattered their money with an abandon hard to conceive.

Perhaps the saddest of other stories is that of Bob Henderson. Embittered and sick, he sold his Gold Bottom claim for $3000. More than $650,000 in gold was eventually to be taken from his ground.

Tappan Adney, the *Harper's* correspondent, who met Henderson when the gold rush was in high fever, asked him whether he was disheartened by all that had happened.

"No," Henderson said, "there are as rich mines yet to be discovered as any that have been found." Adney was "not quite sure" that Henderson really believed that.

In October, 1898, when Adney saw Henderson for the last time, he had just reached Seattle on a ship from Alaska. "Unsuspicious and trusting, he had been robbed on the steamer of all the money he had—$1100. He had one thing left. It was the golden (carpenter's) rule and myrtle-leaves badge of the Yukon Order of Pioneers, of which he was a member. For some reason he insisted on pinning it himself to my vest, saying, 'You keep this. I will lose it too. I am not fit to live among civilized men.'"

Yet, Adney observed, the other miners did not see Henderson as a chronic loser but an uncrowned hero, the real discoverer of Klondike gold. "Siwash George would be fishing yet at the mouth of the Klondike if it hadn't been for Bob Henderson."

Joe Ladue, the ever-buoyant Yukon boomer, never staked a gold claim on the Klondike creeks, but he joined the Klondike millionaires on the *Excelsior*, a millionaire himself. At home in New York he married his old sweetheart, whose parents had refused to let her marry him years before. Ladue had staked out and patented the Dawson townsite on the boggy flats at the mouth of the Klondike and values rose to astounding levels before a year was out. Some lots fetched as much as $40,000 in Dawson's heyday.

Ladue had seen his dream come true, but as with Harper, tuberculosis was to whisk him beyond before 1897 ended.

There were winners, too, and many of them. Beginning their labors in September, with the industrious Skookum Jim sinking the first shaft, hundreds of men began the tedious work of building the dumps of paydirt that would be washed out in the first few weeks of summer in 1897. From these dumps came the gold that the *Excelsior* and the *Portland* carried into San Francisco and Seattle along with the news.

With Bonanza staked virtually from top to bottom, a handful of men who had been prospecting on the major "pup" of the main stream found extraordinary prospects and the staking began. The pup was to be named Eldorado, which proved to be an understatement. Eldorado was soon to become known as the richest stream ever known. Along a stretch less than four miles, 40 claims yielded from $500,000 to $1,500,000 each. Again, there were doubters among those who staked claims, and a number of sales were made, later to be proved improvident; they made latecomers rich and left the first stakers looking for a grubstake.

One such sale was made by an old-timer known as French Joe, who took $600 for Seventeen. (Claims were numbered in order of progression from the discovery claim. The discoverer was entitled to an extra claim. Claims below discovery were called Six Below, Eleven Below, and so on.) Seventeen proved to be one of Eldorado's richest, and the new claimholders, themselves Yukon veterans, graciously, in the spirit of old Yukon gold-field camaraderie, deeded 75 feet of the claim back to French Joe.

Sixteen had been staked, then abandoned before it had been explored. As luck would have it, a young man who had left his job as a YMCA instructor in Seattle and gone north on a hunch, Thomas Lippy, restaked and recorded the claim. It was to yield him more than $1,500,000. While Lippy was a newcomer among the old dogs of the Yukon, he was to become universally liked along the creeks. Not in derision, but out of respect, he was often referred to as Professor Lippy. After all, he had been a teacher.

Save for Berry, Lippy drew more public attention and admiration in the U.S. than any other Klondike millionaire. Along with Berry, Harper, McQuesten, Ladue, Carmack, Skookum Jim, Henderson, and more we have yet to meet, he inhabits the Yukon pantheon.

Cabin life was as boring as the winter diet, but the lonely miner did have a few diversions—reading, daydreaming, writing the folks at home, and cards. This grizzled sourdough is playing a game of solitaire called Red Cross with cards that appear to be as limp as wilted lettuce.

The Bonanza, Dawson's first saloon, went up when the town was nothing more than a handful of buildings. But it was a home away from home for those who had reason to come down from the creeks. Of all the enterprises that sprang up in the mining camps of the West, the saloon was almost inevitably the first. All it took was a few bottles, a plank, and a thirsty clientele.

35

OLD YUKON TALES

Long before the fever died, story-tellers began wrapping the Yukon gold rush in a shroud of myths. The incredible cold, the terrors of the trail, the saints, the crooks, the reckless spenders—all were woven into a fabric of truth, exaggeration, and outright lies that became the Klondike legend. Here are a few of the strands in the weave.

THE YUKON WAY OF BUSINESS
John Sydney Webb, a stampeder in '97, observes the Klondike code of honor

Owing perhaps to the isolation of the country, and to the class of men who have come in, up to the present moment the miners' relations with one another have been marked by the most rigid honesty and fair dealing; and this is all the more remarkable when it is borne in mind that they represent an aggregation of almost every nationality and condition in life. The old-timers say that a man might leave his grub scattered along the trail to the mines for months and months, and no one would touch it.

In fact, a state of things exists today without parallel to those accustomed to the methods in vogue in the East; for the principal place of deposit for gold-dust is on a shelf behind the bars or counters, everywhere in the bar-rooms, where the precious metal lies in buckskin sacks, tied up, bearing the owner's name. No one thinks of disturbing them.

A sample of confidence and trust in one another was shown some years ago, when a cargo of goods was sent to Harper and Ladue, at Sixty Mile. The men were impatient for their outfits, and Harper told them to "sail in" and help themselves, and keep an account of what they took, and hand it in to him. There was a discrepancy of only six cans of condensed milk between the sum total of the taking of individuals and the entire amount of provisions called for by the manifest, and this might have been a mistake of the shipping clerk.

A LONG, LONG WAY FROM HOME
An Englishman named A.F. Ironmonger Sola suffers the anguish of exile

Fortymile consisted of the company's stores, a barber's shop, two bakeries, two restaurants, billiard parlors, distilleries, saloons, opera house, and 80 cabins. The only amusements were gambling, drinking and dancing with the squaws. The principal sport with mining men is found in gambling. Round the table they gather after night-fall and play until the late hours in the morning. They play high, too; sometimes it costs as much as fifty dollars to draw a card. A game with two thousand dollars as stakes is an ordinary event. If a man is fussy and quarrelsome he is told to get out of the game, and that is the end of it; in a few rare instances it ends in bloodshed. The camp, of course, contained some bad men but the most damage they did was with their mouth. . . .

During the first two days of our stay at Fortymile we did little but lounge, smoke our pipes, and take things easily generally. My thoughts were constantly with the old folks in England and with the sweetheart so far away. When I thought how long it might be before I saw her again I could not keep the sadness from my heart; shut out from the civilised world with hardly any means of communication made it harder still.

THE SOURDOUGH'S WEATHER BUREAU
Ingenuity in the Paul Bunyan tradition, as reported by Arthur Walden

We had no thermometers in Circle City that would fit the case [reach low enough], until Jack McQuesten invented one of his own. This consisted of a set of vials fitted into a rack, one containing quicksilver, one the best whiskey in the country, one kerosene, and one Perry Davis's Pain-Killer. These congealed in the order mentioned, and a man starting on a journey started with a smile at frozen quicksilver, still went at whiskey, hesitated at the kerosene, and dived back into his cabin when the Pain-Killer lay down.

A WINDOW OF ICE
Frank Buteau recalls a cosy hibernation on an island in the Yukon River

We then floated down to an island about a mile above the mouth of the Fortymile River, arriving there about the 13th of October, 1886. We immediately started building our cabins—three in all being built. There were sixteen of us located on the island and about five men living near the mouth of the Fortymile River. These five named our island The Sixteen Liars' Island. There was no trading post at Fortymile, and all provisions we had were what we brought with us. We had no stove, no stovepipe, and no windows, and only one-half dozen candles.

There were three of us associated together at this time—Louis Cotey, French Joe, and myself. French Joe suggested that we make a chimney out of wood, extending it through the ceiling in the center of the room and placing an open fire beneath it. He told us that the Hudson's Bay Company where he used to work had done this in one of their camps. We tried it but it was too cold. So we then gathered rocks on the beach and made a stove out of the rocks and mud, and also made a chimney out of the same materials. We used a large flat rock for the top of the stove and cooked in the mouth of it. This rock broke during the winter, and we had to rustle in the snow for another one. For a window, we made a hole in the door, which opened out, and made three wooden buttons which we put around the hole. Then we went down to the Yukon and cut a clear piece of ice slightly larger than the window opening and fitted it over the hole, fastening it on with the wooden buttons. On account of the extreme cold, this window lasted all winter. It did not gather frost but remained clear until spring.

The Dogs of Winter

Development and exploration, indeed survival in the North in the early years, was largely dependent on the trading companies which came up the Yukon with supplies in the brief summer and on the dogs of the North. Native dogs, called huskies or Malemutes, were not registered with the American Kennel Club, but they were as fine a breed of work dog as was ever developed. There was, of course, cross breeding, sometimes with wolves and later with "outside" dogs as they were brought in. Any man with a team could earn a good living, strenuous as the life was, in the hectic days of the Nineties by packing freight and passengers.

The dog above is a splendid example of the native animals. He could have brought as much as $500—a sum equal to the average workingman's yearly wage in the States. The man below has only one dog, but a good dog could pull 300 pounds—almost any dog was a help.

Above, a seven-dog team and their driver prepare to take a
pretty young lady on a pleasure ride. Gene Allan, publisher
of the *Klondike Nugget*, one of Dawson's several newspapers,
also ran a delivery service and distributed the paper and
mail to cabins on the creeks.

Above, a stout nine-dog team hauling a load of freight to the mines. In the background is a row of hand-worked hoists built on cribbing. Below, a fashionable couple wrapped in furs taking a joy ride on the icy Yukon. In the distance, a working team hauls a loaded sled.

CHAPTER III

PITFALLS AT THE GATE

"I have stumbled upon a few tough corners of the globe . . . but I think the most outrageously lawless quarter I ever struck was Skagway. It seems as if the scum of the earth had hastened here . . ."

Beyond Juneau, a hundred miles to the north, lay the end of the inside passage. There, on the upper tip of the Lynn Canal, the rough and ragtag settlements of Skagway and Dyea had sprung up with the news of the great strike.

The first arrivals swarmed onto the beaches in a fever to reach the Klondike, 600 miles away, before the country was locked fast in the eight-month Yukon winter.

Both towns, if they could be called that, were soon to become a chaotic mass of tents, randomly laid-out streets, and hastily put-up frame buildings.

Dyea had long been a small Indian village where John G. Healy had set up a trading post in the mid-1880s. Healy, a tough old Indian fighter and adventurer, had come north at the time of Alaska's first big gold discovery at Juneau in 1880. By the time the first of the 1897 stampeders arrived, Healy had established himself as formidable competition to the Alaska Commercial Company in the Yukon Valley. His company, the North American Trading and Transportation Company, which was backed by the Cudahy family meat-packing fortune, had established Fort Cudahy across the Fortymile River on the Yukon as a direct challenge to Jack McQuesten and the ACC. He succeeded in driving prices down somewhat, and at the same time he destroyed McQuesten's credit system, which was pay if you can, but if you can't you can pay for it next year when you come in for your new outfit. There were too many new faces, too many with money who would rather save on the cash-and-carry policy of Healy. McQuesten was forced to yield.

Skagway had been the site of a single cabin built by Captain Billy Moore, a man with one of the most remarkable pioneer careers in the history of the West. Moore had fought in the Mexican War of 1846, and for 50 years thereafter traveled up and down the coast of the Western Hemisphere from Peru to Canada in the quest for gold. He made small fortunes in the process, but having gone bankrupt when his five-steamboat fleet failed at the end of the Cassiar Rush in British Columbia, he went to Alaska in 1887. It took ten years for him to realize his vision of swarms of men streaming in and out of the Yukon Valley.

When, in midwinter of 1896–1897, William Ogilvie needed a man to carry his communiqué on the fabulous Klondike find to Canadian authorities, he chose Moore to do the job. Moore, then 74 years old, carried the

Welcome to Skagway, 1897—your first taste of gold rush life.

message almost 700 miles in the dead of winter on showshoes from Fortymile to Dyea—a trip no one before him had ever made.

In 1888, Moore had settled at what was to become Skagway, sure in his belief that the crossing above would become the gateway to the Yukon gold fields yet to be discovered. (That crossing was later named the White Pass Trail—and called other things by the thousands who attempted to climb it in 1897–1898.)

Although ownership of that part of the country was under some dispute between the United States and Britain, Moore staked a township and sat there until what he had anticipated came to pass in 1897. It was a most unusual case of foresight, faith, and patience.

Moore was literally inundated by the flood of gold-seekers who came on the first steamers to arrive from San Francisco and Seattle before the end of July. The monomaniac victims of gold madness captured the land, and he completely lost control of his claim in the hectic days and months to follow.

Both towns were controlled before the end of 1897 by a gangster known to all as Soapy Smith, whose reign and ultimate demise are told in Chapter 8. Smith's rule was related in some way, perhaps only symbolically, to the insensate character of the 1897–1898 rush. For in that first great wave, men resorted to almost any expedient to achieve their goal—to reach the Klondike gold fields.

Tappan Adney's description of early Skagway gives some of the flavor of the time:

"We have learned already to place no reliance upon any person's word. Everyone seems to have lost his head, and cannot observe or state facts.

"The very horses and animals partake of the fever and are restless . . . Accidents and runaways are occurring every few moments. Suddenly there is a commotion; a horse starts off with a half-packed load or a cart and cuts a swath over tents up through the town, scattering the people right and left.

"This sort of thing is getting to be so common that a fellow only looks to see that the horse is not coming in the direction of his own tent, and then goes on with his work.

"One man was asleep in his tent, 10 × 14, when a horse galloped through it and carried it off bodily. No one gets hurt, which is amazing. . . .

"A horse in a cart suddenly kicked, ran into a pile of hay, broke loose, and started across town, taking the corners of two or three tents. After

Landing supplies on the beach at Skagway in 1897 was a tedious series of transfers: steamship to scow, scow to wagon, wagon to shore. "The beach is low, and runs out several hundred yards, and then drops off into deep water," Tappan Adney wrote. "At low tide the whole beach is uncovered, so the steamers lie outside and wait for high tide to unload their freight. Our vessel was soon surrounded by a fleet of row-boats and large Siwash canoes, trying to pick up passengers for shore at 25 cents each. In crowds on the deck we stood gazing in wonder at the scene before us. Few of us had the inclination to look at the truly grand scenery . . . Snow and glacier capped mountains, rising thousands of feet from green, sparkling water, burying their lofty heads in soft, cottony clouds, are for other eyes than those of miners excited by the preparation for the real commencement of their journey."

galloping about among the frail habitations, he was finally caught and led back.

"Another horse, tied to a log fifteen feet long and six inches through, began to jerk and jump, and went for a hundred yards cavorting down the main street, dragging another horse that was hitched to the same log."

Of social life, Adney wrote in wonder:

"Across the street the sound of a piano and the moving figures of men and women seen through the windows reminds one that there is a dance tonight, as on every night. This piano is the only one in town, and its arrival is said to have been an event. The four women in the place are not even of the painted sort; paint might have covered up some of the marks of dissipation. Clumsy boots beat time on a dirty floor, but not with much

The beach at Dyea, like that of Skagway, was accessible only at high tide. There were no wharves, no piers, no adequate facilities for landing passengers or animals, and no shelter on land for goods or men. Frequently, a man would endure a dangerous and painful dunking in the ice-cold water before wading with his soaked possessions onto the inhospitable Alaskan shore.

enthusiasm. There is not sport enough to get up as much as a quadrille. The dance-house of a mining-town! Such a thing as shame is not even thought of.

"Among the many who are gazing upon the unaccustomed scene, with the same absorbed interest as the youngest of us, are men whom I take to be old-timers. I asked one of these what he thought of it all.

"Said he, 'I was in the Salmon River mining excitement in Idaho, but I have never seen anything like this. Ten thousand people went in that winter, over a single trail across the mountains; but it was nothing like this. There has never been anything on this coast like it.'

"Another, who is now the mayor of a town on the Pacific coast not far from the Strait of Juan de Fuca, said, in answer to the same question: 'I saw the beginning of Leadville, but it was nothing like this; there has been nothing like this.'

"Still another, a mining engineer from California, said: 'I have never seen people act as they do here. They have lost their heads and their senses. I have never seen men behave as they do here. They have no more idea of what they are going to than that horse has! . . .'

"There is no shady side to life at Skagway; everything goes on in broad daylight or candlelight. After supper every tent is lighted up, and the streets are crowded with muddy men in from the trail. The Pack Train is filled with

The rocky shore at Dyea (above) and the shallows of Skagway (below) were equally ill-suited as ports-of-call for hundreds of adventurers. They were chosen like beaches in an amphibious invasion because of their strategic location—in this case, the starting point on two routes across the coastal mountains to the headwaters of the Yukon. Tappan Adney, astonished, reported: "There are great crowds of men rowing in boats to the beach, then clambering out in rubber boots and packing the stuff, and setting it down in little piles out of reach of the tide . . . Behind these are tents and men and piles of merchandise and hay, bacon smoking, men loading bags and bales of hay upon horses and starting off . . . in the direction of a grove of small cottonwoods, beyond which lies the trail towards White Pass."

people, among whom I recognize several of my friends, who are drawn hither, like myself, by the spectacle. The tent of the biggest saloon in town is thirty by fifty feet. Entering through a single door in front, on the right hand is a rough board bar some ten or twelve feet long, with some shelves against the rear wall, on which are a few glasses and bottles. The bartender, who is evidently new to his business, apologizes for the whiskey, which is very poor and two-thirds water, and sells for 25 cents. After the lecture we received on the steamer from the United States customs officer [the importation and sale of alcoholic beverages was outlawed in Alaska], we are at a loss to understand how whiskey can be sold openly under the very eyes of the officers. But that is a story by itself. Along each side of the tent are the three-card monte, the *rouge-et-noir*, and other lay-outs, but not a faro lay-out in the place nor in the town. The gamblers are doing big business. . . .

"A constant surprise is the number of women. Some of these are at the dance-house, but the majority are the wives of miners. There is but one child in the whole place. It is a town of grown-up people. The women dress,

Rough frame buildings like the Yukon Hotel, which offered relatively luxurious lodgings and "meals at all hours," sprang up in the tent towns along the inlets. Left: The steamer *Willamette*, one of several ships on the suddenly profitable run between the States and the Alaskan panhandle, discharges cargo onto a hastily constructed pier.

Officers of the U.S. Customs set up an office in Skagway and warned arrivals that alcoholic beverages were prohibited. Nobody seemed to pay much attention.

some of them, in short skirts, with leather leggings or rubber boots, or else in out-and-out men's trousers."

But of all the things Adney observed and marveled at, the prevailing prices and wages amazed him most. If the figures seem unreal, remember that a dollar then was worth ten or more of today's dollars:

"Money goes like water through a sieve. It costs a dollar to look a man in the face. Men are like wolves: they literally feed upon one another. Wages for packers—anyone who can carry 75 to 100 pounds on his back and work ten hours—are $7.50 a day upward. 'Experienced' horse-packers are getting as high as—in one instance—$20 a day. The teamsters are making more than that. One was heard growling because he had only made $50 that day; they sometimes make $100. Horseshoe nails are $1 a pound at Skagway; at the 'Foot of the Hill,' 10 cents apiece; and a single horseshoe, $2.50."

Adney dwelt in his writing on horses, madness, morals, and money,

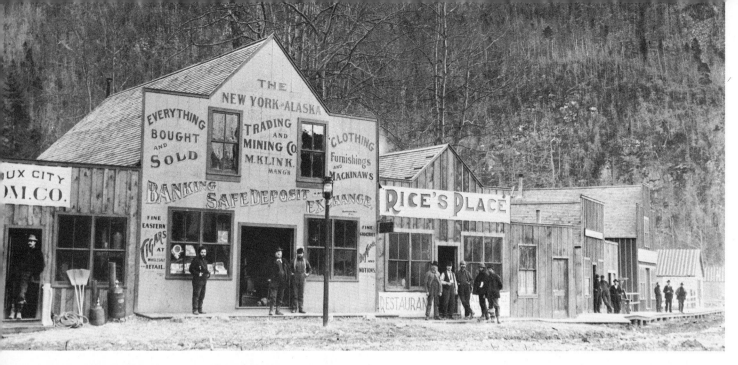

Downtown Skagway looked—and was—rough and raw in the autumn of '97 as wave after wave of Klondikers trudged through the muddy streets and up the trail that followed the Skagway River to White Pass. Enterprising businessmen and women soon learned that many gold hunters had come north ill-equipped. Before long, both Skagway and Dyea could supply basic foods, tools, fuel, boots, and clothing—not to speak of whiskey, roulette, and companions for a night.

because he left too early to see the full-blown lawlessness which was to grip the towns until July of 1898. The earliest arrivals in 1897 were already on the trails before the con men and strong-arm operators moved in to take effective control of municipal government.

Victims of the swindles, banditry, and murder were—almost to the exclusion of all others—transients. It was convenient for the local government, which consisted of a corrupt deputy U.S. marshal and a customs officer, to ignore virtually any responsibility for law enforcement. In fact, to put it simply, there was no control at all.

Observers who came through Skagway and Dyea in that first year, men of good judgment and familiar with earlier frontier settlements, testified to the brutal conditions that prevailed before the law arrived in Skagway and Dyea.

Henry Toke Munn, an experienced frontier and Arctic traveler, wrote: "For the six nights I slept in Skagway there was shooting on the streets every night. At least one man was killed that I knew of and probably others. The shack I slept in had a bullet through it over my head."

Another Englishman, Alexander MacDonald, was astonished at the violence: "I have stumbled upon a few tough corners of the globe during my wanderings beyond the outposts of civilization, but I think the most outrageously lawless quarter I ever struck was Skagway. . . . It seems as if the scum of the earth had hastened here. . . ."

Sam Steele, one of the three original enlistees in the North West Mounted Police, was then a superintendent in the force stationed on the Canadian side of the passes. With at least 25 years of experience in peacemaking and peacekeeping on the prairies of Western Canada, many times in the face of prohibitive odds, he was astonished by what he found. In his words written years later, Skagway was ". . . little better than a hell on earth . . . Skagway was about the roughest place in the world."

In all of the printed accounts I have read on events in Skagway and Dyea during the first year of the rush, I have failed to find a single reference to a sense of camaraderie. The kindest man in that restless crowd of strangers was filled with doubt and worry and had to watch out for his own affairs. I have never found mention of a church or any other institution to which someone in trouble could turn. The literature on the two settlements brings no joy, no feeling of pride or envy. Such is the power of gold to strip away the sensibilities of otherwise decent men.

But the story of life in the gateway towns, hard and dispiriting as it was, proved merely a forerunner to the only truly shameful chapter in all of the Yukon Rush and the subsequent opening of Alaska.

This little tent store at Skagway is typical of the improvised supply posts that dotted the main trails to the Yukon. The name of the town, often spelled Skaguay, was an inexact rendering of a Tlingit word that meant "end of the salt water."

Dyea, three miles from Skagway, had been an Indian village and a small trading post before the boom years 1896–1902 brought in hotels, barber shops, dance halls, and the largest brewery in Alaska. There is virtually nothing left of it today.

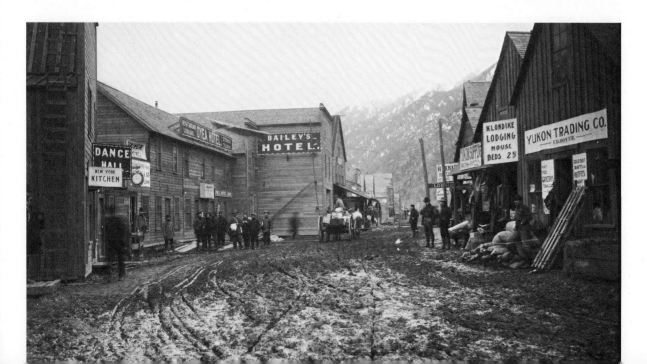

OLD YUKON TALES

Of justice, whiskey, and lonely death

THE CACHE ROBBER
Arthur Walden, the literate dog-puncher,
recounts the fate of an unlucky thief

The one case of stealing in the country happened in this way. Men were in the habit of poking out into the wilderness in the winter, prospecting, leaving caches on the way out to use on the way back. These caches were sacred, as men's lives depended on them; but a destitute man finding one was allowed to use it, provided he replenished it as soon as possible. If he were unable to do this himself, someone else would always do it for him.

The man in question found a cache, took what he wanted, threw the rest on the ground so that it was destroyed by animals, and failed either to replenish it or to report it on his return to town. The owner, coming back, probably sooner than was expected, picked up the man's trail and just managed to get in. He found out who had robbed his cache, but waited several days to give the man a chance, and then laid his grievance before the camp.

A Miners' Meeting was called, and the thief acknowledged his guilt. The unwritten law for an offense of his kind was death, but, as everybody in camp would have to put his hand on the rope and help hang him, a compromise was arrived at whereby the man was given his choice of being hanged or taking a hand-sled, without dogs, and leaving for the outside over the ice. Being a white man he chose the latter course. An Indian would have seen the hopelessness of it and chosen to be hanged.

The morning he pulled out everybody came out to bid him good-bye, and ask if there was anything they could do to help him, and wished him the best of luck and shook hands all round. He could be seen for about six miles, till he rounded a bend in the river, the speck getting smaller and smaller as he made his way up. It was early in the season and the river was partly open, making traveling very rough and difficult. What the man's thoughts were God alone knows. Two men coming back down the Stewart River, where they had been prospecting the summer before, met him 375 miles above Circle City, and were able to spare him some dried moose meat. Not knowing anything about the meeting, they tried to get him to go back with them, which of course he refused. Had he got out we should have heard of it from some of the men who came in from Dyea next spring.

GOOD FELLOWS, A LITTLE WILD
Highjinks on the Klondike creeks
from the memoirs of A.E.I. Sola

Arriving at Miller Creek at ten o'clock at night, and walking down the creek, we passed a tent which evidently contained a noisy and drunken crowd. One man came out and told us to come in and take a drink. Of course, we accepted. We were asked every kind of question, and, I suppose for our benefit, one man offered to bet he could shoot another man's leg off. The fellows told him anybody could do that, and he, being the best shot in the camp, said, "Well, by God, see me shoot his ear off!" He did shoot, and took off a patch of hair. The man he shot at was a man very much disliked in the camp, and he evidently thought it best to get away, so he ran out of the tent, and another man, who evidently had a spite against him, picked up a shot-gun, and fired a charge of buckshot at him. The man kept running, and they say he didn't stop until he reached Moose Creek, a distance of thirty miles.

We had to stay and drink, and before morning one man had his head broken with a pick handle, and numerous shots were fired without doing much damage. They are all good fellows—just a little wild at times. I am pleased to be able to state that the man who got his head broken was the seller of the whiskey. A few months later we forbade the sale of whiskey on the creek.

STUD POKER, HOOCH, AND SHOEMAKER BROWN
John Sydney Webb reports the
social chit-chat from Circle City

Circle City is close to the boundary between the British Northwest Territory and Alaska. As I have said, this was the boom town in August, 1896, and the mines about there, and also at Fortymile, were paying well, and saloons and dance-halls, giving signs of mining prosperity, were wide open. The games of faro and stud poker never closed. If the whisky gave out, there was a "Hoochanoo"—a deadly intoxicant distilled from black molasses or sawdust sugar, as the yellowest of the yellow is called, boiled in kerosene oil cans, and distilled on a rude worm.

Shoemaker Brown was another frontier character. He sold his claim on Fortymile for one hundred and twenty dollars and a Winchester rifle. The man who bought it washed out four ounces (sixty-eight dollars) in one day, and wanted to know why Brown sold such a claim as that for so little. "Oh," said Brown, "they's gittin' too thick for me around here." This was in 1887. [At the time there were fewer than 200 people in the whole valley.]

A YUKON BURIAL
Rafting down the great river, Henry Davis
witnesses the end of one man's grand adventure

We saw other boats coming downriver [May 1887]. One had found a dead man on Cassiar Bar and had him with them in the boat. We all got busy and dug a grave after others had made a large fire to thaw the ground. They buried him. We put lots of rocks over the grave and a head piece with the date of drowning. The man was about thirty-five years of age, dark and about five feet nine inches tall and had a fine gold ring on his finger and a gold watch. There were no other markings anyplace, and we buried all his things with him.

Bounty of the North

For hunters and fishermen, Alaska was—and remains today—a paradise. Bleak and unyielding as the land might be, it is rich in the sustenance needed to support an abundance of wildlife—mountain sheep and goats, caribou, Kodiak and polar bears, wolves and wolverines, seal and walrus, geese and ptarmigan, salmon and grayling, moose and foxes and whales, and more. Right: 300 pounds of king salmon taken from the Yukon. Below: bear hunters with a day's yield.

Mountain goats, probably taken as trophies rather than for their meat, shot at the summit of White Pass.

A big grizzly, whose forequarters and paws were boiled or roasted for the table, lies dead before the hunter. His hide was almost certainly tanned and used for wall decoration or warmth in the winter.

50

Above left, a collection of trophies: caribou, sheep, and moose heads; bear skins and mastodon bones. Above, a catch of the Arctic grayling, a sport fish related to the trout. Left, a day's shoot: 78 ptarmigan, the grouse of the North, in summer plumage.

CHAPTER IV

THE WAY OF DEATH

*"Within a distance of fifteen miles we passed more
than two thousand dead horses. It was a cruel land,
a land filled with the record of men's merciless greed."*

The chain of humanity that streamed through the towns and onto the trails was drawn from every cut of life: farm boys, housewives, merchants, miners, carpenters, writers, card sharks, clergymen, doctors, dancehall girls. All were driven by the glowing vision of Klondike gold—gold in abundance, there for the taking.

There were other routes to the gold fields, but nine out of ten stampeders passed through either Skagway or Dyea in the first year of the gold rush.

The trail from Dyea to the summit of the Chilcoot Pass was only 14 miles long, and much of it was fairly easy going. The summit itself was another story. The 35-degree climb had to be made over a mass of immense granite boulders. Those who could afford it hired Indian packers at whatever price they could negotiate. (Two years before, the going rate was a penny a pound all the way to Lake Lindeman, 25 miles away, but during the height of the Rush the price rose to 40 or 50 cents and occasionally much more.)

But for every man who could afford to pay the packers, a score had to shuttle their own outfits from cache to cache, usually on their backs. Before they reached the lakes, these men had traveled hundreds of miles to make the portage.

As the trails steepened, the pace slowed, and many thousands—no one knows the count—turned back, beaten by the harsh terrain.

Rugged as it was, the Chilcoot Pass proved to be a far easier route that summer than the White Pass trail to the south. There, the muck and fallen trees and the jagged rocky outcroppings broke the spirit of strong men and ravaged the pack animals. The trail had been advertised as an all-weather route to the gold fields, suitable even for wagons. But to those who tried to cross that summer, the opening of the White Pass was not a blunder; in the words of Tappan Adney, "it was a crime."

While many animals were lost on other trails, the path that led from Skagway across the pass has found its way, indelibly, into history as the Dead Horse Trail. The tales of suffering and death of man and beast on the lesser trails—the Ashcroft, Valdez, Edmondton, and others—were far worse than those of the White Pass, but the scale and intensity of the experience in the summer and fall of 1897 on White Pass left behind a written record unmatched in the annals of the time.

The difference can only be ascribed to maddening frustration, not that there was any lack of suffering on the trail. The line of gold-seekers was literally stopped by the fearsome conditions and the ineptitude of many of those who, woefully unprepared, clogged the trail. The psychic surge, the madness of the Rush, never manifested itself more dramatically than it did in those soul-trying months on the Dead Horse Trail.

Men left a sad trail of beasts on their way up the stony path from Skagway to White Pass, advertised as the "easy" route across the coastal mountains to the headwaters of the Yukon.

Tent villages like Sheep Camp mushroomed along the routes from the coast to the mountains. Travelers wrote of seeing emaciated, abandoned horses wandering among the shelters, looking for food and water.

This smithy, with his anvil mounted on a stump beside the trail just outside Skagway, bespeaks a general solicitude for animals that was seldom in evidence farther up the trail. Even the cattle here have been provided with nosebag lunches.

The stories are legion. Arthur Walden was one of many who captured the desperate temper of the times:

"The cruelty to animals was something terrible, and strange to say it was not practiced by the so-called rougher element who knew something about handling animals. The worst men were those who in former life were supposed to be of the better class. These men lost their heads completely. I have seen horses that had stuck in the mud abandoned and left to die. They were not even killed, in the rush to hurry on.

"Men left valuable stuff on the horses' backs, not even stopping to unpack it. I saw one man who, after having made his way over the pass and onto the lakes, where it was all smooth going, got mad at his dogs, and after beating them with a club till they were unable to go, began with the leader and pushed them all down a water-hole under the ice. He cut the traces of the last dog, leaving himself absolutely stranded with no means of locomotion. Then he sat down and cried."

John Sydney Webb wrote in the March, 1898, issue of *Century Magazine*:

"Men who landed at Skagway and Dyea thought the worst of their journey over. . . . But the crush of men and animals on both these trails was terrific, and became the worst feature of the problem. . . .

"Horses, over-loaded or worn out, fell in their tracks; and so warped had men become in their struggle to get over the summits toward the fairyland of Klondike that no friendly hand would be lent to help the owner raise the fallen animal.

"But worse than these delays was the destruction of horses which resulted from the frightful condition of the trails. Many animals died from exhaustion; but by far the greater number were destroyed by falling among boulders, the heavy packs nearly always causing broken limbs. Men, starting with horses as a part of their capital, expected to sell them when their own passage was completed. A few succeeded; but the majority lost their horses, and either hired their goods packed over the trails, or were reduced to the necessity of carrying their outfits, bit by bit, on their own backs. It was then that the bitter, desperate, almost unendurable struggle began."

Tappan Adney wrote: "The story of the Skagway Trail will never be written by one person. It is a series of individual experiences, each unique, and there are as many stories as there were men on the trail." Nevertheless, his chronicle of the painful days of the Dead Horse Trail remains the finest of all written by those who were there. These are some of the entries in his diary:

"The trail along the bed of the river is a continuous mire, knee-deep to men and horses. Here and there is a spot where a spring branch crosses the trail, and in such spots, which are twenty to thirty feet across, there is simply no bottom. One such hole is beside our camp. Of the first train of five horses and three men that I saw go by, three horses and two men got in, and with difficulty got out. After that every horse went in to his tail in the mud, but, after desperate struggles, got upon solid ground.

"There are worse holes than this. The trail crosses the river by two more bridges, and then continues on to the summit by a road equally bad

Backpackers near the village of Sheep Camp have conquered the gentle, riverside portion of the trail from Dyea. Ahead of them lies the almost perpendicular ascent to the Chilcoot, an obstacle that persuaded many stampeders it would be better to take the more southerly White Pass, which came to be known as the Dead Horse Trail.

A fallen horse has blocked the muddy path, creating a clot of nervous animals and angry, frustrated men on a slope of the Dyea (Chilcoot) Trail in the summer of '97. Enterprising investors later corduroyed portions of the trail with logs in a futile effort to improve conditions.

but no worse than what we have come over. Past the summit no one at present knows anything of the trail, only that a few persons have got through to the Lakes, including two or three women. The trail is all but impassable, yet some are plugging along. These men, it is predicted, will lose their horses in three or four days. Some say that something must be done; they are willing to put in work, but are not willing unless others help.

"There is no common interest. The selfish are crowding on, every man for himself. Unless something is done soon the trail will be blocked, and then no one will get through.

"'It's no use going *around* these mud-holes,' says one of my fellows. 'The swamp is all alike. The only thing to do is to make corduroy bridges every foot of the way before there will be a trail. I am willing to start tomorrow and bridge the holes above here.'

"No wonder they are discouraged. Rain, rain, all the time—no sunshine up in these mountains; tent pitched in a mudhole, bed made on the stumps of bushes, blankets and everything else wet and muddy. They are trying to dry out a hair-seal cap and some socks before a miserable fire. Even the wood is wet, and will only smoke and smoulder. . . .

"When the sun and rains of summer shall have melted the snow of the Chilcoot, the White Pass trail will be paved with the bones of horses, and the ravens and foxes will have feasted as never until the white man sought a new way across the great mountain. As many horses as have come in alive, just so many will bleach their bones by the pine-trees and in the gulches—for none will go out . . .

"Everyone is discouraged. Dirty and muddy from head to foot, wet and tired, it is no wonder. Men who have been on the trail two weeks are no farther than this. They tell of parties who have reached even the summit, and there, disheartened, have sold out and come back. Some say boats have been carried as far as the summit and there deserted. Others say boats cannot be taken over at all. The trail is lined from Skagway to the 'Foot of the Hill' with boat lumber enough, as one person said, to make a corduroy road the length of the trail.

"Darkness comes on, and I stop for the night with two old prospectors, alongside a granite boulder as big as a house. Against its flat side, and partially protected by it, they have piled their stuff, in the very spot I should have chosen for my bed. They have a small fire going, and their three horses are tied to bushes near by, munching their oats. The men are well provided with blankets, which, when supper is over, are spread out on the ground beside the pile of goods, while a rope is stretched to keep the horses from tramping on the bed. They are both old miners. One, a man of fifty-four, had been in former mining excitements, and he had seen bad trails. Now every sort of opinion has been expressed of this trail; and when a man tells me a trail is bad, that counts for nothing until I know what his idea of bad is. I asked this man what he thought of this trail. Said he:

Two ministers of the Gospel and their wives, having sagely chosen the Chilcoot Trail, pose at their tent-flap at the end of a day's journey.

A party of self-styled "actresses" fords the Taiya River with the assistance of a hired packer. In late summer and autumn, the glacier-fed stream was only knee-deep, although it was 50 feet wide.

At a camp called Pleasant Valley, a covey of larks migrating to the limelights of Dawson strikes provocative poses among the granite boulders. A few miles south of here, the White Pass was by this time virtually impassable, blocked by quagmires of mud, abandoned wagons, and the reeking carcasses of thousands of horses.

"'I have seen worse trails for a short distance—five or six miles or so—but this is the worst I have ever seen for the distance. I went in over the trail when it was first cut through, and I called it then a *good* trail, but I predict that if the rains keep up it will be impossible to get a horse over.'

"It has stopped raining. We lay our coats under our heads for pillows, and our guns under the coats, and turn in. Of course we cannot take off anything but our coats and boots. We wake up in the middle of the night with the rain in our faces. I put my broad hat over my face, turn over, and go to sleep again . . . .

"Discouraged men are coming down from the trail, and they have but one story to tell—of terrible hardship, horses falling right and left, seventeen in one place; the road, if it can be called a road, in terrible condition; not one in ten will get over.

"I talked with one or two determined fellows who came down to the boat, and who had their pack-trains in on the trail. From these I heard a different story. In all I have talked with five or six good men, but they all agree that there is plenty of trouble.

"'The road is good for four or five miles—it is a regular cinch; after that hell begins.'

"Some say that not one in ten will get over. These are the alarmists and the excited ones. A more conservative estimate is that four out of ten will get through. . . .

"The news of the blockade up the pass is having a discouraging effect on the men. They are earnestly discussing the situation. The mounted police and their 74 horses are all right, and my eight horses for the outfit of three, they say, are all right; and everyone says *we* will get over. We have now authentic information from experienced men who are putting their stuff over the trail.

"I asked them what was the cause of the trouble; and from all whose

Fording the Taiya was time-consuming and toe-tingling but relatively easy in summer. In some places, supplies could be ferried across for $5 a ton; elsewhere, log bridges spanned the stream, and stampeders could cross for a small fee.

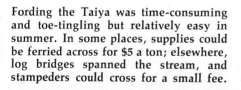

Exhausted by the rigors of the trail, a stampeder naps in a rock-strewn meadow by the Skagway River.

opinion seemed worth any consideration I received but one reply:

"'It is the inexperience of those who are trying to go over.'

"They come from desks and counters; they have never packed, and are not even accustomed to hard labor.

"One party, now within four miles of the top, took in ten horses. They lost four by overloading; then they reduced the weight to 150 pounds per horse. The roads are said to be shelving, and the horses slip and break their legs, and have to be shot. Today two horses mired, fell, and smothered before their clumsy owners could get their heads clear. I have traced the conflicting stories to this:

"This is an army. Those in front are stubbornly fighting their way; they are moving slowly, but they will get over. Behind these are the stragglers, who in turn become the beaten rabble in the rear of the fight. Those up the pass are cool, experienced men, and they are keeping their heads. . . .

Stampeders with Indian guides rest near Stone House, a great outcropping of granite on the upper reaches of the trail to the Chilcoot Pass. Few horses and fewer wagons ever attempted to make it this far up the trail—a blessing, it turned out, for both men and animals.

"The main summit is still six or seven miles distant, and, as it is raining, I put in at the tent of three hardy fellows whom I saw the first day at Skagway, after feed for their two horses. They have been two weeks on the trail. They tell me one of their horses is played out this side of Porcupine.

"'He fell over a bank forty or fifty feet, and was on the trail next day all right, but he must have been hurt inside. He's all shot to hell now.'

"Two of them go back to where they left the horse, and return before night. They have a little fun at first by saying they sold the horse for $125 to a man that came along and wanted to buy.

"'Of course we told him we couldn't recommend the horse, but it was a *horse*!'

"This does not seem unreasonable to us, as any kind of a horse brings whatever one asks for it. At length one of them says:

"'No; but we did offer it to a man for $10. He said he didn't want it. Then we offered to give it to him. He said he didn't want it even at that price. Then we asked him for a gun to shoot it with, and he lent us a revolver and we shot it.'

"I saw one of these men afterwards. He told me they had sold their other horse, as they found it was cheaper to pack their goods on their own backs than to carry horse-feed eight or nine miles from Skagway. A few horses are passing along in the rain. One or two large oxen go by loaded with three hundred and more pounds. It is astonishing what they will carry. And then, when they are there, they can be killed and eaten. Doubtless a horse can be eaten also, but most people have preferences. . . .

"How much of the awful destruction of horses was caused by the trail, and how much by the ignorance and cruelty of the packers, will never be known. One outfit killed thirty-seven horses, and there were others that equalled or surpassed that figure. On the other hand, a Black Hills man . . . packed alone with three horses twenty-four hundred pounds from the 'Foot of the Hill' to Bennett in eighteen days. Each night, no matter how tired, he put his horses' feet in a bucket of water, washed the mud off their legs and dried them, and washed their backs with salt water. He came through when the trail was at its worst, and sold the horses at Bennett for a fair sum. . . .

In a canyon on the Chilcoot Trail, one Klondiker enjoys his pipe while another rustles up a meal of bread and beans. To carry 1000 pounds or more of food and supplies over the Pass, men had to make numerous trips back and forth, leaving the bulk of their possessions in caches along the way.

Confounded by fallen trees, rocks, and bottomless mud holes, horses staggered and fell, often breaking their legs. Most of the beasts were worn-out carriage nags, trolley or dray horses, snatched out of retirement and rushed to Alaska, where they brought extortionate prices.

"Yesterday a horse deliberately walked over the face of Porcupine Hill. Said one of the men who saw it:

"'It looked to me, sir, like suicide. I believe a horse will commit suicide, and this is enough to make them. They don't mind the hills like they do these mud-holes.' He added:

"'I don't know but that I'd rather commit suicide, too, than be driven by some of the men on this trail.'

"Half-way in on the trail goods were actually given away, the unfortunate owners having neither money nor strength to pack them either ahead or back, and the trail being in such terrible condition that outfits not only had no sale value, but could hardly be accepted even as a gift. . . .

"This is what one hears all along the trail, 'We brought a boat with us, but we shed it at Skagway. It cost us $27 in Seattle, and we sold it for $3.50, and were glad to get rid of it!' Yet two Peterboro canoes are on their way to the summit. I saw them myself, as well as a man poking along in the rain with a load of boat lumber on his shoulder so long that the wonder is how it ever got around the turns on Porcupine Ridge.

"Word is brought down the trail that one man, so fortunate as to get

"Thousands of packhorses lie dead along the way," Major J. M. Walsh of the North West Mounted Police wrote in a report to the Canadian Minister of the Interior, "sometimes in bunches under the cliffs . . . sometimes in tangled masses filling the mudholes and providing the only footing for our poor pack animals on the march, a fact we are unaware of until after the miserable wretches turn beneath the hoofs of our cavalcade. The eyeless sockets of the pack animals everywhere account for the myriads of ravens along the road. The inhumanity which this trail has been witness to, the heartbreak and suffering which so many have undergone, cannot be imagined."

Standing dazed among the snags of a creekbed, an abandoned horse waits to die.

over and have his boat built and ready loaded, went to sleep, and in the morning awoke to find the boat stolen and on its way down the Yukon. Surely that is hardship, yet only one out of many. The history of this trail is yet to be written, and will only be heard by the firesides of old men."

Even though Jack London crossed to the Yukon headwaters by the Chilcoot Pass, he saw enough on that trail and heard enough stories about the Dead Horse Trail to have written what is undoubtedly the quintessential summation of the ordeal:

"The horses died like mosquitoes in the first frost, and from Skagway to Bennett they rotted in heaps. They died at the Rocks, they were poisoned at the Summit, and they starved at the Lakes; they fell off the trail, what there was of it, or they went through it; in the river they drowned under their loads, or were smashed to pieces against the boulders; they snapped their legs in the crevices and broke their backs falling backwards with their packs; in the sloughs they sank from sight or smothered in the slime, and they were disembowelled in the bogs where the corduroy logs turned end up in the mud; men shot them, worked them to death, and when they were gone, went back to the beach and bought more. Some did not bother to shoot them, stripping the saddles off and the shoes and leaving them where they fell. Their hearts turned to stone—those which did not break—and they became beasts, the men on Dead Horse Trail."

A light quilt of snow muffles the cruelest episode in the history of the Skagway Valley.

CHAPTER V

BY LAND, SEA, AND MISTAKE

"The worst of the many trails was certainly the Edmonton route. I'm sorry even to think of the poor devils who undertook this journey . . ."

Most of those who reached Dawson in the stampede of 1897–1898 crossed the White and Chilcoot passes. We'll never know the exact number, but the Mounties counted about 28,000. On the other routes, the estimates vary, but perhaps as many as 40,000 were in Dawson and on the creeks before the end of summer 1898. That would include most of the 4500 who were already there before freeze-up in 1897. If so, as many as 7000 must have come by other routes—most of them undoubtedly by riverboat via St. Michael. The figure seems somewhat high, and probably is.

But these numbers do not speak of the thousands who never made it to Dawson on the other so-called trails and the hundreds, only God knows how many, who died in the attempt. Ignorance, stupidity, and greed were at the bottom of the blunders that led many thousands to try the notorious Ashcroft, Valdez, Edmonton, and Stikine trails. American shipping companies and the Canadian railways and the chambers of commerce or their counterparts in all the principal cities of embarkation were guilty of promoting their own interests with slight regard for anything but the money they could extract from the gold-hungry men and women who were driven by dreams.

Before we dwell on the nightmares, it's worth looking briefly at the Dalton Trail and the all-water route, which proved to be the only sane alternatives to the passes.

Jack Dalton, a tough and seasoned frontiersman, forged his trail from Pyramid Harbor, a handful of miles south of Skagway, up the Chilcat River and across the Chilcoot Pass and on across the mountains to Fort Selkirk, the old Hudson's Bay Company outpost that had been burned by hostile Indians in 1852. The route was long, and Dalton charged a toll of $250—which seems exorbitant, but in all likelihood this was imposed only on those who were driving livestock.

Dawson was only 175 easy miles beyond Fort Selkirk, and the route was the most practical for bringing animals in, although that didn't mean it was easy. According to a U.S. Department of Labor Bulletin, 350 head of cattle and 1550 sheep were brought in in 1897, and all who engaged in the traffic made money. However, to repeat, it wasn't a Sunday outing. The bulletin described one man's experience:

"One drover reports that in crossing the Chilcat River he was forced to sit helplessly on his horse and see his herd of eighty-five cattle disappear in the quicksand until in many cases only their heads were visible. Fortunately, the quicksand was shallow, and the cattle were rescued by means of lariats, but in an exhausted condition, which rendered it necessary to allow

Four young optimists from Manitoba pose with their new clothes and camping gear in a woodland of birches on the overland route from Edmonton. Thousands like them started, but only a handful completed the journey to Dawson.

Hudson's Bay Company store, Edmonton, 1897. It was to stimulate sales at outfitting shops like this that chambers of commerce, merchants, and railroads promulgated the cruel lie that the 2398-mile "all-Canadian" trek from Alberta to the Klondike was an "easy" route. Right: A bullock enroute to Dawson hauls his own fodder—and faces the likelihood of death on the grueling expedition.

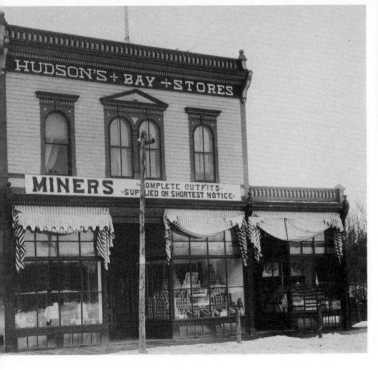

them several days' rest. This drover finally reached Dawson with sixty head, having lost twenty and sold five on the way."

Should anyone question Jack Dalton's reputation as a tough-as-rawhide creature of the West, let him consider a few lines from Edward Keithahn's brief biography:

"Jack Dalton, for whom the famous Dalton Trail was named, and one of Alaska's most colorful characters, was born in the Cherokee Strip in 1855 and died in San Francisco in 1944 at the age of 89. He worked in Oregon as a logger and cowhand until 1882 when he left Oregon to avoid prosecution for 'shooting scrapes.' In 1883 he shipped out of San Francisco for Alaskan waters on a sealing vessel. In 1884 along with fellow crewmen, Dalton spent a year in the Sitka jail when the vessel was seized for fur seal poaching. . . . In 1891 he was engaged by E. J. Glave of *Century* Magazine to accompany him on a private exploration of Chilcoot Pass. Two years later Dalton was tried and acquitted at Juneau for the shooting of Jack McGinnis, a cannery worker."

Some didn't know his reputation, or didn't care, but they quickly learned he was not a man to trifle with. One bunch of drovers who landed at Pyramid Harbor were advised by local people to make the necessary arrangements with Dalton, but as Arthur Treadwell Walden related:

"Their reply was that this was a free country and they guessed they would travel that trail whether he was willing or not.

"Dalton heard of this. The morning they pulled out with their cattle he appeared, mounted, with his six-shooter and rifle, and calmly informed them that he was going along with them the entire journey. Furthermore, he announced, they would be allowed to use the trail where it went through canyons or across fords, where there was no other place to pass; but anywhere else, if man or beast stepped onto that trail he would kill him. . . . Dalton rode the entire distance with them, traveling on his own trail and seeing that they kept off. Where it joined the Yukon he turned around and rode back to the coast."

The remaining sane way to get to Dawson, as history proved, was by the all-water route: steamship to St. Michael near the mouth of the Yukon, there transfer to a river steamboat. A handful of those who tried to reach Dawson before the Yukon froze made it, but most were scattered along the river, locked in the ice until the spring breakup. It was a rich man's route, and for most of those without extensive capital and know-how, it was a futile excursion.

The most humorous story (humorous in the sense that nobody died) in this part of the adventure is that of the ill-fated voyage of the Seattle and

Large corrals at river's-edge hold herds of cattle and saddle horses destined for the Yukon by way of Jack Dalton's trail, a toll road through the Alaskan wilderness.

Cattle grazing along the Dalton Trail had a better chance of reaching the gold fields than did human beings on other routes—but drovers paid a $250 toll for the privilege of following Dalton's route.

An armed camp on the Dalton Trail. Crude canvas tents and heavy bundles of supplies surround men collapsed in exhaustion on the damp ground.

Yukon Trading Company under the command of C. D. Wood. Wood, then mayor of Seattle and in San Francisco at the time the *Excelsior* arrived with the news, immediately wired his resignation and set about raising $150,000, which he did in short order. His party was ready to sail north a scant month after his resignation, but the good ex-mayor almost didn't join them. It seems that he had overloaded the vessel and attempted to leave behind some 50 tons of gear belonging to his fellow sojourners. In turn, some of them threatened to lynch him on the dock. But reason returned, the gear was loaded, and they sailed.

Only when they arrived in St. Michael did they learn that they would have to construct their own riverboat. Another terrible confrontation, but build the boat they did.

The river froze when they were many hundreds of miles from Dawson and they set up a camp dubbed "Suckerville." Wood so despaired of the carping that he left on foot for St. Michael—and made it. It was a sorry and dispirited group that finally reached Dawson in the early summer, and most of the party turned right around and went home—nine months after they had first departed.

* * *

By no measure was the fate of the company a laughing matter, but the travails and tragedies of those who took the cursed overland trails—the Ashcroft, Edmonton, Valdez, Stikine—made the troubles of the *Humboldt* venturers seem like a quilting bee.

Each trail was a blunder, and it is difficult for us today to believe that thousands could have gambled their lives and fortunes, small as the latter might have been, on what anyone could easily discern as, at best, sheer folly. Nor is this merely hindsight. Knowledgeable men of the time knew as

A bearded traveler shows off his dog team on Dalton Trail while a horse-drawn sleigh waits in the background. Photographs of "alternate" trails are rare because few stampeders finished the journey.

well as we do now. Of the all-Canadian routes, woodswise Tappan Adney, himself a Canadian, had this to say about the trails that led from Edmonton:

"The Edmonton route is by courtesy designated a 'trail.' The insane desire of Canada to find an all-Canadian route to her new possessions has led to the suggestion as possible routes those used by the Hudson's Bay Company to reach the Yukon. From Edmonton a wagon-road of 96 miles to Athabasca Landing; thence by small boat, 430 miles, to Lake Athabasca; thence down Slave River, across Great Slave Lake, and down the Mackenzie River, 1376 miles, to the neighborhood of Fort McPherson, near the mouth of the Mackenzie; thence up Rat River and over an all-water connection at McDougall's Pass into the Porcupine; and thence down the Porcupine to the Yukon, 496 miles—a total distance from Edmonton of 2398 miles (Mr. William Ogilvie's figures). There the would-be Klondiker, 303 miles below Dawson and against a hard current, is practically farther away from his destination than if at Dyea or Skagway.

"The other 'route' from Edmonton ascends the Athabasca River to Little Slave Lake; thence by portage to Peace River; ascends that river to a point towards its source; thence overland by a ramification of 'routes' to the Liard; up that river and thence by another portage to the head of the Pelly, and down that river to Fort Selkirk; an exceedingly difficult trail, abandoned forty years ago by the company that first discovered its existence.

"The above briefly describes the 'trails' by which the Canadians, the merchants of Edmonton, and the Canadian Pacific Railway propose to start human beings for the Yukon. It has been termed 'the Athabasca back-door route.' By the same token there are as many other 'routes' to the Yukon as there are water-ways in the northwest of Canada between Montreal and the Rocky Mountains."

Another Canadian, Nevill A. D. Armstrong, added his comments on the trail:

"The worst of the many trails was certainly the Edmonton route. I'm sorry even to think of the poor devils who undertook this journey— Edmonton, Great Slave Lake, Mackenzie River (in scows or boats for hundreds of miles), Fort Simpson, Fort McPherson on the Peel River, up the Rat River (where it was necessary to drag the boats against swift water and rock), then overland many weary miles to the head waters of the Porcupine River, inside the Arctic Circle, where travellers had to relay supplies on their backs, cut a trail and drag boats on wooden rollers to a further river 200 miles down, where stood Fort Yukon. Here they got a small steamer for the final 120 miles to Dawson.

"Look at a map and let your imagination picture a greenhorn doing this tremendous journey. Yet they went in thousands, because this route was extensively advertised.

"I personally knew four Englishmen who dropped their pens in London offices and made this particular trip. Knowing nothing of the conditions out there, they took from England picks, shovels and other essentials (mostly unsuitable), even telegraphing to Winnipeg to have four bales of hay reserved for them! What a pity one of them did not keep a diary; it would have been priceless among souvenirs of the Klondike stampede.

"It may be stated briefly that it took the party eight months to reach Fort McPherson, during which time they had dropped many thousands of pounds of their supplies. Here winter overtook them, so they built a cabin and remained until the following year. It says something for their spirit that they refused to be beaten and kept slogging on for another five months, when they entered Dawson—thus reaching it in 1899, having left London in November of '97!"

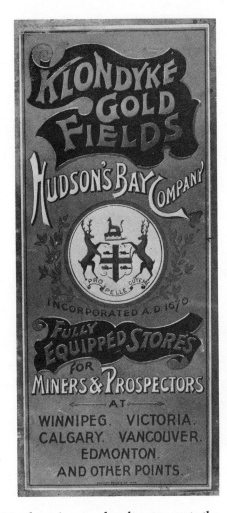

Merchants' posters lured customers to the interminable Edmonton Route. David B. Wharton, in his fine history of the Alaska gold rush, observes: "It would seem that only the most benighted or obstinate Canadian wishing to avoid American customs would consider such a route, and yet many did."

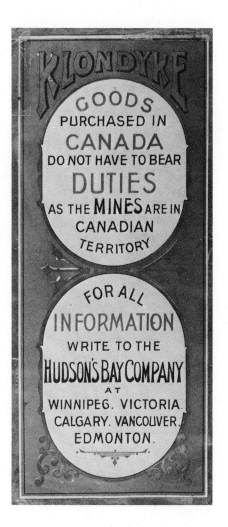

While small boys perch on a fence to watch, drovers in Edmonton pack horses for the 2400-mile jaunt to gold and glory. Admittedly, it was a romantic spectacle. The trouble was, many turned back after the first 96 miles of the "prairie" journey.

In the U.S. Department of Labor Bulletin 19, the author wrote the story of the first successful voyagers to reach the Yukon by the infamous Edmonton route:

"On June 2, two young men arrived at Fort Yukon from Edmonton. They started from that place on August 9 of last year, passing down the Athabasca, Slave, and Mackenzie rivers, and arrived at the mouth of Arctic Red River September 30. They were forced to discontinue their journey by boat at this point by the heavy run of ice in the Mackenzie, and made the portage of 100 miles to La Pierre House, where they spent the winter, their only companions being a few half-starved Porcupine Indians. It required two months of hard labor to sled their outfit across the portage.

"They left La Pierre House on May 30, and the next day, while shooting the rapids at the lower end of the Upper Ramparts of the Porcupine, their boat was capsized and swept away with the remnant of their outfit, and they were left struggling in the ice-cold water. In an exhausted condition they succeeded in reaching an exposed rock in midstream, to which they clung for twenty-four hours, when they were rescued by two prospectors who were descending the river and taken to Fort Yukon, penniless and without a change of clothing. They reported that they passed 800 men last fall en route from Edmonton to the Klondike, but up to June 27 they were the only ones of this large number who had reached Fort Yukon. Here they were greatly surprised to learn that they were still as far from the Klondike, so far as the expense of travel and time are concerned, as they would have been at Dyea or Skagway."

Of the 1500 (some said 2000) who left Edmonton, somewhere between five and 30 made it by 1898, and by 1899, 30 to 200 finally arrived. The numbers depend on which source you accept, but all were at best guesses, and the lower figures are probably closest to the truth. By any estimate, it was, in sum, an unmitigated tragedy. Seventy known deaths were recorded.

* * *

Three to four thousand Americans attempted to reach the gold fields by way of Valdez on the mistaken belief that by taking an "All-American" route they might somehow circumvent the need to pay Canadian customs, but so few made it the point was moot. Others hoped to find gold in Alaska on the way. Altogether, the entourage was as misbegotten a bunch as any who tried the other impossible trails.

The poor devils, lured by advertisements spread by shipping companies and rumors of a secret trail, descended on the beach at Valdez to face an ordeal none could have imagined. From the beach they dragged their massive outfits to the glaciers, and there the struggle began.

The route as conceived was simple: cross the massive Valdez Glacier to Klutina Lake and River, thence to the Copper River and over the Mentasta Pass from whose heights the valley of the Tanana could be surveyed and beyond which lay the valley of the Fortymile River, whose waters would then carry them to the Yukon—from which point it was an easy 55 miles upstream to Dawson and riches. Others planned to descend the Tanana to the Yukon, which if they had gotten that far would have been the better choice.

It was not to be. Perhaps 15 or 20 of those who left Valdez made it all the way, and even this is conjectural.

Few if any had any sense of what they were doing or where they were going. This observation is not made from the distance of years, but from an official U.S. report titled *Compilation of Narratives of Explorations in Alaska* published in 1900: "They had neither the slightest idea regarding the topographical features of the country nor any definite plan of campaign as to their future movements. . . . As to how they should supply themselves

67

with the two most necessary articles for camping, wood and water, they were utterly ignorant."

The story is almost too cruel to relate. Snow blindness, falling out among partners, ravages of weather, impossible geographical conditions, smashed boats, treacherous crevasses in the glacier, avalanches, physical and mental collapse took a fearful toll. As the winter drew to an end, there were men and women spread all along the so-called trail, most of them not only destitute but utterly bereft of hope. Scurvy and frostbite, if not starvation, and death by freezing shattered the ranks. And those who turned back when there was no way to go farther in that winter of 1897–1898 were found huddled on the beach at Valdez, ten to 20 men to the cabin, barely able to move.

The ravages of scurvy are something we rarely see in the Western world today, but it was a killer: general weariness, sore joints, bleeding from the mucous membrane, swollen gums, teeth loosened to the point they literally fell out of their sockets, mottled flesh—eventually death. It was caused, as the British Navy had long before known, by a lack of vitamin C, although it wasn't then called by that name. The term *Limey*, which has come to be a patronizing term for an Englishman, comes from their longstanding practice of issuing lime juice, rich in vitamin C, to sailors on long voyages.

But there was no lime juice in Valdez that winter. There was almost nothing more than the care given by the U.S. Army Quartermaster's Agent, Charles Brown, to the stricken who had struggled back, beaten by the glacier and the almost impassable lands that lay beyond. When April, 1898, came, Army Captain W. R. Abercrombie arrived in Valdez, and he was appalled. His account of the debacle was to tell of the grim events.

Brown greeted Abercrombie with these words: "My God, Captain, it has been clear hell! I tell you the early days in Montana were not a marker to what I've gone through this winter! It was awful!"

Abercrombie estimated that of those who were still living at Valdez, and there was a large cemetery to speak for the dead, perhaps 70 percent were deranged in one degree or another. Stories of a killer "glacial demon" were told, and were widely believed.

In the stinking cabins, the frostbitten and scurvy-ridden survivors who had made it back from the trail were given succor by the Army, and an expedition was sent in to relieve those some five hundred who had chosen to winter on the trail rather than yield their pride and return to the rotting mess at Valdez.

Dwarfed by the vast sweep of the Yukon, a small steamer makes its way downriver. Travelers over the Edmonton Route reached the river more than 300 miles downstream of Dawson, where the gold was. Right: A cavalcade of sleds climbs switchbacks on the horrendous Valdez Trail, perhaps the most disastrous of all paths north.

A store on the trail to the Klondike offered peeled logs, a local commodity of many uses: to corduroy roads, to float rafts, to roll boats on portage—and to build more stores.

No one who embarked from Valdez is known to have brought a penny's worth of gold back from the Klondike.

*   *   *

Of all the tales that have been written on the aberrations of man in the Klondike Rush, one of the most appalling was that told by Arthur Dietz, a YMCA physical education director from New York. In his book *Mad Rush for Gold in the Frozen North* he told the story of the ultimate insanity of the entire stampede. Dietz, then a seemingly rational man, advertised in early 1898 for partners to join him in a novel expedition that was to take them across Alaska's largest glacier, the Malaspina, which lies north of Yukutak Bay at the upper end of southeastern Alaska.

He was careful in choosing his partners. From the 40 or more applicants, he chose 17 from widely varied backgrounds. The planning and studying the group did was admirable, but nothing they bought for the journey was based on anything more than ill-educated guesses.

Their story was an echo of the sufferings on the Valdez Trail. The 18

Travelers peer over the edge of a deep crevasse in the treacherous Valdez Glacier. This massive flow of ice was only one of the hazards of a route plagued by scurvy, snowblindness, storms, and starvation.

Crossing the Valdez Glacier, men and horses court disaster on a route that killed many, drove others mad, and did not lead a single adventurer to his dream of gold.

69

On the icy shores of the Athabasca River, a group styling themselves the Clark Party boards a wooden barge equipped with a steam-driven stern paddle. From here to the Klondike it's a mere 2300 miles, mostly downhill.

Another party of Canadian stampeders, this headed by a Captain Purdy, takes off with a horse-drawn sledge in the style of the plains Indians.

men started out with about 10 tons of supplies and equipment which they had either to pack on their backs or, when conditions were suitable, on sleds—each pulled by four dogs. It took them almost seven weeks to cross the glacier, but not until the elements had taken a fearful toll: all suffered the agony of snow blindness, and three men with their sleds and dogs disappeared forever into crevasses. One, Dietz's brother-in-law, was the company's physician, and with him went all the medical supplies.

During the summer as they struggled on another man died mysteriously, and though they prospected for gold as they went, they found nothing. Despair grew. As winter approached they built a cabin, and three of the party left to see if they could find an Indian village for help. They were swallowed up by the wilderness, never to be found.

The remaining eleven spent the winter in the cabin, and when spring came the survivors sank a shaft in the wild hope of finding gold, but it proved worthless. Another man died of scurvy and three more were lost beneath an avalanche. It was a miracle that any of them survived.

In their flight back to the coast as the first snows fell, the seven had the good fortune to meet Indians who sold them new sealskin coats and footwear. They stumbled on, wracked and broken, half-blind and insane, driven only by the unquenchable will to survive. And for the second time in a year, they attacked the brutal Malaspina Glacier.

Abandoning everything they had except their sleeping bags, dogs, and their dwindling food supply (flour and beans and smoked fish the Indians had given them), they fought their way in madness across the cruel ice mass. For six weeks they were snowbound by fierce storms. Their food gave out and they survived by killing the dogs and eating the raw flesh. But struggle on they did.

They ultimately made it to the coast, and by sheer chance the crew of the Revenue Service cutter *Wolcott* saw their fires and sent a party ashore to investigate. There they found seven bodies, four alive, in sleeping bags.

Dietz, one of the four survivors, recounted that he awoke in the Sitka hospital wondering how he had gotten there. His eyesight and that of one of the others were permanently impaired. The other two were blinded for life.

The ultimate irony of the story came when the four arrived broke and broken in Seattle. There the *Times* reported that the party had brought with them $500,000 in raw gold.

* * *

The Stikine and Ashcroft trails, which merged at Glenora in British Columbia, became the Teslin Trail and together or separately all were disastrous.

The Ashcroft began at the railhead of the town of that name 125 miles northeast of Vancouver, 800 miles from Glenora, or the neighboring town of Telegraph Creek on the Stikine River.

The Stikine Trail began at Fort Wrangell, called by Colonel Sam Steele of the NWMP "a mean and squalid spot, with the usual number of gambling dens and other low dives . . .," and followed the Stikine River, which in summer was navigable but in winter a frozen monster. It was not the first time the trail had been used. Fort Wrangell was the entry in the mid-1870s for a couple of thousand miners and adventurers who made their way to the Cassiar mining district.

It all looked very good on paper, and the merchants of Victoria and Vancouver made the most of it. Five thousand took the Stikine Trail and 1500 set out on the Ashcroft. The trials that lay ahead for every man, woman, and child who set forth on them could simply not have been imagined. Suffering lay ahead for all, and death by drowning, murder, suicide, disease, and exposure for many.

In winter the Stikine froze over, but the temperature rarely dropped low enough to provide a firm surface for the men and beasts who labored up its tortured course. The slush made the going so bad during the winter that fully half of them turned back before they reached Glenora. As spring came the ice became so treacherous that several men broke through and drowned.

Those who made it to Glenora and Telegraph Creek met the hardy survivors of the Ashcroft Trail, which was in fact no trail at all. Beginning at Ashcroft, the trail followed the remains of the wagon road and trail that had been laid out in the 1860s to serve the Fraser River and Cariboo gold fields. What was left in 1898 was at least recognizable, and the countryside was very pleasant. But beyond that, there was no trail save for the remains of the long-abandoned Western Union telegraph attempt to link America and Europe by wire (the successful laying of the Atlantic cable ended the project). Although there were visible remains of the expedition, the line was run up-and downhill without regard to sensible trail-making. It was virtually unusable. And much of the country it crossed was an abomination.

The 1500 who started out brought with them 3000 pack animals, almost all of them horses. Some two or three hundred of those who set out made it to Telegraph Creek or Glenora. Many who turned back did so because they saw their animals die or knew they would had they attempted to continue on.

Hamlin Garland, an American writer and veteran of the frontier, was one who made it through. Garland and his partner Burton brought all but one of their horses through with them. Garland's book *The Trail of the Goldseekers* paints a picture of the hostile nature of hundreds of miles of the so-called trail beyond Quesnel at the end of the old wagon road. The boomers had called the Ashcroft the "Prairie Route"—a sheer fantasy. The Skeena Valley and Mountain country was and still is sheer hell. These extracts from his book were built on the diary Garland kept on the way:

"This world grew oppressive with its unbroken clear greens, its dripping branches, its rotting trees; its snake-like roots half buried in the earth . . . . At last we came into upper heights where no blade of grass grew, and we pushed on desperately, on and on, hour after hour. We began to suffer with the horses, being hungry and cold ourselves. We plunged into bottomless mudholes, slid down slippery slopes of slate, and leaped innumerable fallen logs of fir . . .

"We pushed on with necessary cruelty, forcing the tired horses to their utmost, searching every ravine and every slope for feed; but only ferns and strange green poisonous plants could be seen . . .

"The horses again grew hungry and weak, and it was necessary to use great care in crossing the streams. We were lame and sore with the toil of the day, and what was more depressing found ourselves once more upon the banks of the Skeena, where only an occasional bunch of bluejoint could be found. The constant strain of watching the horses and guiding them through the mud began to tell on us both . . . . We had set ourselves grimly to the task of bringing our horses through alive. We no longer rode, we toiled in silence, leading our saddle-horses on which we had packed a part

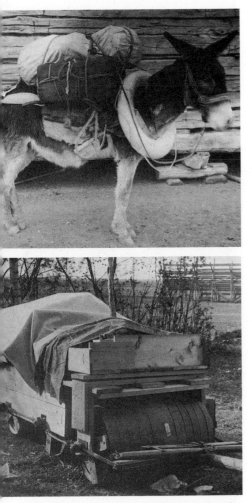

Conveyances leaving Edmonton for the Klondike: A jackass, labeled with postcard wit, "The Prospector's Friend," and a strange, hand-made supply cart mounted on wooden barrels. It seems unlikely that either survived the trip to Dawson.

The B. L. Robinson Party, leaving Edmonton in the winter of '98, carried heavy sledges of baled hay. Such groups were well-prepared to cross the plains but could not transit the rivers, lakes, and mountain ranges that lay beyond.

of our outfit to relieve the sick and starving packhorses . . .

"A part of the time that evening we spent in picking the thorns of devil's-club out of our hands. This strange plant I had not seen before, and do not care to see it again. In plunging through the mudholes we spasmodically clutched these spiny things . . .

"Again we plunged down into the cold green forest, following a stream whose current ran to the northeast. This brought us once again to the bank of the dreaded Skeena. The trail was punishing, and the horses plunged and lunged all day through the mud, over logs, stones, and roots . . .

"The descent of this mountain's side was by all odds the most terrible piece of trail we had yet found. It led down the north slope, and was oozy and slippery with the melting show. It dropped in short zigzags down through a grove of tangled, gnarled, and savage cedars and pines, whose roots were like iron and filled with spurs that were sharp as chisels. The horses, sliding upon their haunches and unable to turn themselves in the mud, crashed into the tangled pines and were in danger of being torn to pieces. For more than an hour we slid and slewed through this horrible jungle of savage trees, and when we came out below we had two horses badly snagged in the feet. . . ."

When Garland and Burton reached the Stikine watershed, the country changed dramatically, and they "descended again to the aspens and clumps of wild roses." The way was still difficult and Glenora was days away, but the land was beautiful.

Along this last stretch, Garland found messages on the white surfaces of blazed trees:

"Some of them were profane assaults upon the road-gang. Others were pathetic inquiries: 'Where in hell are we?'—'How is this for a prairie route?'—'What river is this, anyhow?'"

Garland decided to forsake the Teslin Trail—he had seen his horses suffer too much and he knew the trail was worthless. It was summer, so the trip downstream to Fort Wrangell was simple. But before he left his camp, a tragic moment was to take the joy from his successful journey:

"Among the first of those who met us on our arrival was a German, who was watching some horses and some supplies in a big tent close by the river bank. While pitching my tent on that first day he came over to see me, and after a few words of greeting said quietly, but with feeling, 'I am glad you've come, it was so lonesome here.' We were very busy, but I think we were reasonably kind to him in the days that followed. He often came over of an evening and stood about the fire, and although I did not seek to entertain him, I am glad to say I answered him civilly; Burton was even social.

"I recall these things with a certain degree of feeling, because not less than a week later this poor fellow was discovered by one of our company swinging from the crosstree of the tent, a ghastly corpse. . . .

"In his pocket the coroner found a letter wherein he had written, 'Bury me right here where I failed, here on the bank of the river.' It contained also a message to his wife and children in the States. There were tragic splashes of red on the trail, murder, and violent death by animals and by swift waters. Now here at the end of the trail was a suicide."

From the Stikine, there were those who drove on to Lake Teslin despite all that they had heard. Obsession was the master of reason. Only a few hundred were to reach Dawson, and none of the animals they took with them survived the struggle. An article in the first issue of *Alaska Magazine* tells of the trials of the Teslin route:

"It was 166 miles from Glenora to Lake Teslin—166 miles of solid struggle. Two old men, both over seventy, toiled over it pushing a

A Model Medicine Chest.

We would advise all persons who contemplate going to the Klondyke region to include in their outfits a medicine chest containing the following drugs, the cost of which should be within $10:

Quinine pills	50
Compound cathartic pills	50
Acetanilid tablets	3 dozen
Chlorate potash	1 box
Mustard plasters	6
Belladonna plasters	6
Carbolic salve	4 ounces
Chloroform liniment	8 ounces
Witch hazel	1 pint
Essence ginger	4 ounces
Paregoric	4 ounces
Laudanum	1 ounce
Borax	4 ounces
Tincture iodine	1 ounce
Spirits of nitre	2 ounces
Tincture of iron	1 ounce
Cough mixture	8 ounces
Toothache drops	1 bottle
Vaseline	1 bottle
Iodoform	2 drams
Lint	2 yards
Assorted bandages	½ dozen
Rubber adhesive plasters	2 feet
Absorbent cotton	4 ounces

Monsell's salts for hemorrhages—In quantities in accordance with the person's liability to attacks of the trouble.

wheelbarrow. They relayed their outfit, making four or five trips a day, and finding themselves but one mile nearer their destination at night. After all their endurance one died at Lake Teslin of scurvy, but the other old man reached the land of promise. Let us hope it was to him also a land of fulfillment.

"It may seem incredible, but it is a fact, that one man crossed the pass with a wooden leg. A Polar bear ate off one leg at St. Lawrence Island, Bering sea. Another went 'in' with two little boys, the younger but eight years. They packed in a 1500-pound outfit by relay.

"Some did their own transporting upon their aching backs. There were two and four-wheeled carts, push carts, wheelbarrows, dogs, mules, oxen, horses: in fact, everything that could roll or walk. It was odd to see what men started with and what they ended with. Many 'tenderfeet' came armed to the teeth, to the unconcealed amusement of the old-timers. It was not long before they shed their rifles, their revolvers, and even their knives. For every ounce counts on a mountain trail, especially if one happens to sink to his thighs in black, ill-smelling mud at every step, and if hordes of rapacious mosquitoes, fearing no man, though he be a walking armory, infest the way. . . .

"There are few things more pathetic than to see a faithful, willing, long-suffering horse die, yet scattered along those trails into the land of cold and gold lie thousands of them. On the Teslin trail alone, 2,000 pack animals and scores of oxen are rotting. 'It used to make my heart ache,' said one prospector to me, 'to see our poor animals die. We would notice one covered with cold perspiration, his patient, long-suffering eyes saying plainly, *I'm sorry: I've done my best: but don't be angry: I can go no farther.* Then we'd take off the pack and the poor beast would fall over, take the first rest he had had in weeks, and just naturally die. Our party lost thirty horses and mules that way. Every time we corralled the poor things, we would find from one to three or four dead.'"

These trails collectively probably killed as many animals as the Dead Horse trail did, perhaps more, but the tragedy has largely been buried in memory. Why? I think it is because there were so few who reached the end of the trail, and that among their numbers there were no photographers and very few diarists, Garland being the conspicuous exception. This of course is true of the other trails of madness.

One other Canadian, Stratford Tollemache, however, wrote of his incredible 1200-mile trip from Fort Wrangell to Dawson via the Stikine and Teslin trails. His small party set out on the slushy Stikine River with a full outfit on sleds pulled by 12 dogs. By the time they reached the Yukon headwaters, they had abandoned most of the gear and had killed ten of the dogs one by one to feed the survivors so they could get that far. Tollemache was the author of the blandest remark I have ever seen written by any survivor of any of the death-trap routes. He stated that the trail had been "considerably advertised as being the best, although it turned out to be about the worst."

Walter Hamilton, who in 1967 published his *Yukon Story*, reminiscences going back almost 70 years to his successful traverse of the brutal Ashcroft–Teslin Trail, recalled a verse written on one of the blazed trees on the route, the last line of which expressed for him "the spirit of those who completed the trails of '98 to the Klondike, or died in the attempt." The lines have a lonely and wistful ring tempered by a touch of humor:

> There is a land of pure delight,
> Where grass grows belly high,
> Where horses don't sink out of sight,
> We'll reach it by-and-by.

Typical of the absurd promotion of the all-Canadian routes is this 1897 photograph, captioned: "Lady to go by Edmonton route to Klondike." That the lady never got as far as her target is almost certain; that thousands of other men and women followed her example is a tragic fact of history.

Fort Smith, now the administrative center of Canada's Northwest Territories, was a major stop on the Edmonton-Dawson itinerary. This is how it looked in 1901.

CHAPTER VI

WINTER ON WHITE PASS

"We are beginning to feel rather done up by hard work and exposure. . . . So far I have traveled 270 miles to move our outfit over 35 miles of trail . . ."

Teams of packers, organized into such outfits as the Red Line Transportation Company, carried most of the 1897 adventurers and their supplies over White Pass to Lake Bennett. Gold rush commodities visible here include wheelbarrows, bedding, and crates of dynamite.

WITH THE SNOWS OF WINTER, the cruel rocks and broken carcasses of summer were covered, and the stench of rotting carrion no longer choked the air. But the Dead Horse Trail remained punishing. The exhausting climb, the shortage of feed, chronic abuse, and overloading continued to take a heavy toll of the pack animals. They were sacrificed so that 5000 men and women in that first year could make their way across the pass to the headwaters of the Yukon. By the end of winter in '98, 3000 animals had perished on the Dead Horse Trail.

After the first snows had fallen, the Mounties guarding the Canadian border had established and were enforcing a new rule: Every man headed for the Yukon had to carry food and supplies sufficient to last a year. It meant that, by one means or another, each stampeder had to pack about a ton of food and gear over the tortuous trails, more than half of it food alone.

The trail was choked all through the winter, and the insensate mood that had characterized the summer chaos continued to prevail. Few of the sojourners were really prepared for the arduous trek; they generally lacked experience, and many were not equipped physically or emotionally to see the ordeal through. Stories of the brutalization of animals and the lack of concern for others abound. The story of the man who built a fire under a yoke of oxen, too tired to move further, killing them in the process, has been told many times, as has been the tale of the man who, in utter frustration and rage, beat his dogs and then drowned them under the ice, only moments later to collapse, sobbing in remorse. *On to the Klondike!* was the single burning drive.

Those few who were experienced in living in the wilderness and who knew how to handle animals had what might be called an easy time. But "easy" is a relative term. In his book *My Adventures in the Klondike and Alaska*, published privately in 1960, Walter Starr told of the toils he and his partners went through to get to Lake Bennett.

Starr was 20 years old, a graduate of the University of California, a young man of pioneer stock whose family fortunes and expected future were wrecked following the Panic of '93 when the world price for wheat collapsed. In 1897 he was the possessor of $1,000—a legacy from an uncle—and nothing more save intelligence and good health. His college summers had been spent on long camping trips in the High Sierra, and in his words ". . . I knew how to take care of myself and incidentally how to make camp and cook camp food."

Although the onset of winter vastly improved travel conditions along the nauseating Dead Horse Trail, snow storms at the summit of White Pass tested the stamina of men and animals.

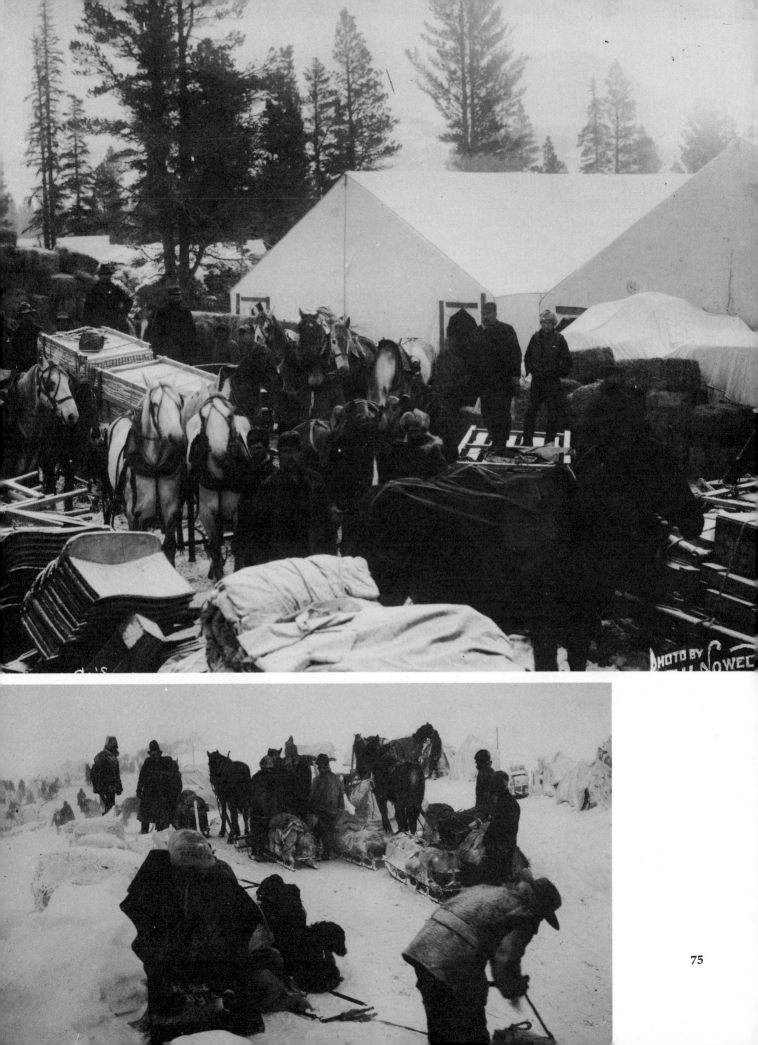

With a mule, three sleds, and half-a-dozen dogs, this prosperous party was unusually well prepared to challenge the 600-mile route from Skagway to the Klondike.

Arriving at Skagway late in February, 1898, he and his two partners, to whom he refers in his diary as Billy and Gil, scouted around and decided to buy two mules and four sleds and tackle the Dead Horse Trail. In his laconic style, Starr recorded the day-to-day demands of the frozen route:

"*March 4* Had trouble hooking up my mule who ran away and had to be caught and brought back. Trail good for seven miles to Sears Canyon. Left one sled here and pulled the other up the narrow and steep canyon. Got stalled and had to lighten load. We all finally landed about nine miles out with part of our loads cached along two miles of the canyon. The trail is a crowded line of sleds pulled by men and all kinds of animals, moving in both directions, which results in many blockades.

"*March 5* We returned to Skagway and made two trips to the foot of the rough canyon, getting all our outfit to our camp there. A man shot himself on the trail. The steamer *Whitelaw* burned in Skagway Harbor.

"*March 6* One mule got kicked during the night, cutting a deep gash in its leg. Billy and I drove back to town to have the wound dressed and made our departure from Skagway with a load of feed for the mules.

"*March 7* Left camp early with 600 pounds on two sleds to each mule. Although trail was rough we made the fifteen miles to the first summit by 3 P.M. where it was snowing. We set up poles in the snow by cutting small trees to mark our cache as it was sure to be buried. Got down to camp by dark after a 30-mile round trip. A man named Beane was murdered and robbed on the trail about an hour after we passed his camp.

"*March 8* Gil and I took two loads about four miles up the canyon while Billy fixed sleds and camp. A thaw made sledding difficult.

"*March 9* Took a load up to the cache in the canyon and moved camp up there in the afternoon, but did not get camp arranged til midnight.

"*March 10* I made the trip of 11 miles to Skagway and brought back a load of feed. Trail becoming very bad.

Photographer Lloyd V. Winter (center) set his camera on a snow bank to record the easeful passage he made with two Indian guides and a couple of heavy sleds over a crude log bridge on an unnamed stream in the valley of the Skagway.

"*March 11* Billy and Gil took up a load to our cache at the summit. I broke through the ice over a shallow lake a couple of miles above camp with two sleds and had to return to camp for dry clothes.

"*March 12* Hauled eleven hundred pounds over the summit and cached at customs house (Canadian). Trail down good but steep.

"*March 13* Took a load to foot of 'Last Hill' and returned to camp. Bought two heavy sleds for ten dollars.

"*March 14* Moved camp and last load to foot of 'Last Hill.' Found no place to camp so took up our residence at the Ford Hotel, a tent.

"*March 15* Made two trips over the pass to Customs House. The only excitement was the frequent rolling of oxen and sleds off the sloping, frozen trail down the mountain side.

"*March 16* Made two trips from the summit and passed our outfit through customs. No duty because all Canadian.

"*March 17* Hauled about 3,000 pounds down Summit Lake six miles to the head of a canyon where we cached most of it and continued on eight miles more to make camp at Log Cabin, the first good place to camp.

A pack horse, fallen through a hole in the ice, wallows in freezing water in Blue Canyon as two packers gingerly try to lead him to safety. Sudden thaws made ice-covered lakes and streams into death-traps for animals and men.

Traffic jams of dogs and sleds, men, and pack animals sometimes blocked the trail up Porcupine Hill, midway between Skagway and the Canadian border. The only rational action, as demonstrated by the man in the center, was to light one's pipe and wait out the blockade.

The trail through Cutoff Canyon, only three and a half miles from the summit of White Pass, was churned to a thick brown porridge of snow and mud by the hooves, boots, and sled runners of a ceaseless caravan pushing toward the lakes.

"*March 18* Returned to cache at the canyon but got caught in a blizzard. I brought back a load but had a difficult time finding the way in the blinding snow and obliterated trail. Billy and Gil returned to camp without a load. To end a bad day a mule broke loose and kicked a hole in our tent.

"*March 19* Went back to the cache below the summit, fifteen miles, and moved the remainder of our outfit to the canyon, bringing two sleds through to camp. Got caught in the dark and had a rough time, not getting to camp until 11 P.M. We are beginning to feel rather done up by hard work and exposure. Temperature ranges from 15° below to 10° above zero. So far I have traveled 270 miles to move our outfit over 35 miles of trail. Billy and Gil have done about the same.

"*March 20* We observed the Sabbath by resting. Billy repaired sleds and harness while I cooked up a stock of beans and bread.

"*March 21* We made a trip to the canyon but got caught in another blizzard and brought back two light loads. The snow was carried by a high wind and ice formed in the eyes due to the low temperature. Both we and our mules found great difficult in seeing. It was a great relief to get back to camp. The thermometer registered 40° below zero. My right hand, used to guide my mule, was partially frozen.

"*March 22* The storm continued and held us in camp. I was not sorry since a bad cold made me miserable.

"*March 23* I stayed in camp on account of my cold and a sore hand while Bill and Gil went up to the canyon to get what remained of our outfit.

"*March 24* I went to Lake Bennett, twenty miles, with about 600 pounds. Found the trail the worst yet, very rough and steep. Billy broke a shaft and had to leave his sled. Found Bennett quite a place, but most of the rush is going on down the lakes to find good timber to whip-saw into lumber with which to make boats and scows.

"*March 25* Made another trip to Bennett. Delayed by a jam on the trail and did not get back to camp until dark.

"*March 26* Got two more loads through to Bennett.

In Box Canyon (below) packers carried load after load on good days (10° above zero) and prayed they would not be caught by storms that dropped temperatures rapidly to 40° below.

"*March 27* To Bennett again. Trail very rough. A jam kept Billy and Gil back all night. I returned to camp and kept dinner hot until 1 A.M. but they did not appear.

"*March 28* Billy and Gil returned in the morning. They had to pay $4.50 at Bennett for 15 pounds of hay, so we decided to return to Skagway for more mule feed.

"*March 29* Billy and I drove the 35 miles to Skagway in nine hours. Found the trail broken and very rough. We went to Adams and Crow's old headquarters for the night. A fight occurred on the trail with Soapy Smith's gangsters and a man was shot.

"*March 30* Found both Dyea and Skagway dull. The rush seems to be about over. Good meals for 25 cents.

"*March 31* We started out on the trail for Bennett at 10 A.M. with 400 pounds of hay and feed on each sled. Two days rain had about finished the trail. We pulled through deep mud, across running streams and up the rough canyons over bare rocks. It was a horrible day's work and we were thankful when we arrived at a camp about 6 P.M. Many poor devils will be stuck in that canyon.

"*April 1* We went over White Pass in a snow storm and made an easy run to our camp at Log Cabin.

"*April 2* Billy and I went to Lake Bennett with a load of mule feed. Sleet and snow fell all day to keep us wet and cold. Trail very rough and well lined with newly dead horses. At Bennett I was surprised to meet Theodore Solomons of the Sierra Club, who went part way with me and Allen Chickering on an exploring expedition in 1896, down the High Sierra from Yosemite Park to Kings River Canyon. We got back to camp very late.

"*April 3* The storm continued, so we took a Sunday rest in camp. Four hundred and sixty miles of sledding to date.

"*April 4* Pulled up stakes and hauled camp to Bennett where we made our headquarters at the tent of Crow and Adams. News came in of a disastrous snow avalanche on Chilcoot Pass. So far over 70 bodies have been dug out."

This handful of brief paragraphs tells of what but one man went

Yukon photographer Asahel Curtis, carrying a heavy glass-plate portrait camera, paused with a companion at a canvas "roadhouse" (above) on the Skagway–White Pass Trail late in 1897. A few miles farther on, at the foot of the Pass, Curtis photographed a stampeder named Wesley Young and his six companions (below), who had been caught in a snowstorm that almost buried their shelter. "Men took desperate chances to beat the coming winter," Curtis recorded, "and two members of this party lost their lives before the close of the day."

The Alpine beauty of Cutoff Canyon (left) had no charm for packers rushing toward the winter camp at Lake Bennett, where they could begin work on boats to take them down the Yukon to the gold fields.

At "The Ford," half a mile below the summit, the canvas-roofed Pack Train Hotel and Feed Stable (above) welcomed travelers to the shores of Summit Lake. Many camped here, looking back with relief at Cutoff Canyon (below) before tackling what Hamlin Garland called "the unclean ribbon" of the winter trail, winding up the hill to the Canadian customs station.

A forlorn bullock turns his back on the cavalcade of pack mules (left) inching toward the border station. North West Mounted Police (below) try to screen out bandits, con men, and indigents. The Mounties' basic rule in the winter of '98: Every man headed for the Yukon must carry a year's food and supplies.

through to cross the White Pass that winter. His words are spare and used with an objectivity rare in the annals of the time. In truth, the scene fairly throbbed with drama, a fact that even Starr's dispassionate, telegraphic entries could not conceal. Not that he tried to, but after all he had a single purpose: to get his outfit over the pass and on to the lakes where the rushing Yukon would carry him to the fabled gold fields of the Klondike.

Gazing on the scene after the summer of 1897 and the winter of '98 had passed and the Dead Horse Trail had given way to a wagon road, which was in turn to yield to the White Pass and Yukon Railroad in another year, Hamlin Garland wrote in another dimension:

"Down there in the gully, on the sullen drift of snow, the winter trail could still be seen like an unclean ribbon and here, where the shrivelled hides of horses lay thick, wound the summer pathway. Up yonder summit, lock-stepped like a file of convicts, with tongues protruding and breath roaring from their distended throats, thousands of men had climbed with killing burdens on their backs, mad to reach the great inland river and the gold belt. Like the men of the Long Trail [Ashcroft Trail], they, too, had no time to find the gold under their feet.

"It was terrible to see how on every slippery ledge the ranks of horses had broken like waves to fall in heaps like rows of seaweed, tumbled, contorted, and grinning. Their dried skins had taken on the color of the soil, so that I sometimes set foot upon them without realizing what they were. Many of them had saddles on and nearly all had lead-ropes. Some of them had even been tied to trees and left to starve."

Echoes of that shameful year still reverberate in the valley of the Skagway River today.

Bearded John Gorst, one of some 30,000 gold-seekers who traveled over the Coast Range from Skagway and Dyea in 1897–98, was photographed on the cutoff to Lake Lindeman, next stop on the route to the headwaters of the Yukon River.

KLONDIKE TALL TALES

Perhaps it was the isolation, the long winters, the sourdough pancakes, or the gut-rot hooch. There was something about the North that spawned these whoppers...

THE GLACIER BEAR

Judge James Wickersham tells a tale he heard one night at a cabin on 12 Mile Creek, which sat by the dog trail between Circle and Fairbanks

Our hosts for the night are Gus Miller, one of my Puget Sound friends, young Norton from California, and Bill Woodman, a grizzled frontiersman and a mighty hunter. What a fine batch of sourdough hot cakes old Bill made us for supper and breakfast! And how we enjoyed his hunting stories! May he live long and prosper!

Among the "bar" stories Bill told us while we smoked and talked after dinner this evening was one which his old Juneau friend, Dick Willoughby, told tourists, so often that, Bill said, Dick got so he believed it himself.

One day a group of Boston tourists were being entertained on the Juneau streets by Dick, who told them of certain great glacier bears he often saw around his cabin on an island in Glacier Bay. One of the tourists suggested that such gigantic animals must be slow in their movements, but Dick gave his personal assurance, from an intimate acquaintance with these bears, many of which he had watched in their daily fishing and hunting exercises, that they were not slow, but on the contrary were the most agile large animals known to man. In the heat of the argument that followed Dick told them this story to illustrate the agility with which these great bears could move around:

"I rolled out of my bunk one morning as the rays of the rising sun filled my cabin through the east window, and when I was dressed I went to the front door and threw it open for a good breath of fine salt air. My cabin stood on an island, near the mainland, in Glacier Bay. There were many salmon streams nearby and consequently a great number of these large salmon-catching bears. As I stood in my door filling my lungs with the morning air, I noticed a monster bear, probably fourteen feet long from tip to tip, approaching my house, following the trail I used leading from my house to a salmon lake, where I always caught my fish for breakfast. The bear was an elephant in size and was coming straight toward me. I reached above the door and took down my trusty buffalo gun which I had carried on the plains and through the Cassiar mining camp, examined it to see that it was ready for action and waited till the bear should approach nearer so that I would not have to carry his hide so far. About fifty yards from my house the trail crossed a little rise of ground, and when the bear reached that point, he evidently saw the house for the first time. The bear's eyesight is not sharp, and this one exhibited

his surprise at seeing the house and me standing in the door by stopping, raising his head, and opening his mouth. Just at that moment I rested my gun against the right door jamb and fired. The bullet struck the bear along the top of his tongue and went through him ranging just below his backbone. And that bear was that quick in turning around that, while the bullet was in his body between the tip of his tongue and its exit beneath his tail, he turned so exactly half around that when the bullet came out, the other end of the bear was toward me and the bullet came back and split the door jamb within three inches of my face. I've always been thankful that the bear, probably by reason of his age, was just the fraction of a second slow in turning, else that bullet would certainly have hit me in the eye."

I looked into Bill's honest face and asked: "Now, Bill, did you believe that story?" "Believe it," he answered, "*believe it*, why, of course I did. I knowed Dick Willoughby for years, and I've heard him tell that story to a hundred tourists, and of course I believed it. Why, I'd believe *any* story Dick Willoughby would tell a lot of Eastern tourists."

FOOD AND DRINK

Arthur Walden, a fine storyteller as well as an expert dog-puncher, believed in the ancient journalistic doctrine, "Never check a good story to death."

The saloons were almost like clubrooms, patronized alike by temperance men and drinkers. The custom now began among the saloonkeepers of shutting down for a few hours or days while they made minor changes or repairs. Then they would hold what was called a "Grand Opening," and everybody seemed to patronize them the more to help them recover from the time when they were closed. But with all this activity there didn't seem to be the insane feverishness that you meet in a large city.

An incident happened the next winter which I think I shall mention here in connection with the Dawson saloons. One very popular saloonkeeper had a "Grand Opening" which was, you might say, too successful, because he was so well patronized that they drank up all his available whiskey. Being a man who could rise to an emergency, and seeing that he was losing trade, he made a speech to the gathering, something like this:

"Gentlemen: I opened tonight with the expectation that I could give a good welcome and plenty of refreshments to my friends. But fate is against me. I have twelve dog-teams coming down the river, which are expected today, loaded to the gunwhales with the finest whiskey that man ever drank.

"You remember when I was out last summer I visited my old home in Kentucky. As a boy a legend floated around there of a hidden cave, 'way back in the times of the Civil War, which was raided by the government officials, and a hundred and forty barrels were found in it. The distillers themselves were killed in the fight, and the heads of the hundred and forty barrels were stove in, and this priceless fluid was spilled on the floor of the cave. The cave's mouth was then roughly rocked up and soon overgrown with the verdure of that country, and in those harrowing times when men's hearts bled and women's tears ran, all trace and memory of the cave was lost.

"By chance a boy, a rabbit hunter, chasing his fleeting game through this howling wilderness, saw his prey disappear into these deep rocks, and being a boy and knowing that he would get a licking from his father if he didn't get the rabbit, he pried out some of the rocks and discovered the cave of the legend. This was done just when I got back to Kentucky. And, gentlemen, those hundred and forty barrels of whiskey spilled on the barren rocks of the cave had drained into a hollow, and there by evaporating for some forty years had reduced down in the sterilized air of the cave to only ten barrels, and I, gentlemen, bought every drop of it and am now having it shipped to the brave men of the Yukon.

"Now, gentlemen, my dog-teams are somewhere on the ice, if they are not under it, but rather than disappoint you I will give you a little of my private stock, which I scooped out with my own hands from the deepest depression of the pocket. This, gentlemen, I will give you tonight at the same reduced price you have always paid."

With that he turned to one of his bartenders, who was wearing a broad grin, and said, "Johnny, bring in my private stock." The bartender, rising to the occasion, dipped two buckets of Yukon water out of a barrel, produced several demijohns of alcohol and different ingredients and made his whiskey before our eyes. It must have been pure, because we all saw it done, and what's more, everybody went up and had a drink to see what the stuff did taste like. But I don't think any saloonkeeper in the place but Pete Macdonald could have got away with it.

WHALE'S MILK

Scotty Allan, a renowned dog-puncher during the pioneering days in Nome, recalled a "rumor" that convulsed one of the godforsaken, snowbound camps in the cruel clutch of winter.

Ed was a great debater in the dark months when men were shut up for many weeks by bad weather and bitter temperatures. And when there was nothing to argue about he used to start rumors of his own. Some of these rumors were unique. I remember one idea that he created out of the whole cloth years afterward, which I overheard when it was first launched. Within twenty-four hours the "news" had the whole camp by its ears. Of course Ed ran about and listened to his own yarn retold over and over.

As I remember, Ed's conversation on that memorable night was with another miner named Mat and ran something like this:

"Well, Mat, I expect we will be getting canned milk at our own price pretty soon."

"How come, Ed?"

"Don't you ever read the papers, Mat?" Ed's very tone was an insult.

"Darned seldom. I can't get a paper to read."

"Well, you should read what you can get and try to keep posted on the outside world." By this time several other miners had stepped up to listen.

"Maybe I should. But I'm hanged if I can see what that has got to do with the price of canned milk."

"Well, it has. Did you ever hear of Japan?"

"Sure I've heard of Japan. Japan is next-door neighbor to China." There were growls of approbation at this sign of knowledge.

"That's right. I see you do know something of your geography. Now I want to tell you that the little Japanese is a darned smart race."

"What have they done beat us to now?"

"They are going to control the canned milk industry, I'm telling you."

"Why, I thought they were short of cows on their island."

"'Tisn't cow's. It's whale milk." Ed looked around to make sure his audience heard. "Whale milk," he repeated solemnly. "They round them up with submarines and corral them."

"What!" cried Mat. "But say, Ed, allowing the submarine can chase whales all over the ocean and into a corral, what kind of a corral have they got?"

"It's like a drydock," lied Ed, pulling his tousled, red whiskers. "They chase them right into it, and it's easy because a whale is wise and after she has been corraled once the next time she sees a submarine coming around about milking time, she hits right out for the corral. After they get them all in they close the gates and empty the dock or corral, and there you have all your cow whales ready to go to work on!"

"But say, Ed, they can't milk a whale with their hands, can they?"

"Certainly not."

"How do they do it then?"

"They put a big vacuum pump on her and suck it right out of her just like drying out a wet mine—simplest thing in the world!"

"Well! well! At that, by gosh, I don't believe I want any whale milk. I'll bet it tastes fishy."

There was a chorus of approval from the large audience.

"No, they say not, but it does taste salty and keeps for a long time, and it is very strong food. A little of it goes a long ways. I believe it would be great stuff on the trail for a long mush."

By morning the crowd outside Ed's cabin was ten deep, all wanting to hear more about whale milk. But right in the middle of the excitement someone burst into camp with news of a fresh gold find and a stampede started. And by the time things settled down again Ed and his whale-milk story had given way to some new and equally fantastic gossip.

CHAPTER VII

THE THREE-MONTH CLIMB

"The mountain is alive. There is a continuous moving train . . . zigzagging across the towering face of the precipice, up, up, into the sky . . ."

As winter approached in 1897, the tides swept across the shallow delta at the mouth of the Dyea River, and with each change the ships and barges from the south disgorged their human cargo and what grew to be a mountain of gear and provisions. Something on the order of 60 million tons of goods were packed over the Dead Horse and Chilcoot passes in the first year of the rush, and the great bulk of it all went the way of the Chilcoot Trail.

Dyea, Skagway's counterpart three miles to the northwest, carried most of the traffic, even though Skagway got virtually all the publicity. The reason was simple: The Chilcoot Trail was the poor man's trail, and although Soapy Smith's men worked both the Chilcoot and the Dead Horse, the town of Dyea was slim pickings compared to Skagway.

From Dyea the river, which flowed with twice the volume of the Skagway, meandered through a lovely valley for a distance of six miles. From there the trail entered a canyon closely bound by rocky cliffs on each side until it broke into another generous gap in the mountains where the town of Sheep Camp had sprung up. This was the last stop with any pretense of comfort along the trail between Dyea and Lakes Lindeman and Bennett, the staging areas for the final assault on the Yukon and the long downstream voyage to Dawson.

The first steep climb lay beyond Sheep Camp on the way to The Scales, so named because for years the final weighing of cargo was made there by professional packers before they were to lug their loads over the last and most taxing legs of the trail between Dyea and Lake Lindeman. The distance from Dyea to the top of the pass was 14 miles, and the lake lay nine miles beyond.

Tappan Adney, one of the last to get through early enough to make it all the way to Dawson before the Yukon froze that winter, expressed more awe and wonder about the Chilcoot Trail than anything else he saw in his year-long adventure:

"From Sheep Camp the valley is a huge gorge, the mountain-sides rising steep, hard, and bold to a prodigious height. The valley begins to rise rapidly, and the trail is very bad. A mile above Sheep Camp, on the left hand, a huge glacier lies on the side of the mountain, jutting so far over and downward that every moment one expects a great chunk to drop off and tumble into the river. But it does not, and only a small stream of water from its melting forces its way to the bottom. A mile farther on is Stone House—a large square rock, crudely resembling a house; it stands on the

Passing over the Chilcoot summit in the winter of '98, these heavily bundled sledders get their first glimpse of Canada's Yukon Territory in a classic photograph by E.A. Hegg.

The ubiquitous Hegg, sledding along the Chilcoot Trail with a team of long-haired rams, accomplished the dual purpose of photographing the great adventure and promoting sales of his "Views of Alaska."

85

The perils of the Chilcoot Trail were real enough—especially for inexperienced gold hunters—but professional myth-makers embroidered the experience with elements of romance for the parlors and theaters of America: Dramas in the tradition of Buffalo Bill's Wild West Show (right); stereopticon views like the one below, which was distributed from New York, St. Louis, Liverpool, Toronto, and Sydney; and carefully staged photographs (bottom) of portages and encampments in woodlands hung with icicles.

HEART OF THE KLONDIKE

THRILLING RESCUE OF THE CHILD AND HEADLONG FALL OF THE VILLAIN INTO THE DEPTHS OF CHILKOOT CAÑON.

river's brink. At the base of the mountain is a great mass of slide rock, some of the boulders being nearly as large as the one by the river. . . . The valley here makes a sudden turn to the right, and the trail begins to grow steep. The valley is filled with great water-and-ice-worn boulders. The trail climbs from one to another of these. There is no vegetation, save a few alders here and there, and these cease just above Stone House.

"The trail enters a cul-de-sac, climbing higher and higher. The valley seems to end; a precipitous wall of gray rock, reaching into the sky, seems to head off further progress, seaming its jagged contour against the sky—a great barrier, uncompromising, forbidding—the Chilcoot Pass.

"Horses and men with packs are ahead of and behind us. The sun has broken clear, and shines down on a strange scene. In a pocket under the cliff are some score of tents and huge piles of baggage. The tents are held to the earth by rocks on the guy-ropes. Men are busily at work making up the goods into packs and unloading packhorses. Adding to the animation the rocks are covered with bright blankets spread out to dry.

"The men take up the packs, and this is what happens: They walk to the base of the cliff, with a stout alpenstock in hand. They start to climb a narrow foot trail that goes up, up, up. The rock and earth are gray. The packers and packs have disappeared. There is nothing but the gray wall of rock and earth. But stop! Look more closely. The eye catches movement. The mountain is alive. There is a continuous moving train; they are perceptible only by their movement, just as ants are. The moving train is zigzagging across the towering face of the precipice, up, up, into the sky, even at the very top. See! They are going against the sky! They are human beings, but never did men look so small."

Adney was over the pass and on his way before the first heavy snows fell, snows that would turn the pass into a white-bound amphitheater and the goal and temporary home for thousands in the months to come.

But he wasn't over the pass before he witnessed the result of the first of two natural disasters that were to visit the gorge of the Dyea in the 1897–98 season. It was in the latter part of September that he recorded the following:

"Next day it begins to storm down the valley—such a storm as I never saw before. It blows until it seems as if the tent, which is held down by heavy rocks on the guy-ropes and the edges of the tent, would be taken bodily and thrown into the lake. Goods have to be piled endways to the wind or else be blown over.

"The storm continues for several days, with wind, snow, and rain, the sun shinning clear each morning through the rain. We engage some men to pack our stuff over, doing considerable ourselves. . . .

"Having waited several days in vain for the boat to come over the summit, we start back to Sheep Camp, and on the way we hear that Sheep Camp has been washed entirely away, and many persons lost. At Stone

Camped in a ravine half a dozen miles from Dyea, this pack train was still on the "easy" portion of the trail. Horse-drawn sleighs and wagons carried heavy supplies to the foot of the grueling pass, but from there on, transport was mostly by man-back. In narrow gorges like the one below, horses pulled, men pushed.

In narrow gorges horses pulled, men pushed.

It was at Sheep Camp, a cluster of saloons, supply stores, and hotel-restaurants 1000 feet above tidewater, that most cheechakos spent their first night on the Chilcoot Trail. Miners here formed a committee of vigilance (above) in the winter of 1897–98 and arrested an Irishman named Wellington and his Danish partner, Hansen, for plundering an unguarded cache of supplies. Terrified of being hanged, Wellington shot himself. Hansen, sentenced to 50 lashes on his bare back with a half-inch rope, was reprieved when the local doctor interceded after 15 terrible blows had been struck by a left-handed muleskinner named Billy Onions. The elders of Sheep Camp sent Hansen, half-dead, down to Dyea next morning wearing a chestboard labeled "Thief."

House the square stone is gone. Several parties camped there tell us the first they heard was a roar, and, looking across the valley, saw a stream of water and boulders coming off the mountain top, the boulders leaping far out in air as they tumbled down, an immense torrent, and it poured into the Dyea River, overwhelming a young man who had gone to the river for water, undermining the big rock, flooding the tents, carrying away several outfits, and speeding towards Sheep Camp, bearing trees and wood with it. Sheep Camp, when we reach there, is a spectacle. The big saloon tents and many small ones are wiped out, and the main street, lately a trail of black mud, shoe-top deep, is as clear and solid as sand can make it. The catastrophe occurred on the 18th [September], at seven o'clock in the morning, before many were up. Numerous outfits were either buried or have been carried away by the flood. People are digging in the sand, wringing garments and hanging them out on the bushes to dry. Only one life is known to have been lost.

"This disaster has decided many who were hanging in the balance. Whether they have lost their outfits or not, it has given them a good excuse to go back. From this time on only the strong-hearted continue on their way."

The problem of caring for animals was as great as it was on the Dead Horse Trail; only the numbers differed. Pack animals could be taken over the Chilcoot only at great expense and risk, and few tried it. Feed was for practical purposes unavailable, and as the season wore on, an animal was worth little more than he could earn for a packer in one day. Again, Tappan Adney:

"The cruelty to horses is past belief; yet it is nothing to the Skagway trail, we hear. There are three thousand horses on the Skagway trail—more to kill, that's about all the difference. Sheep Camp is filling up with broken-down brutes. Their owners have used them and abused them to this point, and are too tender-hearted (?) to put them out of their misery. Their backs are raw from wet and wrinkled blankets, their legs cut and bruised on the rocks, and they are as thin as snakes and starving to death. A Colorado man says to me, 'Of all the cruelty to horses—and I've seen a good deal—the worst is on this trail; they are killing them with sticks.' They are

Street life (if these be streets) in Sheep Camp that winter included con men playing the notorious shell game; housewives slogging to market with the family sled (below, left); and bargain-hunters at Courtney's Store. A U.S. Cavalry sergeant, traveling the Chilcoot in March, 1898, reported that the town consisted of one street, 16 feet wide and a mile long, winding along the east bank of the Taiya River; two drug stores, a hospital, 15 hotels and restaurants, numerous coffee stands, two laundries, a bath-house, several stores, and innumerable saloons.

hobbling about among the tents, tumbling over guy ropes, breaking into caches, making great nuisances of themselves. No one will take the responsibility for shooting them. Someone may come along and demand $50 for the dead horse perhaps. That settles it. So we drive a batch of them out of town, where the poor creatures may find a little feed.

"A wretched, thin, white cayuse came to my tent. He had been driven from four miles above, where his owner deserted him. It was raining a cold rain. He put his head and as much more as he could inside the tent, trying to get next to the stove. He stayed there all night and was around all next day, and he had nothing to eat. I am certain he never felt the 44-caliber bullet back of his ear that evening. Thereupon a general killing-off began, until carcasses were lying on all sides."

As winter came on, with its miserable winds and blizzards, the trail became choked. No one knows for certain how many crossed the pass that season, but it was somewhere between 22,000 and 30,000. Disease and frustration took a toll of those who left Dyea and Skagway, and thousands turned back, if they didn't die on the trail. Harry Munn, who crossed the White Pass as nearly as I can determine even though in his book, *Prairie Trails and Arctic By-Ways*, he refers to his route as the Chilcoot Trail, left a glimpse of the stark specter of death that hovered over each:

"On my way back from Bennett on one of the many trips I made to hurry our canoes and goods over, I saw a light in a tent, went over to it and, putting my head inside, asked if they had a mug of tea to spare, the freemasonry of the trail always giving you this. A man sitting on a box beside the little sheet iron stove, with his head between his hands, nodded. 'Help yourself,' he said curtly, and resumed his staring at the ground in front of him. His partner was under the blankets on the far side of the bed. 'Your partner's taking a sound sleep,' I said when I had slaked my thirst. The other man looked up. 'You're right,' he said dully, 'he's dead.'

"Cerebro-spinal meningitis was said to be the disease which took a heavy toll of life on the trail of '98. Feeling ill, shivering fits, unconsciousness and often death in twelve hours. My host, returning with a load from his cache back on the trail, arrived to find his partner dead. He had only complained of feeling ill the day before."

Sheep Camp at the time of Adney's passage boasted a few saloons (tent, two crates on end with a six-foot board suspended on them, and a bottle of whiskey) and a hotel. His description of the hotel is probably generous, if one is to judge by other accounts of similar roadhouses that sprouted that winter:

"Sheep Camp has a hotel. If anyone is in doubt on that point, a huge cloth sign on the front of the building announcing the fact in letters three feet high is sufficient evidence. That the proprietor, a Mr. Palmer, is a modest man is evident in that he has not placed his own name in letters equally large in front of the simple but gigantic word 'Hotel.'

"It is one of the two wooden buildings in town, built of rough boards, and in dimensions about twenty by forty feet, comprising a single room. A portion is partitioned off at the back by a calico curtain, and here live the proprietor, his wife, and a large family of small children, and here the meals are prepared for several hundred hungry packers three times a day as fast or faster than the pack-train can bring the grub from Dyea. At noon, but more particularly at evening, the floor of the hotel is crowded by a wild, dirty, wet, unkempt crew of men from Chilcoot, who advance in relays to a long table, where the beans, tea, and bacon are thrown into them at 75 cents each, payable strictly in advance. The fare depends greatly on what the pack-train has been able to pick up at Dyea. There is always enough, although sugar or milk may be a bit scarce. The men eat like wolves. 'Still,

Above Sheep Camp the trail ascended steeply for four miles to the summit at 3500 feet. It was rare, indeed, to see pack animals on this portion of the Chilcoot, as E.A. Hegg did, pointing his camera downhill on a winter afternoon in 1898. In the lower picture, taken from a great rocky overhang called "Stone House," about a mile from Sheep Camp, hundreds of two-legged beasts of burden are laboring upward, carrying 50-pound packs or dragging heavier sleds.

there are some who kick at the price,' says Landlord Palmer. 'Why, the price they pay hardly pays the packing on what some of them eat.'

"When supper is over, the floor is thrown open for guests. All who have blankets unroll them and spread them on the floor, take off their socks and shoes and hang them on the rafters, place a coat under their heads, and turn in. By nine o'clock it is practically impossible to walk over the floor, for the bodies. The first night I spent in Sheep Camp I spread my blanket under the table, sharing it with a fellow traveller who was not so provided. No charge is made for the sleeping privileges of this hotel. In the morning the lavatory arrangements are of an equally simple sort. One simply walks outside to a brook that flows under one corner of the building, and, after ablution in water from a glacier up the mountainside, lets the water dry on his hands and face. I noticed most of the men did not take even this much trouble."

But despite the suffering and meanness, the fear of defeat and the overwhelming compulsion to push on at any cost, those who crossed the Chilcoot that winter were participants in one of the most dramatic migrations in recent history. It took each man on the average of three months to pack his outfit from Dyea over the pass to Lake Lindeman. The distance was only 27 miles, but the man on foot trudged many hundreds of miles back and forth along the trail, moving his gear from cache to cache.

The final climb produced one of the most moving photographic images in American history. No staged version of this event could ever match the incredible drama created by the thousands of men and women who

The Scales was the last staging point before the three-quarter-mile climb to the summit.

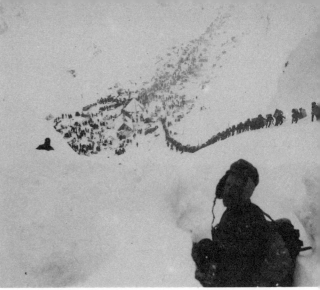

struggled up the 30-degree incline to cross the Chilcoot Pass that winter. The average man carried about 50 pounds each trip up the 1500 steps carved into the icy face below the pass, and it was rare when he could make more than one trip a day. For some, then, it meant as many as 40 bone-wearying climbs in 40 frozen days to get their outfits over the top.

Whether gold lay at the end of their trails or not, they had crossed the Chilcoot, an achievement that for many was the crowning event of their lives.

Once over the top, the first sight to greet them was the Union Jack and the Canadian Mounties, who kept a rigid, benevolent grip on affairs from that point on. There had been a good deal of public grumbling about Canadian "highhandedness" in the ranks of the Klondikers and in the American press. High tariffs, an as yet to be resolved border conflict (had there not been so many Americans on the scene, the Canadians would have undoubtedly taken both trails and Skagway and Dyea, each of which they had long claimed), national pride, and other ingredients led to some friction. But there was scarcely a man in the long parade across the border

The Scales (above, left) at the height of the stampede had a superficial resemblance to a ski resort in high season. Most of the tents were coffee houses, dispensing "hot stuff" at high prices. Up the hill, near an unprepossessing cabin-restaurant, was the office of a gasoline-powered tramline that would haul a miner's outfit to the top for two cents a pound. From above, stampeders could look forward to an easy slide to the base of the hill to carry up another load.

Clutching a guideline with one hand and a walking stick with the other, thousands of Klondike adventurers trudged the 1500 steps of the "Golden Stairs" from the Scales to the summit. Resting places, dug into the snow at the left of the stairway, are visible in the upper picture on the opposite page.

who did not welcome the sight. Soapy and lawlessness lay behind, and the incorruptible rule of the Mounties lay ahead. None ever had reason to regret his appraisal.

How did a handful of Mounties manage to control the seething, single-minded mob that poured over the pass? It was simply a matter of principle and will, faithfully executed by men of tremendous stamina and unshakably high character. Harry Munn recites an encounter which sums it all up:

"I pushed on to Lake Bennett with my precious load and found Major—as he then was—Steele there in command, the same officer I have referred to once before. He offered me the hospitality of his cabin, and during the evening we heard a couple of shots outside. 'Sergeant,' sung out Steele, 'go and see what that was and report.' Word was brought back it was an American who claimed to have been cleaning his revolver when it accidentally went off. The Sergeant added he thought he was 'one of the gang.'

"'Arrest him and lock him up and go through his things,' said Steele. Next morning the Sergeant reported he had found he had three dogs, a tent, blankets, and a few provisions, a complete thimble-rig outfit, some marked 'monte' cards, and also that one of the men of the Detachment recognized the man as one of 'Soapy's lot.' He was brought before Steele and asked who he was. 'I'm so and so,' he began very indignantly, 'and I'm an American citizen, and I'll have you know you can't lock up U-nited

Hundreds of supply caches were established at the summit by backpackers hauling their outfits bit-by-bit up the "Golden Stairs" (left). From here, there was a short, steep descent to Crater Lake (right), down which winter travelers could ride their sleds. The men in the picture below, having conquered the Chilcoot Pass, are coasting down the east slope in April, 1898.

States citizens and get away with it. My God, sir! The Secretary of State himself shall hear about it,' and so on. The man worked himself into a fine passion. Steele let him talk on for a few minutes, then said quietly, 'You say you are an American citizen?'

"'Yes, surr, I am, and . . .'

"'Well, that'll do. Seeing you are an American citizen. I'll be very lenient with you'—the man began to smile—

"Then, very sternly, 'I confiscate everything you have, and I give you half an hour to leave the town.' The man's jaw dropped, but before he could say anything the Sergeant sung out, 'right wheel,' and he was hustled out of the room. In half an hour he was walking back the twenty-two miles to the summit, with a policeman at his heels telling him to step lively. When they left the room I said to Steele, 'Major, forgive my curiosity, but how can you do that? You haven't martial law here, have you?'

"'I *can't* do it, Munn,' he said, 'but I'm not going to have any of those thugs robbing and murdering on this side like they are doing down at Skagway. I've been waiting for just such a one over here to make an example of him. By the time he's walked to the summit, and been told to beat it down the Pass, he'll have had enough. We shan't see any more over here.' Nor did they. Nor was anything further ever heard about the incident. Steele was the right man for those jobs. He never feared or shirked responsibility."

This was the milieu into which they marched, fiercely independent, utterly interdependent—strong men and babes in the woods whom fate had thrown together in one of the most fascinating adventures of the century.

On the frozen, snow-covered surface of Crater Lake, enterprising sourdoughs rigged their sleds with canvas sails.

The restaurant at Crater Lake offered all the comforts of civilization—or, at any rate, hot coffee, a board-and-barrel bench, a canvas roof, and some bright, feminine smiles.

Avalanche!

Hundreds were camped at the foot of the Chilcoot Pass on the night of April 2, 1898, waiting for the day to break and one more struggle over the pass in the seemingly endless task of carrying their outfits, pack by pack, on to their goal. Weeks of storms had built a wet, six-foot snow pack on top of the early winter snow and ice that covered all of the pass and surrounding mountains, and the threat of avalanche was very real. Indian packers and other old-timers refused to climb and retreated to lower stretches of the trail. At noon on the third it happened. Hundreds of thousands of tons of the snow mass thundered down the pass, and at least 70 were trapped. Suvivors dug for a week, saving somewhere between six and ten, but many of those lost were not found in their icy graves until summer.

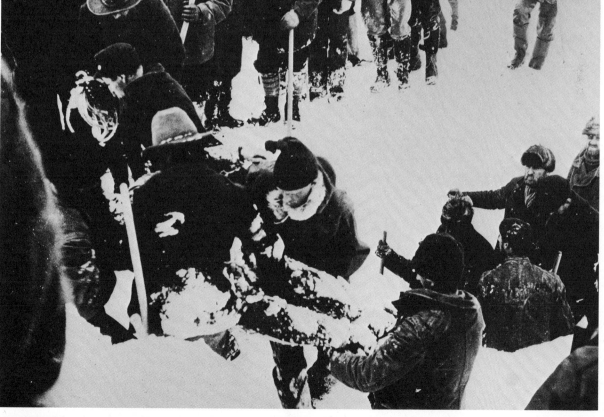

The scene following the immense slide was one of single-minded concern for those trapped in the snow. Above left, sticks were placed to delineate the areas of search. Below left, the summit of the pass. How E. A. Hegg, the photographer, managed to get to the top is something of a mystery. If Hegg had left a written record to match his superlative photographic record, the history of the Rush would be even richer than it is. Above, the hastily established morgue at Sheep Camp, the instant and soon-to-vanish city which grew two miles from the foot of the pass. Right, the graveyard established at Dyea that was set aside for avalanche victims. The simple markers give no hint of the dramatic impact the catastrophe had on the world.

CHAPTER VIII

RASCALS ON THE TRAIL

"Soapy and his men are on the rampage, and Hell's a-popping down in Skagway"

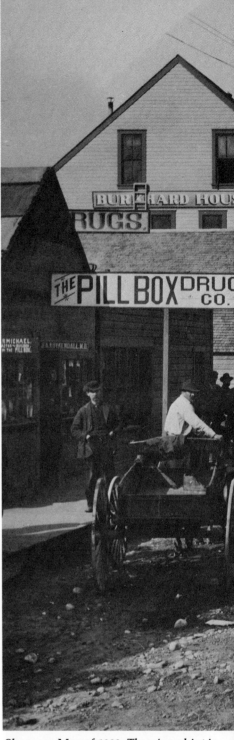

Skagway, May of 1898. There's no hint in this picture that the town was in the firm grip of Soapy Smith and his gang of thugs and con men, but until the eighth of July he controlled everything—not only the streets and trails, but the law itself. The sleepy dog didn't care, for Soapy was a friend of strays.

Soapy Smith was America's last frontier badman of legend, and by any measure a nonpareil of the genus. He was baptized Jefferson Randolph Smith and called Jeff by those close to him, but Soapy was the name he was stuck with until his untimely death and all the years that have followed. The name came from the days he spent in Leadville and Creede and Denver, Colorado, selling bars of soap to willing buyers who were convinced by the charming flimflam man that somehow $20 bills were concealed under the wrappers. To this day, having read the story in many versions, I still cannot understand how he did it.

For all his notoriety in Colorado, Soapy Smith's lasting fame rests on the year he spent in Skagway and Dyea. Pioneer Judge James Wickersham tells the story:

Soapy ". . . landed at Dyea in 1897 and quickly gathered under his command a band of cappers, crooks, card-sharps, and cut-throats un-equalled on the Pacific Coast since the Vigilante days at Virginia City. He came of a wealthy and prominent Southern family, was a hail-fellow-well-met sort, and spent his earnings freely. Any criminal, male or female, who was unfortunate enough to be caught in the net of the law was sure of immediate sympathy and assistance from Soapy. His men covered the towns of Dyea and Skagway and both trails to the boundary line on the Chilcoot and White Pass summits, beyond which they dared not go for fear of Canada's Mounted Police.

"In 1898 the mountain trails from Dyea and Skagway were crowded with men, women, horses, dogs, all going towards the summit without organization or police protection. Packers carried valuable merchandise on their backs, and each of these unprotected travelers necessarily carried a considerable sum of money on his person. This horde, well supplied with money, but with no organized protection, afforded thugs and highwaymen ideal opportunities for fraud, theft, robbery and murder. The whole area between Lynn Canal and the headwaters of the Yukon, including the Dyea and the White Pass trails, had but a single deputy United States marshal for protection, and he quickly became a silent partner of Soapy Smith's. Soapy's boldest highwaymen were stationed in the towns and at advantageous points along the two parallel trails in 1898. Open violent robbery was a daily occurrence. Sure-thing games—the 'shell game' being the most prominent—were played at every stream crossing and at every over-night camp. What the crooked gamester missed, the highway robber got. . . .

"Terror reigned in the towns and on the trails. Law-abiding citizens

BROADWAY · SKAGWAY · ALASKA · MAY 20th 1898

were intimidated, though the bandits were careful to prey upon transients rather than local residents.

"The businessmen of Dyea and Skagway were too much engrossed in their own affairs to provide law enforcement. Transients did not stay at any place long enough to organize for their own safety. They were intent upon getting to the gold fields and amassing a fortune as soon as possible. Soapy's gangsters, on the side lines, chose their victims, and boldly robbed them on the unprotected trails. If complaints were made they fell on deaf ears, for the editor of the principal local paper and the deputy U.S. marshal and the justice of the peace, the only law officers in the towns, were notoriously friendly to the criminals and refused to protect travelers or their property.

Left: Soapy stands in his saloon surrounded by his crooked minions. The bar and the back room were the scene of many skillfully executed robberies. Below: The heart of the gang in formal pose. Soapy is in the center, passionless, staring at the camera with his cold gray eyes. With a little imagination, you can separate the strong-arm men from the shell-game operators.

''If a traveler passing through the towns, or along the trails, displayed or appeared to have money, word would be sent ahead to confederates, and he was almost certain to lose his money, if not his life, before reaching the safety of the Canadian policemen on the summit. Bandits along the trails were honest-appearing prospectors, with big phoney packs, filled with hay or shavings, to mislead the unwary. Each of these desperadoes carried dangerous weapons and gambling devices, and was always ready to seduce the innocent traveler to join a game with their cappers or confidence men.

''A Presbyterian missionary came to Dyea in the fall of '97 en route to Dawson to establish a church there. He was accompanied by a lay brother, who carried the church fund. The latter was both inquisitive and social, and readily talked with strangers about the trails, the scenery, or matters of current interest. One day on the trail he fell behind his shepherd and met a well-dressed and agreeable gentleman who was giving three roughly-garbed men, carrying heavy-looking miners' packs, information about the trail to the summit. Being naturally interested, the guardian of the church fund stopped and joined in the conversation. It appeared that the very agreeable gentleman had been eating English walnuts, for some shells were on the ground at his feet. A short piece of board also happened to be nearby. Picking up the board and three half shells, the agreeable gentleman sat down on a boulder and laughingly explained to the simple-minded miners a childhood game called 'Where is the pea?' Before the inquisitive

Memories of Soapy linger still in Skagway, and this grave marker is but one reminder of his reign. The legend reads:

**NOSCITUR
SHOT IN THE MOUNTAINS
May 1st 1898**

102

lay brother solved that simple problem he had lost the church fund he was carrying to Dawson!"

Soapy was a curious mixture of a man: he was the benefactor of stray dogs; he could fleece a man of all his money and then turn around and give him enough cash to get back home; he surrounded himself with the most ruthless con men and thugs who could be found on the continent; he sought and gained public approbation through his philanthropies and patriotic gestures.

It may be casual for a layman to diagnose the problems of a man across these many decades, but Soapy must have had a severe character disorder of some sort. Something was clearly out of whack, not because he was a con man (God knows, con men can reach the highest offices in government), but because he was willing to consort with killers and strong-arm men when artifice was all he needed to separate the innocent from their money—and he was a master at that. He didn't even really want the money. He apparently gave away as much as he stole. Gain was not his motive. Power beyond the law was.

If Soapy Smith wasn't ingenious, he wasn't anything. He may remain condemned for the armed robbery and murder some of his men were guilty of, but most of his confidence games and larcenies would have given him a prince's ransom if money itself had been his end. To fully appreciate the man, you have to know of some of the inventive touches that he added to the history of the "sure-thing game," a term Soapy himself is credited with coining. As he observed in his Colorado days, he was not a gambler, but a sure-thing man.

The most beguiling of all his tricks was the telegraph office he set up to allow homesick Argonauts to wire home—on a nonexistent telegraph system—before they set off on the remote trails that led to the Klondike. For five dollars one could "send" a short message to any place in the States or Canada. Invariably a message would come back to the sender asking him to send money—by wire, of course!

The work of Smith and his men was so thoroughgoing and well-publicized that the businessmen of Skagway and Dyea finally got the message that Soapy and his gang were hurting business. The word was abroad: don't bring your gold back from the Klondike through Skagway.

Even the Mounties had to resort to subterfuge to get the sizable fortune they had collected in customs at the top of the trails past Soapy in Dyea. Soapy's confederates somehow missed the shipment as it went through town. But learning that it had slipped by them, they attempted to board the ship that was carrying the money. The piracy failed, but the episode clearly showed the brazen, totally uncontrolled grip Soapy's men had on Skagway and Dyea. Smith himself was not a coward, but as events would prove, his men were. And cowards don't go about highjacking big money shipments from the North West Mounted Police in any waters unless their numbers and firepower were overwhelming.

One need not be a student of Greek drama to draw a line on Soapy's end. He struck the high point of his civic career on July 4th, 1898, when as grand marshal of the parade and other festivities he had summoned forth all the best of American patriotic instincts and made it a day to remember. He had even prevailed on Governor John Brady to come from Sitka to participate in the celebration, no small coup in its own right. But Soapy was the star of the day.

Mounted on a fine and spirited gray horse, dressed to the teeth with a ten-gallon Stetson to top it all, Soapy had his finest hour. Four days later he would lie dead.

Earlier in the year he had organized a company of militia and offered

Skagway celebrated the Fourth of July in 1898 not despite but with the wholehearted support of Soapy. Indeed, the Fourth was the high point of his civic career. Astride a gray mount, wearing a tall Stetson, he led the parade as Grand Marshal. It was only a matter of days before his empire crumbled and he lay dead.

Another group of Soapy's men, smug in the knowledge that, for practical purposes, Soapy was the law in Skagway and the pickings were easy.

his and his men's services to the Secretary of War in the fight against the Spaniards. While he was turned down (his reputation was not unknown outside Alaska), his gesture earned him grudging respect from at least part of Skagway's permanent residents. And respect, with power, in my guess, is all he ever wanted. He was not a drinker, although the day he died he was half-drunk. He didn't chase women, but while there is no evidence that he wasn't normal in this department, one might wonder.

No matter what, he was a compelling figure whose imprint on American folklore was and remains immense. I suspect that when the nation's tercentenary comes along, Soapy and Jesse James will survive as the best of the country's 19th Century outlaws—or worst, depending on how you count—not only for their style and success, but also because they weren't all bad. Billy the Kid, an adenoidal moron, Belle Starr, the Dalton boys, Butch Cassidy and the Sundance Kid were all pikers in comparison.

Enough speculation. Let us turn to the details of his dramatic departure, for if ever a man's life closed in as stunning and seemingly preordained fashion as his did, one would have to turn to Shakespeare or the Bible for precedent.

Judge Wickersham, one of Alaska's most distinguished pioneers, continues the story in his book, *Old Yukon*:

"A simple-minded Klondike miner named Stewart brought in over the trail a small poke of gold dust worth about $2700. Having safely walked through the danger zone from the summit to Skagway, he deposited his little fortune in a merchant's safe. Upon hearing the news, two of Soapy's lambs formed an acquaintance with Stewart and persuaded him to take his poke to Jeff's Place for examination. There a quarrel was started by cappers, the poke was seized, and Stewart was thrown into the street. Stewart at once complained to his merchant friend who ran to the secret committee of the Vigilantes with the facts. A small group of business men sent for Soapy and begged him to return the poke and gold dust to the owner. He refused to do so, stating that Stewart had lost his gold in a square game. Thereupon the Vigilantes declared war.

"Frank H. Reid, a prominent citizen, civil engineer, and official town surveyor, was one of the most courageous and active members of the Vigilantes. Soapy feared him and looked upon him as the leader of the law and order forces. . . .

Jeff Smith's notorious parlor decked in patriotic bunting for Fourth of July festivities. Soapy's men always seemed ready for the photographer.

"The robbery of Stewart, following upon so many similar crimes by the bandits, stirred the Vigilantes to action. The members were notified that there would be a meeting that night at nine o'clock, at the Sylvester dock warehouse, to consider active measures for the suppression of the criminals. When they met, four of the members were stationed at the town approach to the dock with instructions not to allow any one except members of the Committee to enter the warehouse. One of these outer guards was Reid.

"When Soapy learned of the meeting from a spy, he gathered fourteen of his men and marched down to the wharf. Two big revolvers hung from his belt, and a double-barrelled repeating Winchester rifle lay in the crook of his arm. He insolently shouted to the people standing on the sidewalks to 'chase yourselves home to bed'; passed on and stepped upon the end of the dock facing the Vigilante guards. None of these guards were armed except Reid, who still carried the revolvers with which he had armed himself to kill Soapy.

"Soapy walked rapidly past the two outer guards, for he saw Reid twenty feet further on. As he approached Reid, the latter said to him, 'You can't go down there, Smith.' The outlaw replied, 'Damn you, Reid, you have been at the bottom of this,' and struck at him with his rifle barrel. The Vigilante chief caught the descending weapon with one hand, quickly thrust his other hand into his coat pocket and attempted to discharge his revolver from that position. Smith jerked his rifle back from its position near Reid's head, who held on as it was lowered. When the rifle was forced down to the middle of Reid's body, Smith pulled the trigger and at the same time Reid fired. Each fired four shots in as many seconds and both fell together on the wharf—Smith dead, Reid mortally wounded. . . .

"When Soapy fell his henchmen drew their revolvers and rushed forward to avenge his death. Reid's companion guard, a brave little Irishman named Murphy, seized Soapy's Winchester and faced the advancing gang. Just then the Vigilantes came running from their meeting,

Above: The long pier where a citizen's committee met on July 8th to consider what to do with Soapy and his men after they had pulled one too many strong-arm robberies at Soapy's parlor. Soapy attempted to break up the meeting and was killed at the entrance of the pier. Below: The armed committee which gathered to round up the rest of the gang.

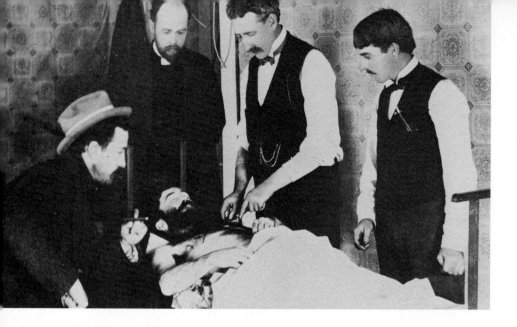

Dr. F. B. Whiting removes the fatal bullet while witnesses observe the autopsy on Soapy's body. That the event was photographed is indication of the stature—or notoriety—Soapy had attained.

calling as they came, 'Get your guns, men, and kill them.' The gang broke and ran, without discharging a gun.''

Shortly after the shooting, Dr. F. B. Whiting, physician for the White Pass and Yukon Railway, and Mike Heney had climbed into their beds at the company's executive bunkhouse at Rock Point, six miles beyond Skagway. He and Heney, the superintendent of construction, had lit their pipes and were discussing the events of the day when, as he wrote in his book, *Grit, Grief and Gold*, ''. . . the door burst open and in rushed Dan O'Neil, the night watchman. He was much excited and out of breath.

''They want you at the telephone down in the commissary,' he addressed Heney. 'Soapy and his men are on the rampage, and Hell's a-popping generally down there.'

''Heney sprang out of bed and hastily kicking his feet into an old pair of shoes, ran on down to the commissary without dressing. He soon returned, his face beaming with excitement.

''Get up and dress right away,' he exclaimed, 'they're rounding up Soapy's gang, and he's already been killed. Saddle up the horses, Dan, and we'll be right down behind you.' . . .

''At the upper end of town we encountered the vigilantes with a prisoner, and we continued on down to the city jail with them. There, hundreds of excited citizens swarmed about the place, a crude building made of roughly hewn logs, the front part of the city hall, the back part of the jail. Winchester rifles and revolvers were carried openly without the least effort at disguise. Now and then, men were seen with coils of rope in hand, like cowboys at a round-up. Some ten or twelve were by now captured, and the surrounding country was being combed for the rest. The marshal, who had long been known to be in league with the outlaws, was encountered at his home and promptly relieved of his star, and a well-known citizen, who could be depended upon, was selected in his place, much to the relief of the former, who had expected somewhat rougher treatment. The new marshal began his strenuous duties promptly. The U.S. commissioner chartered a small boat and disappeared during the night, never to return.

''Later, during the night, it was discovered that the three ringleaders of the gang had been secretly transferred up into the garret on the third floor of a nearby hotel for safety from the increasingly dangerous mob outside, bent upon satisfaction at any cost.

''We stood at three the next morning out in front of the Hotel

Soapy was buried without ceremony and without mourners, but Skagway will never forget him.

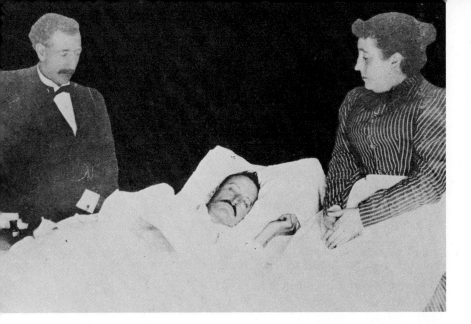

Frank Reid, the man who challenged Soapy at the wharf, was shot in the groin and lingered for days in agonizing pain before he died. He was and remains Skagway's greatest hero.

Burkhard, with hundreds of others, at the foot of the stairway leading up to the top floor. Here, at the entrance stood the newly appointed marshal, pleading earnestly with the mob to be calm and let the law take its course. On the top floor, in a musty garret, stood three deputies with glistening Winchester rifles, braced to resist the onrush of the mob from below. Behind them, huddled together in one corner, were the three prisoners, expecting momentarily to be taken out and strung up. As the mob prepared for the final rush, one of the deputies poked his head out from a window and announced the escape of one of his prisoners by a back window. This was taken as a ruse by the gathering in front. However, a large man ran around behind and there stood 'Slim Jim' [one of Soapy's men] with his back against the wall, glancing about anxiously for an avenue of escape. The large man covered him with his gun, and grabbed him by the collar, half dragged him out into the open. Out at the end of the alley stood a man with a coil of new rope in one hand and a Colt's revolver in the other, apparently undecided as to which to use, grasping the situation and realizing the opportunity of using either. Just then, however, a squad of U.S. soldiers rushed in and took charge of the prisoner, martial law having been invoked in the meantime, and the troops summoned from Dyea . . .

"The three ringleaders were later tried before the Federal court and given heavy sentences in the penitentiary, the remainder of the gang sent to the States under a 'blue ticket,' with the warning not to return.

"Thus ended the colorful career of Soapy Smith, the hardest character Alaska had ever known."

These words were published 35 years after Whiting witnessed the end of Soapy's gang and while some of the details, as in all retelling, may never tell the story precisely as it was, the spirit of the moment is certainly here. His closing words to the story, overwritten as they are, have always moved me:

"Many seasons have since come and gone. The deep snows of Winter have fallen alike upon the just and the unjust. The chilling Arctic blast shrieks down the gulch and moans a solemn requiem over the silent city of the dead beneath the sombre spruces. The gaunt timber wolf emerges at night from the darkness out into the moonlight, glances furtively down at the few remaining lights in the deserted village below, crosses over the graves, leaves his tracks in the cold, dry snow, and slinks once more back into the darkness. Beneath all lie the earthly remains of Frank H. Reid and Jefferson R. Smith, sleeping on in peace throughout eternity."

Carved upon the monument erected over Reid's grave by the people of the town are the words: HE GAVE HIS LIFE FOR THE HONOR OF SKAGWAY.

The Pride of Canada

No doubt about it: there was far less crime and disorder in Canada's Yukon Territory than in America's Territory of Alaska. The reason was not to be found in some inherent difference between the two countries. To the contrary, the polyglot mixture of gold hunters from around the world was the same on either side of the border. The reason was the Mounties.

As one stampeder put it: "It seemed almost as if, after stepping off the mud into the snow, which was near the boundary, everything was absolutely changed. Here a little bunch of North West Mounted Police held sway. How they managed it goodness only knows, but they did.

"The little group of police in this part of the country were the pick of the Mounted, themselves a picked body. They handled the situation, not by brute force, which would have been a physical impossibility, but by common sense, tact, and fearlessness."

Three Mounties in one place constituted a showing of *force majeur*. "A single policeman would rise to an emergency and make his own law for the time being," wrote one gold miner, "and they were always Johnny-on-the-spot."

Col. Sam Steele, superintendent of the Mounties at Dawson, looked pompous in gold braid, waxed moustache, and feathered shako, but in action he was an efficient administrator and tireless overseer. At right, Steele relaxes with associates and their associates outside the NWMP barracks at Dawson on a sunny midnight in June, 1899. Left to right they are: a Miss Scott; Inspector Starnes of the Mounties; Mrs. Starnes; and Captain Henry Burstall of the Yukon Field Force (later Chief of the Canadian General Staff).

A force of well-armed Mounties, alert to the threat of highwaymen of Soapy Smith's persuasion, prepares to escort a cartload of dust out of the Yukon during the summer cleanup period. In the small, tubular canvas bags is roughly $400,000 in gold.

Mountie graveyard in Dawson (a contemporary photograph) is an austere, grassless plot surrounded by a chain-link fence. The average age at death was under thirty.

CHAPTER IX

WAITING OUT THE WINTER

"For those who have not laid in a winter's supply to remain here longer is to court death. . . . Starvation now stares everyone in the face who is hoping and waiting for outside relief . . ."

While the huge head of human pressure continued to build at the lakes, Dawson slipped into the long Yukon night, which is not to say a long winter's sleep. In those glorious years, Dawson was probably the most vibrant, changing, ever-fascinating small community in the world.

The big problem that seemed to face the town was the matter of food for the winter. Supplies were low, and many of the new arrivals had come in with the understanding that they could buy what they needed from the two big trading companies. And these newcomers amounted to perhaps three-quarters or more of those who were to winter in Dawson and on the creeks.

It wasn't a new problem. The winter of 1896–97 had been a true "starvation" winter. Those caught without provisions ended that season on a diet of straight flour, and when the sound of the whistle of the tiny steamer *Bella* was heard coming upstream in spring, the town became a madhouse. Arthur Walden recalled the scene. The whistle ". . . was answered from all over town by yells from the men and howls from the dogs. Everyone knew that the camp was saved. In less than an hour the old *Bella* was tied up to the bank, loaded equally with liquor and food, which were rushed ashore immediately. What few saloons there were opened up with free drinks: the ban was off, and *everybody* got drunk. This included the temperance men. But the crowd was good-natured, and there were no fights except among the dogs, who seemed to realize that something of importance was up and celebrated in their own way."

Between the first of the year and October of 1897, Dawson had grown prodigiously. From three or four houses in January the number had jumped to four or five hundred in October, not to count the rather extravagant buildings that had gone up along the river front. Dawson from the very beginning never lacked facilities for an evening's pleasure, and dancehalls and saloons—often the two together—were seemingly at every turn. One early observer stated that along the business blocks, every third door opened on a saloon.

In fall of '97, with the memory of the preceding winter foremost in the minds of all, a pall fell over Dawson.

Charles Constantine, head of the Mounties in the Yukon, announced in September that the Canadian government had found that there was insufficient food to sustain the population through the winter and those who were not already supplied with provisions should make haste to get to

Dawson City, locked in the iron grip of winter, was mecca to thousands of gold hunters struggling north from Skagway and Dyea. Its site at the confluence of the Klondike and Yukon Rivers was the heart of the mining district.

By the time the first Canadian mail service left the new town, Dawson had grown so prodigiously that it took 24 dogs and six men to handle the postal shipment—6000 pounds of letters.

The pleasures and vices of civilization quickly blossomed in the Yukon, fertilized by easy gold from Bonanza and Eldorado Creeks. The best bar in Dawson (above) offered bracing Tom and Jerries and had a mahogany buffet and a brass rail that would have done credit to a saloon in Seattle or San Francisco. Even the simple establishment below provided assorted liquors and pin-up pictures on the canvas wall.

Fort Yukon, where, he stated, rations were ample. In his impassioned plea, Constantine said:

"In a few days the river will be closed, and the move must be made now, if at all. It is absolutely hazardous to build hopes upon the arrival of other boats. It is almost beyond a possibility that any more food will come into this district. For those who have not laid in a winter's supply to remain here longer is to court death from starvation, or at least a certainty of sickness from scurvy and other troubles. Starvation now stares everyone in the face who is hoping and waiting for outside relief."

The town was full of fear and resentment—the companies were always suspect in the days after the Klondike discovery—and confusion reigned.

Captain Hanson of the Alaska Commercial Company echoed Constantine, but Captain Healy of the North American Trading and Transportation Company disputed both of them. Healy was right, as things turned out, but it wasn't until hundreds had undertaken the trying trip downstream, many of whom turned back to Dawson as the lesser of two perils, that Healy was found correct in his assessment.

Many had hoarded or overpurchased in anticipation of what Constantine predicted, and the surplus emerged as the picture grew clearer. No one starved to death for want of food in Dawson that winter; indeed the only ones to suffer were those with a tooth for luxury and without the means to buy more than bare subsistence.

One of the charming side stories of the whole affair was of what may be the only law-abiding, peaceable hijacking ever held on American soil. The story was recorded by several men who were in the country at the time, and although details vary in each account, Arthur Walden summed up its substance and spirit:

"Conditions at Circle City at this time were as follows: There were only eighty men left in the district, and they were all in the town itself, as the mines had to be closed down for the winter. No food had been left at Circle City by the passing river steamers since the year before. It had all been taken upstream to Dawson, where prices were higher, each boat promising that the next boat would leave provisions. So these eighty men were marooned, with no food, and with the season practically closed. There was no danger of actual starvation, as they could make their way back to Fort Yukon, eighty miles down the river. But if they did that they couldn't work their mines the next summer, as it would take them all winter to get their food up to Circle City and the summer to pack it on their backs out to the mines.

"The rising of the river gave them some hope that another boat would get up, but whether the boat would leave provisions or not they had no means of knowing. A Miners' Meeting was called, I think the last Miners' Meeting on the Yukon, and it was decided that if another boat came up and stopped at Circle City, the captain would be asked politely to put eighty outfits of food ashore. If he refused, the eighty miners would compel him to do it. In case the boat didn't stop, it was to be headed off at Fish Camp, where the river narrowed down, a move that could easily be done by shooting a shot or two through the pilot house, as the boats made very slow time at this point. The food was to be paid for at Dawson prices.

"I think it was the next day that the *Portus B. Weare* came around the bend and headed straight for shore. It reminded me of some large animal approaching the hunter. There was always the chance that at the last moment she would turn and run downstream. Unsuspecting, she pushed her nose into the bank, and a deck hand made her fast with a cable. The gangplank was swung out and the superintendent of the company walked ashore.

"He was immediately surrounded and the case was put to him, very politely. Refusing to comply, he turned and ordered the captain to have the line thrown off. A deck hand, walking up a couple of hundred feet to the place where the hawser was hitched to a stump, to carry out the order, was very much startled when twelve men confronted him with Winchesters over their arms. He walked back with his hands stuffed deep into his pockets, his head high in the air, whistling loudly. One of the pilots, approaching the fore part of the boat with an axe to cut the rope, was warned by the same twelve men and went back in a hurry.

"Negotiations were then opened, but instead of giving in with good grace the superintendent refused to allow the men any food on the ground that it was all bonded for the British side. The boat was held three days, every minute of which was valuable because the season was already late and, if the ice once began to run in the river, it would be absolutely impossible for her to get anywhere.

"It was eventually settled by the miners themselves going into the hold and unloading eighty outfits of food, which were taken into the company's store and immediately paid for in cash. Each man was paid by the storekeeper for the time he had worked in unloading the boat. I think this was the most decorous hold-up I have ever heard of. It must be understood that the steamboat and the store were under the same company."

All life is filled with contrast, but somehow the contrasts of life in the Yukon in the first years seem unreal. Men rich beyond dreams lived out

Prices at Jake's Saloon and Restaurant reflected the inflated money system. An oyster stew cost $15, which accounts perhaps for the woeful expression of the customers. Jake kept a gold-dust scale on the bar to handle transactions in the local specie.

"The Combination" theater and dance hall, sketched here by Tappan Adney, the versatile *Harper's Weekly* correspondent, was Dawson's most expensive night-club (admission $1) and the only one in a wooden building. (The competitors were in canvas tents.)

lives of drudgery and privation in the winter of 1896–97 and many others suffered through the next winter. One observer noted that the life of those on the creeks was meaner than that of "Negro plantation workers in the American South."

Scurvy, typhoid, exposure—all took their toll. Rich as the stakers on Bonanza and Eldorado were in gold and on paper, more than one died before he could enjoy a penny of his hard-won fortune. The bitterness of the elements and the brittle remoteness of the early days remained. Tappan Adney quoted Arthur Walden on his last winter run to Circle City in early 1897:

". . . When grub was high, I went down with a dog team to Circle. The wind blew so hard at one time that it blew the trail-sled, piled with stuff, clean over, and blew the dogs out in a string. You sweat like everything when you are travelling, and the Mackinaws freeze like a board. My coat froze, and I turned it to the fire and burned a hole in the back. I sews that up, but that made it so I couldn't button it in front; so I lets in a piece of gunny sack in front. I had gunny sacks around my legs and a mukluk on one foot and a moccasin on the other. I froze both feet, the tips of my fingers, and my nose, face, and ears. I was a pretty-looking sight when I got into Circle. The boys didn't know me. It is impossible to cover up the face so it will not freeze when it blows on the river. I didn't want any more of that, and I came up with a load and gave up freighting between here and Circle."

And while this was going on, a jackass by the name of Swiftwater Bill Gates was throwing his money away in Dawson at the gambling tables and at the feet of the ladies of demimonde, who did little to discourage him. Gates had been a swamper in a greasy-spoon restaurant in Circle City when he overheard the news of the Klondike find. The story of his life was written in 1908 by one of his several mothers-in-law, and while I'm sure her account is somewhere near the truth, at least in general, we will never know all the details. This we do know: He struck it rich on the Klondike creeks; he was a scraggly five feet four or five, had a Napoleonic ego, and would do virtually anything for attention; he squandered not only his own money but that of others with what seemed a religious fervor. He bought two wives, sisters, in succession, each of whom knew a good thing when she saw it; he seduced and finally married a fifteen-year-old, by whom he had two children; and then without benefit of divorce he married his teen-aged niece. He was pursued in Mack Sennett style up and down the Pacific Coast

Men and dogs worked underground through the winter, hauling out ore that would be washed for pay dirt come spring. The diggers above are working the celebrated No. 16 Eldorado claim of "Professor" Thomas Lippy, the young YMCA instructor from Seattle. At right, No. 17 Eldorado. Men are visible, working bucket winches atop each dump.

The tallest ore dump at No. 29 Eldorado contained an estimated $450,000 in gold when this photograph was made.

by outraged women who in the process always seemed to come out second best.

He was all talk, all color, and because of his posturing and gall he is remembered as one of the great characters of the time. In my book he was a contemptible show-off who served a purpose of sorts in the entertainment-starved days of Dawson. Underneath he was nothing more than a toady and con man who long since should have been banished from anything but circus histories of the great Klondike days. Unfortunately, such was his notoriety that he can't be ignored altogether.

But consider another, not so well remembered—a man who in the short time he had to do his work in Dawson was to endear, indeed enshrine, himself in the hearts of everyone who ever touched his life. His name was Father William Judge, a Jesuit priest who had already spent a dozen years in the Yukon. Father Judge—soon to earn the sobriquet "Saint of Dawson"—undoubtedly to his embarrassment if he ever heard it—labored with ascetic devotion to alleviate the suffering that grew from poor sanitation and grossly inadequate diet.

In 1897 he built a chapel and a hospital in the shadow of Moosehide, a huge landslide that dominated the north end of a steep escarpment towering above the town. He worked without surcease, sometimes 16 hours a day. He wouldn't sleep in his own bed if there was a sufferer in need of it. Typhoid fever and scurvy were the scourges that plagued Dawson and the creeks, and the sick had nowhere else to turn.

The hospital, which he named St. Mary's, cost more than $35,000 to build—money that was advanced without collateral or interest by the Alaska Commercial Company. The miners held a pass-the-hat fund-raiser and gathered the money needed and more. When fire took the small church, the hat was passed again. Father Judge didn't break his heart trying to meet the staggering responsibilities he had assumed, but the years of hard labor, concealed privation, and the toll of age left him without the strength to fight off pneumonia in January of 1899.

For all his saintliness, he was never out of touch with the men within his all-embracing ministry. The ubiquitous Arthur Walden told a story which, like all of his, speaks for itself:

"Whenever Father Judge had to make a visit to an outlying district, we

Mushing in a load of logs to brace a mine shaft, the men below struggle to hold their sled on a downhill slope. At bottom: the bucket winch at a mine head.

Inspector Charles Constantine, chief of the North West Mounted Police in the Yukon District, had a force of only 20 men when the gold rush began, but he proved himself to be a tough, business-like officer.

A window of bottles in a cabin in Dawson let in light, kept out winds at minus 50° Fahrenheit.

Enterprising Indians purveyed moose meat, fresh from the sled, outside the door of Dawson's log cabin bakery. Despite warnings of a winter of starvation, the bakery turned out fresh bread, rolls, and pies every day.

drove him across with our dog teams. Although he always wanted to pay us, we never accepted it. I was driving him one day, and, while running along beside my team on the hard trail, I happened to stub my toe. I am afraid my language was more or less questionable, and I apologized to the old man for having forgotten whom I had for a passenger. His reply was this: 'See here! A priest is no different from any other man, and your language to me shouldn't be any different. I know very well you didn't mean any disrespect to the Almighty, and He probably won't lay it up against you: it was just letting off steam. He will probably forgive you if you keep your word, are true to your partner, and don't get drunk any oftener than you have to. Men who do that are the kind of men we want.'

"He broke me of swearing for some time. This old man certainly understood us, and everyone who came his way got some benefit from him. Later on Alex MacDonald, known as the 'King of the Klondike,' built a chapel for him, under the altar of which the old man was subsequently buried."

Good hearts abounded in the Yukon, and although the mutual trust and code of the north which had seen the old-timers through more than 20 years without the formality of police and court rules had vanished, old traditions did not die. Under the strong and benevolent hand of the ramrod Mounties, Dawson was from the very beginning as law-abiding a town as could be found in North America. Gambling, dancing, drinking, all-night carrying on were part of everyday life (except for the Sabbath) as long as one man's frolic didn't impinge on the rights of others. The tables were straight; the girls, while aggressive, were not thieves; and the saloons gave fair measure, although it was early established that in the weighing of dust most of the error was in favor of the house.

So the winter of 1897–98 wore on. The fortunate claimholders and the men who labored for them built massive new dumps to wait the spring thaw. In the dead of winter, the Land of the Midnight Sun might have been called more aptly the Land of the High Noon Moon. The gloom, the cold

seemed endless, but for men with a poke and a hankering for some
diversion, Dawson did its best to provide what they wanted.

Until legitimate theater arrived in Dawson—and we will never know
quite the level of quality that the theatrical troupes brought north—the
cultural pickings were rather slim, as witness Tappan Adney's description
of nightlife in the latter part of 1897:

"During midsummer tour variety theaters were running, with the usual
adjuncts of bars and gambling lay-outs. They were respectively the
Pavilion, Monte Carlo, Mascot, and Combination. The last named was a
wooden building, but the rest were simply tents. The entrance to all was
through the barroom, but at the Monte Carlo there was an additional bar
inside the theater for the greater convenience of the patrons. The stage was
commodious, and in some there was real painted scenery, but in others the
'scenery' consisted solely of a screen of striped bed-ticking or similar goods,
which was also used abundantly for wall coverings. The audience seated on
boards placed on stools; but Eldorado kings, government officials, and
other 'dead game sports,' spending their money, occupied boxes on one or
both sides of the pit, and raised sufficiently to allow the occupants, who sat
upon hand-made board stools, to see over the heads of the common herd.
The price of admission was 50 cents (including cigar or drink) in all but The
Combination, where it was $1. For the boxes there was no extra fixed
charge, but occupants of such were expected to receive female members of
the troupe, or any lady friends they themselves might choose to bring in, to
help them dispose of champagne, which varied in price from $40 a quart to
$40 a pint.

"At the opening of the Monte Carlo one man spent $1700 for wine
during one night. The same evening two girls opened forty-eight bottles of
wine, receiving $4 commission on each bottle. The orchestra consisted
usually of piano, violin, trombone, and cornet, and musicians were each
paid $20 a day. The actors and actresses received various salaries, $150 a
week prevailing. At the Monte Carlo girls for the 'grand balls' after each
night's performance were specially employed at $50 per week and commis-
sions. The running expenses of the latter place were $500 a day."

The winter of 1897–98 in Dawson was a seller's market if ever one
existed. Food, hardware, companionship, warmth, entertainment of any

Turning his back on a spectacular view of
Dawson, the Yukon valley and the Klondike (left), a hunter on snowshoes goes
after small game for the tables of Dawson City.

Captain Hanson, swathed in furs and
formidably armed, represented the power
and glory of the Alaska Commercial
Company at Dawson. His warning to
U.S. and Canadian authorities that the
Yukon faced starvation helped avert that
danger—but it also panicked some miners into disastrous flight.

Big Alex McDonald, known as the "King of the Klondike," was a rough nugget who pyramided a single claim into a string of mines and had his hand in almost every business venture in the Dawson region.

kind were sold at prices that completely dazzled Canadian and American newspaper readers. They dazzled the people of Dawson, too, but none who had the money had complaints. Wages were high and a man could put a bit away if he didn't fall for all the temptations offered. If he were a Klondike "millionaire," he might well have taken part in the 1897 auction that Arthur Walden described:

"It was advertised at one of the dance-hall saloons that fall that a young girl [a 22-year-old French Canadian by the name of Mabel LaRose] would auction herself off to the highest bidder. Of course this was rather a unique event, so there was a large attendance at the saloon. When the auction opened, the girl was dressed in the usual garb of the dance hall, which was the latest Parisian fashion. She was assisted onto the bar and stood there while the auctioneer expounded the terms of the auction, which were, as far as I can remember, that she was to live with the highest bidder as his wife for the winter, doing his housekeeping. He and she were to act in every way as a married couple for the duration of that time. The money was to be deposited with one of the big companies, not to be paid to her till after the expiration of the time allotted. If this proved unsatisfactory to either party, the one breaking it lost the money put up. Courtesy and good treatment were called for on both sides.

"The bidding was sharp, as even the men who didn't want her liked the idea of being in it. It gradually got down to a few, and when the bidding showed signs of lagging, the girl was asked to walk up and down the length of the bar. There was nothing indecorous on either side. It was her right not to accept a bid if she didn't like the man. She was eventually knocked down for somewhere round five thousand dollars. How they came out I never heard."

And so the winter moon waned away in 1898, and even before the brilliance of wildflowers that burst forth each spring had shown their color, the vanguard of the horde that was to descend on Dawson began to trickle in. These were the men who had been trapped in the frozen Yukon vise near Dawson in October. When the ice finally broke that spring, Dawson was never again to be the same.

Winter travel to Dyea, on the coast of the Alaska panhandle, required courage and skill in handling a dog team. Every departure was a major event.

Waiting for the mail at Jimmy Keery's Palace Saloon and Billiard Hall on the frozen river front of Dawson City could occupy hours and sometimes days. Some of the men in the top picture have taken shelter behind a signboard inviting one and all to drop in at the Dawson Mining Exchange, one block east. The Exchange promised "room for everyone" (an important consideration at 30° below) and such services as "Mining and Real Estate Interests Bought and Sold on Commission . . . Money Loaned . . . Collections made (and) General Mining Business Transacted."

A considerable number were back in line the second day (right) and even more on the third day (below), March 5, 1898, all hoping to make what the Mining Exchange called "Outside Connections."

"The Armstrong Sawmill"

In the recorded history of the Rush, it is fair to say that of all the vexing trials the gold-seekers had to undergo, save for serious physical punishment of one kind or another, whipsawing took the prize. Or perhaps it was a tossup between whipsawing and the mosquitoes of summer. Both were known to drive men to a frenzy.

While a few had carried in knockdown boats or finished lumber, almost all had to saw planks from the slender spruce which grew on the slopes leading down to the lakes. It was an exacting job, one that taxed the tempers of all who tried it.

The method was simple: one man stood below and pulled the saw on the outgoing stroke. The man above guided the saw along the chalk lines on the log and lifted the saw in the non-cutting stroke. It took a great deal of coordination, and the man down below, who invariably got sawdust in his eyes, was usually the first to blow up.

It was said that the experience ended more good friendships than any institution except marriage. One observer wrote, "It should be suppressed. Two angels could not saw their first log without getting into a fight. It is more trying than the Chilcoot Pass."

CHAPTER X

DOWN RIVER TO DAWSON

"In all the history of transportation I doubt if there could be found at one time and in one place such odd and varying craft . . ."

From the Chilcoot and White Passes, at least 28,000 had descended on Lakes Lindeman and Bennett and Tagish Lake. The shores of the lakes for the next two years were to be crowded with the eager and innocent, the greenhorn and the old hand, the dreamer, the artisan, the hustler, and the merchant—men and women who were to carve a community deep in the Yukon wilderness and eventually open all of Alaska to the world.

To get from the lakes to Dawson with all the required food and equipment, the traveler had to buy or build a boat or barge of some sort. Some brought in knockdown outfits, and others bought lumber that was cut by the primitive mills that had been rushed into service. But most had to turn to the soul-testing process of whipsawing to produce the boards from which they would fashion their mongrel vessels for the trip downstream.

Every conceivable type of craft was built—some of them by professional boat builders, others that looked as though they had been put together by men who had never held a hammer or saw before. More than 7000 boats and barges were constructed during the winter and spring, and each was carefully recorded and given an identifying number by the Mounties.

In an early issue of *Alaska* magazine, one observer described the scene:

"In all the history of transportation I doubt if there could be found at one time and place such odd and varying craft as the boats which carried the intending prospectors, who went in over the trails, across Lakes Laberge and Bennett and down the Yukon. Men who had never been the distance of a country side to where a boat was being built, men who had scarcely traveled upon one, essayed to build one that would actually run the terrors of White Horse Rapids and stem the devilish current about Five Fingers. The boats looked like those a small boy whittles out with his first pocket-knife. The results were what might have been anticipated. Dozens, hundreds of them, many more than ever were reported, were lost without a moment's warning. At Lake Teslin scows were swamped containing 600 carcasses of cattle. Still a larger proportion than one would think possible carried their builders and outfits in safety to Dawson, where I saw them on shore, cut in half, and used for sheds, caches, etc. The story of these half boats is often the sign of a quarrel among partners. One of them was occupied as a laundry and a family lived in another."

A few of the early arrivals in the fall of 1897 managed to get their boats ready for the run to Dawson before the winter set in. Fortunately for many, winter was late that year, and the Yukon didn't freeze until the very end of

All the exhilaration and terror of the Yukon River run is caught in this view of a strange double-oared barge wallowing through White Horse Rapids. Although the picture was taken almost a decade after the height of the gold rush, the rapids of the Yukon continued to challenge boatmen—as they still do.

After a winter of sourdough society at the Ham Grease Saloon, the greenest chee-chako was ready to brave the river that led to the Klondike.

An enormous tent camp, presumptuously named "Lindeman City," sprang up on the shore of Lake Lindeman. Here, thousands of stampeders, having surmounted the Chilcoot Pass, stopped to build boats for the 500-mile journey to Dawson.

In summer the Canadian Post Office at Lake Tagish sorted letters outdoors; in winter, deliveries sometimes were delayed until frozen sacks thawed.

October. Tappan Adney was one of them, and his descriptions of the trip were typical of the adventures of those who were to follow him in the spring:

"I was laid up for a week—the constant wet and cold had been too much. Work stopped on our boat. On the 4th of October the snow went off. On October 5th our boat is finished; we had decided to remodel her, giving her six inches more width top and bottom. The last seam is calked today, and she is carried down to the lake, and the next day we load the goods into her. She stands 23 feet over all; 6 feet beam; 16 feet by 30 inches bottom; draught, 18 inches with 1500 pounds of cargo.

"We start amid a salvo of revolver shots. The lake is as smooth as glass—what Brown [his stalwart partner on the trip] calls an 'ash breeze.' So he gives her the ash oars until a real breeze springs up, when we hoist a sprit-sail, and in a short while are at the foot of the lake, where several other boats are about to be lined through a nasty thoroughfare into Lake Bennett. It has raised a great load of anxiety from our minds that our little boat carries her load so well; above all, even when loaded she responds to the oars in a way that delights Brown."

The first test they faced was to get through the rapids between Lake Lindeman, where Adney had assembled his boat, and Bennett. It was a short, fierce run, and it took a good boatman to make it through without a dunking or worse. J.B. Burnham, who witnessed the passage, later wrote in *Forest and Stream* magazine:

"Adney was an expert at river nagivation; and his companion, though inexperienced in this kind of work, was a champion oarsman, cool-headed and gritty. On a later occasion I happened to be on the trail near the point referred to, when I heard some men calling out from the top of the canyon-like bank that the *Harper's Weekly* man was shooting the rapids. I ran across just in time to see the boat swept by with the speed of a bolt from a crossbow, leaping from wavecrest to wavecrest, and drenching its occupants with sheets of spray. Adney and Brown were standing erect in bow and stern, each wielding a single oar used as a paddle, and from their masterly course it was evident that they had their boat well under control. It was all over in a very small fraction of time. They had avoided by the

narrowest margin jagged boulders that it seemed impossible to pass, and in a slather of foam shot out into the smooth water below."

The story was told of one poor man whose boat struck the rocks and sank. He returned to Skagway or Dyea, gathered another outfit, packed it over one of the passes and built a new boat only to smash it to pieces on the second trip through. Safe on shore, he cried, "What will become of Jane and the babies?" and then put a bullet through his head.

Essentially the same story was told about a man who struck what was known as "Casey's Rock" at the end of Thirty Mile River, another of the tougher parts of the descent to the Yukon River proper, and so we will never know for sure if the account above is accurate. The story is clouded in detail, but if one is to judge by the well-substantiated and terrifying stories of others, it is probably not apocryphal.

Of all the hazards of the river trip, none was worse than the pair of rapids that lay beyond between Lake Marsh and Lake Laberge, both downstream from Lake Bennett in the waters that led to Dawson. Miles Canyon was the first of them, and the even more treacherous White Horse Rapids lay two miles below. Adney's account of their trip through was typical of the many that were recorded:

A bearded adventurer shapes a tiller with a draw knife while a young woman stands primly by with a hand saw in this carefully posed scene of boatbuilding on the edge of Lake Lindeman. Note three tipis in the background.

At Lake Bennett, just north of Lindeman, the White Pass trail from Skagway joined the Chilcoot from Dyea. Here, too, stampeders created an instant city (long ago vanished) and an inland boatyard. Although saw mills sprang up, most boatbuilders economized by painfully cutting their own planks with the two-man whipsaw. One can count at least ten groups (left) sitting or standing triumphantly on partly finished hulls.

125

Lake Bennett (above) provided a relatively easy interlude of sailing, whereas Lake Marsh (below) sometimes was clogged with floes of melting ice. These boaters (photographed by E.A. Hegg) were waiting for the ice to move.

"After an hour's run in the swift current we pass a fine boat smashed on a rock in mid-stream. Soon we hear a shout, followed by another, 'Look out for the Canyon!' and on the right hand see boats lined up in a large eddy, below which is a wall of dark rock and an insignificant black opening. We pull into the eddy alongside. Some of the men are those we saw at Tagish, and some we never saw before. They have all taken a look at the Canyon, and most of them are unloading part of their goods and packing it around—a distance of three-fifths of a mile. We go up the trail to a spot where we can stand on the brink and look directly down into the seething waters of the gorge.

"Miles Canyon, named in honor of General [Nelson] Miles, is about a hundred feet wide and fifty or sixty feet deep, and the whole body of the Lewes River pours through at a high rate of speed between the perpendicular walls of basaltic rock of the hexagonal formation familiar in pictures of the famous Fingal's Cave. Halfway down, the Canyon widens, and there is a large eddy, which the boats are told to avoid by keeping to the crest of the waves, and then continuing as before. A boat starts in as we are looking, manned by two men at the side oars, and with a bow and stern steering oar.

"After our trip through Lake Bennett in the storm we feel pretty sure of our boat, so we conclude not to carry any of our stuff around. We tuck the

A "nasty thoroughfare," in the words of *Harper's* Tappan Adney, was the narrow chute of water between Lakes Lindeman and Bennett (left). It was the first hazard faced by voyagers who built their crafts at "Lindeman City," and provided a short but brisk inauguration for beginning boatmen.

There was a festive air in the squalid camp at Lake Bennett (right) on a day in late May, 1898, as these stragglers put finishing touches to their boats and prepared to join others who had hoisted sail for Dawson.

Farther north, Klondikers found smooth sailing on Lake Marsh (below, right) and Lake Laberge (above), the vast, notoriously windy inland sea celebrated in the poem of Robert Service as the place where Sam McGee from Tennessee found comfort at last in being cremated.

tarpaulin down close and make everything snug, and when Brown has seated himself at the oars, and said, 'All ready!' we push off and head for the gateway. I think I notice a slight tightening of Brown's mouth, but that is all, as he dips the oars and begins to make the long stroke; but perhaps he can retaliate by saying some unkind thing of me at this time. As soon as we are at the very brink we know it is too late to turn back, so when we slide down the first pitch I head her into the seething crest. At the first leap into the soapsuds the spray flies several feet outward from the flaring sides. A dozen or two huge lunges into the crests of the waves, and we know that we shall ride it out. All at once—it must be we are not exactly in the middle—the boat's nose catches in an eddy and we swing around, head up stream. It is a simple matter to turn her nose again into the current, and then we go on again, leaping and jumping with terrific force. Brown, who manages the oars splendidly, keeps digging them, and in a few moments we emerge from between the narrow walls into an open basin."

Jack London, whose great literary career was founded on his experiences in the Yukon country, wrote of his trip through the canyon:

"Lashing the steering oar so that it could not possibly escape, I allotted my comrades their places; for I was captain. Merritt Sloper, direct from adventures in South America and who knew a little of boating, took his

Capsized in the swirling, rock-strewn shallows of Thirty Mile River, these unlucky navigators succeeded in salvaging most of their outfit, then faced the task of repairing and reloading.

On a calm stretch just above Miles Canyon, boaters rested in anticipation of the ordeal ahead.

A horse-drawn tram with log rails trundled boats past Miles Canyon and the White Horse Rapids—for a price. Several of these resourceful transport engineers, not missing a trick, are wearing mosquito netting attached to their hats.

position in the bow with a paddle. Thompson and Goodman, landlubbers who had never rowed before this trip, were stationed side by side at the oars. . . .

"'Be sure to keep on the Ridge,' cried the men on the bank as we cast off.

"The water, though swift, had a slick, oily appearance until we dashed into the very jaws of the Box, where it instantly took on the aspect of chaos broken loose. Afraid that the rowers might catch a crab or make some other disastrous fumble, I called the oars in.

"Then we met it on the fly. I caught a glimpse of the spectators fringing the brink of the cliffs above, and another glimpse of the rock walls dashing by like twin lightning express trains; then my whole energy was concentrated in keeping to the Ridge. This was serrated with stiff waves, which the boat, dead with weight, could not mount, being forced to jab her nose through at every lunge. For all the peril, I caught myself smiling at the ridiculous capers cut by Sloper, perched in the very bow and working his paddle like mad. Just as he would let drive for a tremendous stroke, the stern would fall in a trough, jerking the bow clear up, and he would miss the water utterly. And at the next stroke, perhaps, the nose would dive clean under, almost sweeping him away—and he only weighed one hundred pounds. But never did he lose his presence of mind or grit. Once, he turned and cried some warning at the top of his lungs, but it was drowned in the pandemonium of sound. The next instant we fell off the Ridge. The water came inboard in all directions, and the boat, caught in a transverse current, threatened to twist broadside. This would mean destruction. I threw myself against the sweep till I could hear it cracking, while Sloper snapped his paddle short off.

"And all this time we were flying down the gutter, less than two yards from the wall. Several times it seemed all up with us; but finally, mounting the Ridge almost sidewise, we took a header through a tremendous comber and shot into the whirlpool of the great circular court.

"Ordering out the oars for steerage-way, and keeping a close eye on the split currents, I caught one free breath before we flew into the second half of the canyon. Though we crossed the Ridge from left to right and back again, it was merely a repetition of the first half. A moment later the *Yukon Belle* rubbed softly against the bank. We had run the mile of canyon in two minutes by the watch.''

Arthur Walden was also on the scene, and his account of the Miles Canyon run adds a lighter touch to the record:

"The water above the canyon is about a quarter of a mile wide with a six-mile current; this narrows to a hundred feet or less, between sheer blank walls of rock that tower far up into the air, the water sucking down into this natural sluice-box at about eighteen miles an hour. The current is ridged up in the middle five or six feet high, and on top are tremendous

At Miles Canyon, the Lewes River (upper Yukon) pours through a narrow gorge of perpendicular basalt rock. The trick here, as Jack London learned, was to keep to "the Ridge" (i.e., away from the canyon walls). The mile-long run took London only two breathtaking minutes.

White Horse Rapids, as these pictures amply illustrate, was the raw material of short stories, novels, grandfather-tales, and Yukon legends, Although a few inexperienced or ill-fated boaters lost their lives, thousands of average men survived and even carried home E.A. Hegg photographs to record the experience, whether it included waving one's hat, like the man in the Peterboro canoe at the left, or merely hanging on, as in the pictures above and below.

rollers, so that a boat is always standing on one end or the other.

"Halfway down, the canyon bends sharply to the left, and there is a large whirlpool on the inner side. It is about two hundred feet across, and in it the water goes around at a terrific pace. The rim is high and the center many feet lower; there is, however, no suction toward the center, and if a boat is not dashed to pieces on the walls there is not much danger, as there are no rollers."

"The trick of going through the canyon was to keep the boat straight and cross the whirlpool as far on the right as possible without hitting the wall; if this was not done, you were likely to get into the merry-go-round and had to trust to luck to get out. I remember two Swedes who had this experience and were carried round and round for over two hours, in spite of all their efforts to get out. At last they gave themselves up as lost and lay down in the bottom of the boat, but after a time they were suddenly swept out and down the rest of the way without mishap. There is a saying in the Yukon, 'As lucky as a Swede.'"

The most dramatic run of all was the trip through the White Horse Rapids, which like the canyon had claimed many lives in the years before the big rush. The figures are uncertain, but we know that at least 10 drowned and scores of boats were wrecked and lost in the first three days of the spring run in 1898. The Mounties, once perceiving the magnitude of the peril, ordered everyone on the river either to demonstrate river-running competence or to hire professional pilots to get his boat through the treacherous rapids. Their action raised some hackles but without question saved many lives.

Both Adney and London left vivid impressions of their passage through the White Horse. Something of each man can be discerned by a careful reading of his words. The "Mane" that London alludes to is the churning, white-capped section at the end of the rapids:

"When we struck the 'Mane,' the *Yukon Belle* forgot her heavy load, taking a series of leaps almost clear of the water, alternating with as many burials in the troughs. To this day I cannot see how it happened, but I lost

130

control. A cross current caught our stern and we began to swing broadside. Then we jumped into the whirlpool, though I did not guess it at the time. Sloper snapped a second paddle and received another ducking.

"It must be remembered that we were travelling at racehorse speed, and that things happen in a tithe of the time taken to tell them. From every quarter the water came aboard, threatening to swamp us. The *Yukon Belle* headed directly for the jagged left bank, and though I was up against the steering sweep till it cracked, I could not turn her nose downstream. Onlookers from the shore tried to snapshot us, but failed to gauge our speed or get more than a wild view of angry waters and flying foam.

"The bank was alarmingly close, but the boat still had the bit in her teeth. It was all happening so quickly that I for the first time realized I was trying to buck the whirlpool. Like a flash I was bearing against the opposite side of the sweep. The boat answered, at the same time following the bent of the whirlpool, and headed upstream. But the shave was so close that Sloper leaped to the top of a rock. Then, on seeing we had missed by a couple of inches, he pluckily tumbled aboard, all in a heap, like a man boarding a comet.

"Though tearing like mad through a whirlpool, we breathed freer. Completing the circle, we were thrown into the 'Mane,' which we shot a second time and safely landed in a friendly eddy below."

Having surveyed the stretch, as did all who were to run the fabled waters, Adney lightened his boat to increase the freeboard, and he and the redoubtable Brown headed their boat, which was built on the lines of a Canadian bateau, into the current and entered the passage of no return.

"For a quarter of a mile it lashes itself into a perfect fury, and then, with a jumping and tossing, it bursts through a gorge a span wide with banks level with the water, and then spreads out serene, once more the wide, generous river. . . .

"Following the roughest water, to avoid rocks, we are soon in the dancing waves and pitching worse by far than in the Canyon. As we jump from wave to wave, it seems positively as if boat and all would keep right on through to the bottom of the river. The water even now is pouring in, and it is plain that the boat will never live through. One thought alone comforts us: the fearful impetus with which we are moving must surely take us bodily through and out, and then—we can make the shore somehow. I count the seconds that will take us through.

"The water even now is pouring in, and it is plain that the boat will never live through," wrote Tappan Adney. Both he and the boat made it.

With oarsmen fore and aft and a sturdy passenger clinging to the mainmast, an awkward scow from the great shipyard at Lake Lindeman waddles into the maelstrom at White Horse.

Defeated by the rocks of White Horse Rapids, six men sit stoically while other Klondikers haul their sinking barge to shore. The consequences would be weeks of labor repairing the vessel, drying out salvageable supplies (right), and repacking for the journey—precious time lost from the search for gold.

"The effect to the eye, as we enter the great whitecaps, is that of a jumping, not only up and down, but from the sides to the middle.

"Now we are in. From sides and ends a sheet of water pours over, drenching Brown and filling the boat; the same instant, it seems, a big side-wave takes the little craft, spins her like a top, quick as a wink, throws her into a boiling eddy on the left—and we are through and safe, with a little more work to get ashore.

"Men who were watching us from the bank said that we disappeared from sight in the trough. Brown is wet up to his waist. Everything is afloat. We jump out leg-deep into the water near shore, and when we have bailed out some of the water, drop the boat to the usual landing place, a little sandy cove, where we unload, pitch tent, and watch the other boats come through. They are all big ones, and all get through without mishap. Our goods are not damaged, because the sacks were tight and they were wet for so short a time. . . .

"There have been no drownings in the White Horse this year, so far as known. But probably no fewer than forty drownings are to be credited to this bit of water since the river was first opened to white men.

"The trail around the rapids is lined with trees blazed and inscribed with the heroic deeds of those gone before. They are written on trees, on scraps of paper, on broken oar blades. Some are amusing, while all are interesting.

Warping a river steamer through Five Finger Rapids (below) required use of hawsers and tow-barges and brought curious spectators to the cliffs above.

At the junction of the Yukon and the misty Stewart River, stampeders brew coffee, cook flapjacks. and rejoice, knowing it is now only one day's run to Dawson City.

Jack London, seen here in the nautical surroundings of his later novels, completed his downstream passage in autumn, 1897, just before ice closed the river, but spent the winter at Stewart River, soaking up tales of the Yukon that later made his literary reputation.

"A load of anxiety is off our minds now that we are safely through. Next morning, before starting, we watch some boats come through. It is a great sight as they come dancing into view at the turn; and as they go flying past we give them each a rousing cheer."

London and Adney were both to make it downstream before winter locked the river, but London wintered at the mouth of the Stewart River, a day's run from Dawson. Many of the tales he heard through the long winter were to form the bases for the extraordinary stories on which his reputation was to rest.

Once winter set in, the business of boat building and planning for the spring breakup began for those who continued to pour in over the passes.

Toward the end of May the ice in the lakes began to loosen, and on the 29th it began to move. This was the moment the waiting Klondikers had been looking for. In a couple of days the ice cleared and they were off by the thousands. The 600-mile voyage was filled with adventure for all. From the bottom of the White Horse Rapids the last 475 miles downstream to Dawson was fairly simple, and the stampeders, almost to the man, rushed ahead with all the power they could summon.

For many it had been six months or more of hardship and suffering, but by the time they reached the mouth of the Stewart River—just one more long day's run to Dawson and the rich Klondike diggings—the past was put aside and the dream of gold burned as brightly as ever.

Sourdough flapjacks were sustenance at the end of the trail, but for Klondike miners the 600-mile voyage from the coast to Dawson was only a beginning of the grand adventure.

OLD YUKON TALES

Of the code duello in the frozen North

HIGH NOON AT CIRCLE CITY
*Arthur Walden's account of a
shoot-out that hung fire*

Back in the summer of '96 there was a man in Circle City who had been in the country fourteen years, and had come from Montana, where in his younger days he had hunted the last of the buffalo. But having killed a man there he left the country and came to Alaska, gradually working his way into the interior.

He was in no way a bad man in the present sense of the word, but being a product of the early West he was a law unto himself. He was not in the least quarrelsome; in fact we always found him very good-natured. You could play almost any trick or joke on him and he would not take offense. But any insult he resented, as in the early days when the West was wild. He was absolutely honest and a great respecter of women, although he knew very few. I shall call this man Stanley, as he is still alive.

There was another man in Circle City whom I shall call Higgins. He had a very bad disposition and was generally feared when he was liquored up. Guns were not packed at that time, for everybody had to carry his stuff by dog-train in the winter and on his back in the summer, and a six-pound gun meant two days' rations. Also the climate was against quarreling.

As it happened, Stanley and Higgins got into a row, and as they were not fist-fighters they ran for their cabins to get their revolvers. Stanley getting out first, Higgins took a crack at him through his window, shooting through the glass and missing him. Then Stanley ran around behind Higgins's cabin, pulled out the moss from between the logs, squinted in, and, seeing nothing but Higgins's legs, he creased him across the calf, not doing him any harm.

There had been a duel in Circle City the year before, and the Canadians at Fortymile had made cracks about the lawlessness on the American side. The men of Circle City, not wanting to justify this name, called a Miners' Meeting on these two men to stop their fighting. This Miners' Meeting was held in Jack McQuesten's trading post, a log building over a hundred feet long. A chairman and clerk of court were chosen as usual, but proceedings came to a halt because neither man would make an accusation against the other.

Some men spoke of their shaking hands and making it up, some wanted to see a fight and kept quiet: but the majority didn't know what to do. . . Finally, the chairman gave up his chair to another man, and addressed the meeting. "Mr. Chairman and Gentlemen! I make a motion we let these two men fight. If one is killed we will give him Christian burial; if both are killed we will give them both Christian burial. But if one survives, we'll hang him!"

Another man took the cue, and stepping forward said, "I'll make the amendment that if either man is found dead under suspicious circumstances, the other shall be hung without trial." Unanimous verdict.

Then Higgins stepped forward and said, "I'll not fight under any such conditions as these, as I know I'll kill Stanley and I don't want to get hung."

This ended the trial. But to my own knowledge these two men met each other on the sixty-five-mile trail to the mines and no harm came of it. Each man knew that if either turned up missing, the other would be hanged. And I actually believe that if either man had fallen down a prospect hole or into the Yukon, the other would have pulled him out. Yet each hoped for the other's death by some means or other not traceable to him. They were brave men both, yet each was always afraid the other would either forget or take the chance.

Later, Higgins got into a row with Kronstadt, a bartender, and, sending him warning through his friends that he was going to kill him, appeared in the doorway of the saloon with his uplifted gun. Kronstadt instantly drew his gun from under the bar, and, instead of raising it, fired from the level of the bar, striking his man under the eye, the bullet going out through the back of his head. By shooting in this way, he gained a fraction of a second on his opponent.

Immediately afterwards Kronstadt wrote his own notice out, calling a Miners' Meeting on himself, walked across to the trading post, pinned it up, and everybody followed him in. He was tried and acquitted in twenty minutes. Of course the ban was off Stanley, owing to Higgins's death, and to celebrate he deposited all the dust he had with a saloon-keeper: it was free drinks for all as long as it lasted. Then he put on his best clothes and went to the funeral.

RULE, BRITANNIA
*William Ogilvie, surveyor and administrator,
recalls an instance of imperial solidarity*

At Fortymile there was a challenge issued for a duel through a dispute over a woman. An Englishman and an American quarrelled because the American's squaw accepted too many attentions from the Englishman, so they were to shoot over it. The time was at five in the morning, the place on the ice in front of Fortymile. As the story went, the Englishman appeared at the time and place appointed, armed with a Winchester rifle, and brought with him, in what capacity no one knew, a big Canadian, armed with a double-barrelled shot-gun, who remained on top of the bank.

The American came along soon after, armed with a large six-shooter. He looked to the front, and there was the Empire [British, lest one wonder]; he looked to his left flank, and there, too, was the Empire, one of the five nations furnishing, we may assume, a voluntary contribution to the defense. He was uncertain as to what part that shot-gun would take in the dispute, and the owner was a very sphinx, so he abandoned the field. There was peace after, proving that a well-prepared defense makes for good understanding.

Red-letter Days in Dawson

While there were diversions aplenty in Dawson, perhaps none was more welcome than the occasions which arose spontaneously or were formally organized to bring throngs to the streets. Usually it was a holiday or some civic celebration planned in advance, but it could have been nothing more momentous than the arrival or departure of a riverboat, or the public reading of a newspaper account of high interest. Left, one of several readings that were given during the summer of 1898 of the news on the Spanish-American War, in this case the story of the American victory in the Battle of Santiago. Below, the Mounties fire a salute to mark Queen Victoria's birthday.

Above, another reading for the news-hungry multitude, this time the news of Admiral Dewey's smashing victory over the Spaniards. Right, Captain Jack Crawford leading the color guard through the crowd after delivering a stirring patriotic address from the speakers' stand in front of the notched-log skyscraper in the background.

200 YARD RACE
DAWSON JULY 4th 99.

On the Fourth, there wasn't a vantage point to be found for the relays, obstacle races, sprints and all the other track events that were part of the celebration. The day had begun at one minute past midnight in the light of the midnight sun with the most God-awful racket the Americans (who made up 75 to 80 percent of the population) could generate. Tappan Adney estimated that 5,000 pistols, rifles and shotguns were fired repeatedly in the pandemonium. The dogs in town went crazy and ran wildly in an attempt to get away. It took days for many owners to find their terrified animals.

While there were no thoroughbreds in Dawson, the Klondike Derby generated just as much enthusiasm as the big race at Churchill Downs, and a lot of money changed hands after it was run.

The vaulter flies over the bar which may have been set as high as eight feet—not much in these days of fiberglass poles and 18-foot marks. But, given the circumstances, not a bad jump at all. The 1896 Olympic champion won at 10″9³/₄′.

Queen Victoria's Birthday races drew crowds just as large as did the Fourth of July festivities.

No Western town was without its hose team or teams—the object of civic pride and even more so of those who made the team, as the expressions on the faces of these young stalwarts clearly reflect.

While this noontime parade lacks the lotus-land glitter of today's Tournament of Roses spectacle, it's the real article—home made and as charming a sight as you could find anywhere.

CHAPTER XI

BOOM TOWN
IN THE BOG

"Buildings of every description sprang up like mush-rooms in a night. . . . Three sawmills, running night and day, were unable to supply the demand . . ."

Dawson was a boom town like nothing the world had seen since San Francisco in the days of the 49ers. As the newcomers poured in, the population jumped to somewhere near 40,000. Whatever the exact number, Dawson, almost overnight, became the largest North American city west of Winnipeg and north of Seattle.

Many stampeders lived on their boats after they arrived before deciding what they were going to do, because if they learned nothing else when they first touched shore, it was that every inch along all the known gold-bearing creeks had long since been claimed. There were no nuggets free for the picking. Klondike fortunes were still to be made, but they would be made by men who were on the ground first or by others who had the capital to buy them out.

But for all the disappointment, Dawson was still an exciting, bustling town, and street life was a continuing show. Many quickly found that there were more ways to make money than to dig it from the ground. Virtually any service and commodity available in Canada and the States could be found in Dawson before the middle of summer. And in every place of business, large and small, there were gold scales to weigh the precious dust as it passed from hand to hand—carefully measured at the prevailing rate, 16 dollars an ounce.

Prices were outrageous that summer, as they had been through the winter, the only difference being that with the supplies that came over the passes and up the river from St. Michael, almost anything could be had for a price. Tappan Adney caught the color of it:

"It was a sight just to walk along the waterfront and see the people, how they lived. Some slept in tents on their scows. One stumbled over others on the ground under robes or blankets.

"Outfits of all descriptions were placarded 'for sale,' and these were surrounded by representatives of eating places buying provisions, or old-timers buying underwear and tobacco. Tinned goods, butter, milk, fresh potatoes were eagerly asked for.

"The first to get in with provisions made small fortunes, for by good luck they brought the very things that would sell best. The first case of 30 dozen eggs brought $300. Soon the market was better supplied, and eggs fell to $150 a case, and in two weeks came down to $3 a dozen; milk, $1 a can; tinned mutton, $2.50 a pound; oranges, apples, and lemons, $1 each; potatoes brought 50 cents a pound; a watermelon, $25. Regular market stands were opened for the sale of vegetables of all kinds, and the waterfront looked like a row of booths at a fair.

"Every conceivable thing was displayed for sale—clothing, furs, moc-

Dawson had all the familiar, raunchy characteristics of a 19th-century boom town on the North American frontier—raw streets, flimsy saloons, stray dogs, loveable tarts, and horrendous prices.

The wooden hulls that had carried thousands of fortune hunters downstream served as dwellings during the summer of '98, when rooms were scarce in Dawson City and houses commanded a hundred times their price in the States.

Front Street, the main boulevard, was no thoroughfare for a team and wagon during the warm summer rains. Boggy lots sold for as much as $20,000, and a load of lumber, fresh from the sawmill, brought 20¢ a foot—a dazzling figure in those days.

Venetian Dawson, at the junction of the Yukon and the Klondike, was more than normally inconvenient for pedestrians in flood time.

casins, hats and shoes, groceries, meat, jewelry. There were hardware and thoroughly equipped drug and dry goods stores. Here is one of the signs:

```
DRUGS   DRUGS

Rubber boots, Shoes, Etc.

Bacon, flour, rolled oats, rice, sugar,
     potatoes, onions, tea and
        coffee, fruits, corn
     meal, German sausage,

        Dogs   Dogs
```

"In the brief space of a few days there seemed to be nothing that could not be purchased in Dawson, from fresh grapes to an opera glass, from a safety pin to an ice cream freezer. . . .

"When meals dropped to $2.50, what a treat it was—no longer obliged to stand up before a rough board, nor to live on homemade flapjacks, beans and bacon, until, as one man expressed it, he was 'ashamed to look a hog in the face.' Instead, we sat down at tables covered with clean linen. What a feast, the fresh vegetables and the curried mutton! They have tried to tell us that when a man left this country he didn't feel he had a square meal without bacon and beans. The man was only joking. We could understand now how Pat Reagan felt when describing an outfit which a Dutchman lost in Five Fingers the year Pat came in. 'It was a foine outfit,' said Pat. 'He had two whole cases of condensed milk.'"

The prices for real estate were enough to stagger all but the high rollers. In the States a comfortable cottage could be built for $500, and a flat in San Francisco might fetch $4 a month in rent. But in Dawson, the boggy land went for unheard-of prices. Adney's seemingly exaggerated account of what he found in 1897 might be questioned, but government reports not only substantiate his figures but show that the boom continued on without surcease all the way through 1898:

". . . buildings of every description sprang up like mushrooms in a night, from the black, reeking bog. Many of them were of substantial logs and lumber, but the greater part, both large and small, were mere coverings, intended to last only through the summer.

"First a frame of rough scantling went up, then a covering of white or blue drilling hastily stitched together into the form of a tent and thrown over, with openings for windows and doors; fitted with seats and tables for restaurants, with shelves and counters for stores, and with the appropriate furniture for gambling houses and saloons. Several buildings of dressed lumber, intended for use as stores, hotels, and theaters, were as handsome as one would care to see. The river front was leased by the government officials to a favored individual for about $1 a foot per month, and re-leased by him to builders at $8 to $13 a foot per month; and this was solidly packed with tent-covered frames, excepting a few hundred feet reserved for the landing of steamers and at the ends of two cross-streets.

"As high as $20,000 was paid for a desirable corner lot for a saloon, while a two-story log building in the center of town was worth with the lot anywhere from $30,000 to $40,000. The government surveyed what public land had not been previously granted to townsite claimants into 40-by-

Motley but amiable, the street crowd usually included some swaggering Australians, Englishmen in tweeds, Americans from every state, and even a few women—in this case, a lone precursor of Rose Marie, wearing the hat of a North West Mountie.

Arrival of the riverboat *Seattle No. 1*
under the midnight sun brought a curious
crowd to the river's edge to look over the
new "cheechakos"—tenderfeet—who
usually were as broke as the old-timers.

The Gibson brothers, displaying their
bounty of ducks and hares on the eaves of
the Montana Steam Laundry, were
among the many Dawson residents who
saw more opportunity for gain in trade
than in mining for gold.

A meeting of the Miners' Association at
the Presbyterian Church on December 6,
1898, had as its modest aims pure government, improved mining regulations, and
the abolition of royalty.

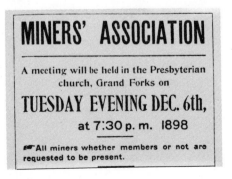

MINERS' ASSOCIATION

A meeting will be held in the Presbyterian
church, Grand Forks on

TUESDAY EVENING DEC. 6th,
at 7:30 p. m. 1898

☞ All miners whether members or not are
requested to be present.

144

60-foot lots for cabins, and assessed locators from $200 to $500 each, prices which they justified as being only half the market value.

"Three sawmills, running night and day, were unable to supply the demand for lumber, which was worth at the mill $150 to $200 per thousand feet. Men stood with teams waiting, taking the boards as they fell from the saw. Nails were so scarce that a keg of 100 pounds brought $500; a single pound cost $6, and $3.50 per pound was paid for burned nails from the ruins of the 'Opera House.' So that a building of the size of some of these that went up cost $5,000 to probably $10,000 for the shell alone. One of the trading companies had a large stock of cotton drilling, worth perhaps 8 cents a yard, which it disposed of at 75 cents a yard."

Those who had wintered in Dawson were not overawed by the men who came in on the spring flood, even though they couldn't wait to see the new faces, to hear the news from outside, and perhaps to prosper in some small way from the influx of new money.

But most of the cheechakos were as broke as those who had failed to find gold the year before, and their disappointment was evident. Even the compassionate Adney had this to say:

"Who is there that can describe the crowd, curious, listless, dazed, dragging its way with slow, lagging step along the main street? Can this be the 'rush' that newspapers are accustomed to describe as the movement of gold seekers? Have the hard, weary months of work on the trails exhausted their vitality? Or is it the heavy shoes that make them drag their feet so wearily along the street?

On the Dawson waterfront the Seattle-Yukon Transportation Company (S.Y.T.) boasted a commodious wooden shed, a stockpile of canned goods and grain, and a restaurant that called itself Delmonico.

Even the outdoor bakery was equipped with a set of balance scales with which to weigh out gold dust, legal tender in the Yukon at $16 an ounce.

"It is a motley throng—every degree of person gathered from every corner of the earth, from every State of the Union, and from every city—weatherbeaten, sunburned, with snow glasses over their hats, just as they came from the passes. Australians with upturned sleeves and a swagger; young Englishmen in golf stockings and tweeds; would-be miners in Mackinaws and rubber boots, or heavy, highlaced shoes; Japanese, Negroes—and women, too, everywhere. It is a vast herd; they crowd the boats and fill the streets, looking at Dawson. Some are disappointed. 'This is not as big as Skagway,' they say. The old-timer (we are all old-timers now) is lost. The mere recognition of a face seen last winter is now excuse for a friendly nod and a 'How-de-do?' The crowd is good natured, elbowing and slowly tramping back and forth."

Kathryn Winslow, in her book *Big Pan Out,* synthesized contemporary observations. It was not a joyous scene:

"Few arrived in Dawson wearing puff ties and spats. Most of the 1898 cheechakos looked, and were, no more prosperous than the disappointed men they saw crowded to the water front. First impressions of the town were of its steaming muddy streets—for it rained frequently early in the summer and the temperature was seldom under eighty; of its hundreds of British and American flags blowing as if for a holiday; of its dog-drawn funeral carts, endlessly passing by on their way uphill to the cemetery; of the enormously high prices which kept most men from buying even a square meal. A canned oyster stew was $15 a bowl. A cucumber was $5, a radish $1. Porterhouse steak was $8 at the Arcade restaurant, one of the few places where they served beefsteak. Moose was commoner."

Health problems remained serious in 1898, although scurvy was greatly diminished because of the great variety of vegetables, fresh and canned, that came into the district after the ice broke. But typhoid and dysentery remained epidemic. Adney:

"As had been predicted, the town was in a terrible sanitary condition. There was no drainage, and, except by giving warning about cesspools, the government did nothing but provide *two* public conveniences, entirely inadequate for a town of nearly 20,000. Fortunately, good drinking water was had at several springs. Still, as could not be otherwise in a city built upon a bog, by midsummer, the hospital was filled to overflowing, men were lying on the floor; and there were many in cabins, suffering from typhoid fever, typhoid–malaria, and dysentery. The number of deaths were three to four a day, in one day reaching a total of nine. At this juncture, when the amount of sickness had become a cause for general alarm, the Canadian doctors, who were greatly outnumbered by Americans, began prosecutions against the latter, and several of the highest standing, but who had come unprovided with licenses to practice in Canada, were haled before the magistrate, jailed, and fined. While Americans should have expected this, it was admitted by most persons that a more unfortunate moment for the prosecutions could hardly have been chosen. The American physicians continued practicing, however, without signs or asking fees. In all there were about seventy physicians in the camp, only a few of whom, however, found lucrative practice."

At the portals of the Yukon Board of Trade, four young performers on donkey-back stirred up enthusiasm for the opening of Dawson's newest theater.

The arrival of a dog team could signal a new girl in town or a box of canned oysters. Either was welcome.

Refuse from the creeks that came down the Klondike combined with the garbage and excrement that Dawson poured into the waters to raise a noisome stink. The daytime heat of summer (and it was daytime almost all the time) exacerbated the problem.

Still, life in Dawson was far from being all death, diarrhea, and high prices. The redeeming quality of faith in others was not totally snuffed out by the passing of the old Yukon days of complete trust. Businesses thrived, and newspapers blossomed in the summer, replacing sketchy communication by word of mouth, ancient "outside" newspapers, and posted notices on the bulletin boards of the Alaska Commercial Company.

In July the *Klondike Nugget* recorded this remarkable blessing that was visited on Dawson:

THIRTY DOLLARS A GALLON

The first milk cow ever in Dawson arrived on Wednesday. She is not very well pleased with her surroundings and did not give much milk, but that first milking brought in just $130 in Klondike dust. She will be treated to the best that Dawson affords—flour and packing case hay—and is expected to do better as the days grow shorter. One hundred dollars a milking is not too much to expect of her, as she comes of good family and will not do anything to make her ancestors turn over in their graves—or more properly speaking, in the stomachs of their patrons. H. I. Miller is the man who brought her in along with 19 male companions. The gentleman is more favorably known as Cow Miller, and as Cow Miller let him be known from this on.

Cleaning Up in Summer

When Spring came and the sun rose high and lingered in the sky, the ground began to thaw and the ice in the streams and tributaries of the Yukon began to move. The great day came when the ice broke up in the big river itself—a thrilling and deafening spectacle for all. For the miners it meant the beginning of summer cleanup, the end of a long winter's labor. Gold in the huge dumps of paydirt that grew during the seven or eight frozen months before could not be separated from the clay and gravel until water from the creeks could be diverted into the simple flumes which carried it to long sluice boxes. In placer mining, separation of free gold relies on a simple principle: wash the paydirt with water in a trap of some kind where gravity will leave the much heavier gold behind as other material is carried away. The simplest device is the pan, in which, with a swirling motion and the addition of more water when needed, the miner settles the gold to the bottom as the worthless dirt is washed over the lip. The men above are using the pan to test a sample of paydirt before it makes its way through a sluice box. The sluice box itself is the principal tool used in gathering free gold, whatever the means of collecting paydirt might be—underground workings, hydraulic washing, or simple surface shoveling. In the sluice box, as shown here, the miners nailed riffles—converging lengths of saplings, slats or bars—which slowed the passage of the water/paydirt mixture and held back the heaviest particles, the gold, which in turn could be scooped out for further refinement.

Sizable crews were required to clean up the winter's diggings. Above, the gang at Antone Stander's exceedingly rich Eldorado Creek claim. Left, a sluice box on a Bonanza claim. Below left, shoveling directly from the dump into the fast-flowing stream in the sluice bed.

While there were no Chinese miners, and as far as I can determine no Chinese in any occupation in the Klondike region during the Rush, there were conspicuous numbers of American blacks and an international agglomeration that gave Dawson a cosmopolitan flair that belied its remoteness and relatively small size. The decades of brutal treatment of the Chinese in Western mining camps would probably account for their absence, but despite Jim Crow, the blacks were not relegated to the back of the bus. One black freight handler made enough in the winter of 1898/99 to follow the rush to Nome and open a hotel. The men above and left stand for the camera with a self-assurance that speaks for itself.

151

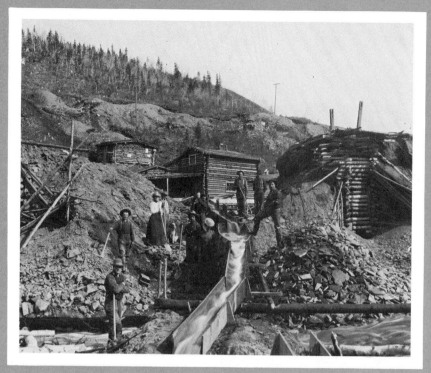

Much as the cleanup operations shared in common, none quite matched the others. The works were crude, the men behind them were resourceful and pragmatism was evident at every corner. This is not to say that their extraction methods were as efficient as they might have been, for they weren't. The gold they left behind was still being dredged from the creek beds 70 years later. But the original miners, using the methods shown on these pages, took many tens of millions before the big capitalists began to consolidate claims into larger workable units. Below, the crew of miners hired to work one of Clarence Berry's treasure-laden claims.

153

A back-breaking load of rock had to be
hauled to the surface from the drifts of
many of the mines, not because it was
worth anything, but because there was no
other way to get rid of it. The pile shown
above is merely the tip of the iceberg, but
the gold that came up the shafts by
handpower with it would have moved
mountains. Right, cleanup on one of
Clarence Berry's claims; Berry is the one
holding the pan of gold taken from the
sluice box. From left to right, his
sister-in-law, his brother and partner
Henry, four miners and on the far right,
his bride, Ethel, who spent the winter of
1896/97 in the 12x16-foot windowless
cabin on their Eldorado Creek claim,
working with him in the darkness and
hardship and in the happy knowledge that
the gods had smiled on them.

CHAPTER XII

NIGHTS OF FIRE AND ICE

"The flames increased. . . . Window sashes burst, and gallons of liquor flowed out, only to be at once frozen in the open air, for it was 45 degrees below zero . . ."

Dawson may not have shared the shoot-em-up tradition of other 19th Century gold-rush towns, but it was very much in stride with most of them in one respect: It burned down more than once. San Francisco, for example, burned down six times between 1849 and 1851, and Nevada City, where my home is, was nearly leveled seven times in the 1850s and 1860s; and these are only two of hundreds like them.

Dawson's first fire came on Thanksgiving Day in 1897. The fire was started by a dancehall girl who, in a fight, threw a lighted kerosene lamp at a rival in one of the river-front fleshpots.

Along with many other buildings, Joe Ladue's sawmill burned, and the nearest replacement was at Circle, hundreds of miles downstream. Whipsawing once again became the order of the day, and the town rebounded, despite the severe lack of nails—a chronic problem until 1898. Nails sold for as much as 25 cents apiece in the height of the shortage, but there was no lack of buyers. In a town where table salt was once literally worth its weight in gold, anything was possible.

Arthur Walden, who was witness to the fire, wrote of it and added a touching anecdote characteristic of the early Dawson days:

"Early this winter a fire broke out one evening in one of the saloons in Dawson, and before it had burnt itself out it had destroyed the heart of the city. All the building were of logs, and some of them three stories high. The fire was very hot while it lasted and, as there were no chimneys or foundations, the city being built on perpetually frozen ground, there was absolutely nothing left.

"The Alaska Commercial Company saved their building by opening bale after bale of blankets, covering the whole building over, and keeping the blankets saturated with water. The only water supply was that which could be dipped up by pail from the Yukon River.

"In the saloons and business houses, the ashes of the place where the cashier sat and weighed out gold dust were panned out, so that practically no gold was lost. But a lot of provisions were burned up, making the scarcity of food a great deal worse. The fire was hardly out before rebuilding of the town began.

"There was a pet donkey in town called 'Wise Mike,' who was the survivor of a burro train of the previous summer. At one time he had traveled with a circus and he knew many tricks. He had spent his time before the fire traveling from saloon to saloon. He was always welcome, was fed by the different saloon men, and would lie down by the stove like a big dog. It became the custom, when some miner from the creeks arrived in town and had had a few drinks, for the saloon-keeper to ask him if he

The great fire of April 26, 1899, (above), began at about 7 o'clock in the evening in the quarters of a Dawson dove named Helen Holden, upstairs at the Bodega Saloon, and destroyed more than 100 buildings before it sputtered out at 2 A.M. Victims began searching ruins (lower right) for gold dust and other valuables before the ashes had cooled.

wouldn't kindly kick 'that damed jackass' out, as he had been there all day. Then the fun began.

"At the first kick Wise Mike would rear up in his wrath and attack the man, much to the amusement of the surrounding crowd. As there was no use trying to punch him, it generally wound up in a wrestling match, the donkey standing on his hind legs and striking at the man, squealing, but never attempting to bite, and the man trying to throw him off his pins and lug him out.

"A really sober man was never asked to do this, and the sympathy of the surrounding crowd was always with the donkey. I have seen a bystander play foul in the donkey's favor by tripping the man up. After vanquishing his opponent, Wise Mike would either saunter out slowly, just to show he could go out by himself if he wanted to, or he would go back and lie down by the stove and go to sleep again. After the big fire, since Wise Mike had no home, and since food was very scarce, some kind friend shot him."

Dawson's second fire broke out on October 14, 1898, and that one took with it much of the town. Starting in an upstairs room of the Green Tree

Only charred logs and steaming ashes remained of the Bank of British North America after the fire of April, 1899. Big Alex McDonald, the owner, set his loss at $14,000, not counting records and papers consumed in a supposedly fireproof vault. Below: the *Klondike Nugget* reports the fire of Octover 14, 1898, concluding laconically: "Came at last. Might have been worse. Organize the fire department at once. Fortunate it happened in daylight, too. Providence intervened luckily when the wind shifted . . . "

THE KLONDIKE NUGGET.

VOL. I. No. 44   DAWSON, Y. T., SATURDAY, OCTOBER 15, 1898   PRICE 25 CENTS

DAWSON ON FIRE.

Forty Buildings Burned to the Ground.

A HALF-MILLION DOLLAR BLAZE SUBDUED WITHOUT A REGULAR FIRE DEPARTMENT.

Citizens, Policemen and Soldiers Fight To Save Dawson.

Saloon and Hotel, the fire quickly spread and took 40 buildings before the heroics of the Mounties and volunteers succeeded in stopping it with pail brigades and demolition. Curiously, these first two fires were caused by the carelessness of the same lady of the evening, Belle Mitchell.

The fire acted as a catalyst, and in anticipation of another catastrophe the city acted to forestall it. Russell Bankson, in his story of Gene Allen, publisher of the *Klondike Nugget*, told of the reaction:

"The first big fire proved the incentive for hastily pushing forward the organization and equipping of the department, and on October 27, 1898, a volunteer crew was organized and began drilling and running the apparatus up and down the streets. At about this time a finance committee of citizens likewise signed notes for $12,000, which lifted the debt from the fire apparatus, and a board of fire commissioners composed of a group of leading citizens was appointed. A chief and assistant were elected, and three captains were appointed, with a department membership of 100 men."

Dawson saved its best for the big fire in April of 1899. Jeremiah Lynch wrote the story from a very personal viewpoint but in terms that convey the intensity of the experience and the resourcefulness of the men who bent the wilderness to their will.

Lynch was a former state senator from California and a man of means who arrived in Dawson in the summer of 1898 by steamer from St. Michael. After surveying the busy Dawson panorama, he decided to bide his time before attempting to buy a claim on the creeks. With the ample capital he had, he bought 5000 50-pound sacks of flour at $5 apiece and built a warehouse on swampy land behind the main streets of town. It was out of fear of fire that he chose to build out of the mainstream of Dawson's commercial life, and as he put it, "People were amused . . . but no insurance could be obtained, and I was resolved to take no chances. I did not come to the Klondike to be burnt out."

As events were to prove, his foresight was rewarded. This is his story:

"At eight o'clock on the night of April 26, 1899, I came down town from my cabin. I had gone home after an early dinner at the restaurant, and was returning to the warehouse. Passing Monte Carlo, the largest building in Dawson, I observed smoke issuing from the half of the second story fronting the street. A few seconds later someone cried out 'Fire!' as a thin red flame shot out like a serpent's tongue from one of the upper windows. That was a fearful sound to utter on that cold winter's night, more dreadful than storm or hidden rocks to the seaman. In a moment the street was thronged, packed. Monte Carlo was in the center of the principal block— the heart of Dawson. Adjoining on both sides were other places of like character, from all of whose portals poured the gamblers and loafers.

"'Where are the engines?' shouted a man.

"'Down on the river,' replied another voice.

"'Come down, all of you, and help to stretch the hose.'

"Down the steep bank and over the frozen river rushed hundreds, eager, fighting to do some good, some service.

"By public subscription, a couple of steam-engines had been purchased and brought to Dawson last October just before the freeze-up. One was small; but from the other we expected great service, as it was of the latest model, and supposed to be perfect and complete in every detail. Both engines were stationed on the river ice and covered by double tents. A large hole had been excavated through the ice, 10 feet down to the flowing water beneath. When this aperture was closed by the ice, as occurred every six or seven days, the apparatus was moved to another point a few feet distant, and a second hole dug. So there were numerous little mounds like small pyramids clustered together on the river ice about 100 yards from shore, extending down the stream. A man was supposed to be always there, and to keep a fire in the boilers perpetually. But, alas! there had been some trouble in the local council as to the pay of the four or five men who were engaged as firemen, and when the foremost of the crowd came to the engines there was neither fire nor firemen.

"But these Klondikers were men of resource. Some ran back to the shore, and, gaining access to the stores, returned in haste with cans of kerosene, while others carried dry birch and sawdust, which make quick and fierce fires. There was not a pound of coal, except a little blacksmith's coal, in the whole country. The hose was unrolled, stretched, and carried with a hurrah from the engines, along the river ice, and up the steep bank, the nozzles resting in the middle of the narrow street waiting for water. But the fire had waited for no one.

"In this cold latitude the buildings are excessively inflammable. The intense heat of the big fires in the big stoves, that are never extinguished all the winter long, thoroughly dries the log walls and floor, lumber and timber, that make the building. The roof is covered with moss a foot thick, which when dried forms a good covering and coating against ice and cold. But this moss dries—indeed, almost evaporates—near the chimney itself, where the latter emerges from the roof. The chimney itself, made of thin sheet-iron, is worn through by springtime. Nothing that man can frame can endure the continual action of fire.

"The flames increased in number and size; the smoke obscured the clear starlit sky; window sashes burst, and gallons of liquor flowed from the broken packages within to the side-walk without, only to be at once frozen in the open air, for it was 45 degrees below zero. The street was enwrapped in a thick fog, so dense that the huge flames, flashing vertically—for there was no wind—could be seen only like lightning gleams. It was remarkable that the heat as well as the flames ascended. The atmosphere was so dry and cold that heat was immediately dissipated, and men that night stood so close to flames as to have their fur clothes burned and destroyed without appreciably feeling the scorching. The area of the fire increased, and the whole block was evidently doomed. People, both men and women, were running with articles in their hands or on their backs to the vacant frozen marsh in the rear, covered with snow. I walked leisurely to my warehouse, which stood apart like an isolated castle, for I knew that it was safe; and I congratulated myself on my expensive forethought, for this night was my reward.

"At last, at last! the frenzied efforts of the men at the fire-engine had sent water through the frozen hose from beginning to end, and a great cheer went up amid the fog and flames as a small stream of water spurted

The April, 1899, fire occasioned another special edition of the *Klondike Nugget*, declaring: "It has come at last. The really great fire which Dawson people had been dreading . . . transpired last night. The scene of its origin, the wind, the hour and scores of other elements seemed to favor the city's old-time enemy, and within half an hour of the time that the first smoke of warning was seen there was no room to question the extent of the disaster . . ."

THE KLONDIKE

VOL. 2 No 35   DAWSON, Y. T., THURSDAY, APRIL.

Extra Edition!

DAWSON IS ONCE AGAIN IN ASHES.

Queen of the Yukon Is Once More Attacked
by Her Old Time Enemy.

THE CITY'S LOSS WILL BE FULLY A MILLION DOLLARS.

One Hundred and Eleven Buildings Gone Up in
Smoke and Flame.

Incompetency in Operating the Fire Steamer Charged With Being the Cause
of the Heavy Loss—Police and Soldiers Do Heroic Service—List of
Some of the Principal Losses—Four Business Blocks Involved at
One Time.

By the time of this fire in Alex McDonald's hotel on a November day in 1901, Dawson had acquired a working fire engine and a volunteer fire company, and the disaster was limited to one building—although an upright piano and some troupers' trunks had to be rescued from the nearby Savoy Theater.

The Alaska Commercial Company perfected an all-weather, waterless method of fire resistance by draping its storehouse in damp cloth during the fire of January 10, 1900. Although this was not the origin of the term "wet blanket," it afforded an elaborate demonstration of the effect of a moist bedspread on an otherwise hot time.

feebly from the nozzle. But the temperature was 45 degrees below zero, and the line of hose was 400 feet long, lying exposed on the river ice. The power from the engine was not strong enough or not sufficiently developed, and the water slackened gradually until it stopped altogether.

"'My God! the water is freezing in the hose,' cried someone.

"In fact, the water in the hose, from engine to nozzle, had turned into solid ice. Though at various points the expansion of the water when freezing had torn the hose as if with giant scissors, yet the ice remained smooth and compact without breaking, even where the gap in the hose permitted it to be seen. Men gazed at each-other through the icy films pendent from eyelashes and eyebrows.

"'What is to be done?' shouted Tom Chisholm to Captain Starnes, who commanded the police patrol.

"'Blow up the buildings in front of the fire,' was the prompt response.

"'But where shall we get powder or dynamite?'

"'I know,' said Schoff, the druggist. 'The A.C.C. has a fifty-pound box of Giant powder in Warehouse A.'

"'Take a dog team and go for it,' ordered Captain Starnes, turning to Sergeant-Major Tucker.

"'Very well, sir,' responded Tucker.

"With a crack of the whip the patrol team of three dogs darted like an arrow down the narrow side-street, between the ruddy fires now casting colors above and beyond, while Tucker and Brainard crouched side by side on the sleigh. A voice, and the dogs stopped as suddenly as they started in front of Warehouse A, 200 yards distant. A word to the alarmed and expectant watchman. He remembered the box. It was found, carefully placed on the sleigh, and in ten minutes Sergeant Tucker saluted Captain Starnes, adding:

"'There is the box of dynamite, sir.'

"'Are there any miners here who know how to use Giant powder?' cried Starnes.

"'Aye, aye, sir!' came from a score of throats; for the crowd included miners from California and South Africa, to whom firing dynamite was as familiar as lighting their pipes.

"Starnes selected McMahon, Thilwall, Armstrong, and Olsen.

"'Take the box,' he hurriedly said; 'open it, and blow up the Aurora, Alex McDonald's building, and the Temenos.'

"These were three large cabins of two stories each, right in the pathway of the blaze. For hours hundreds of men had been rushing to the marsh carrying goods from these buildings, but thousands of dollars in value still remained in them. Men were offered 10 dollars an hour, a two-horse team and driver 100 dollars an hour. But even these Klondike prices did not secure adequate assistance. Everyone was helping himself or his friend. No one was idle that fateful night. But the buildings had to go.

"A few minutes later, and the explosions overswept the fire, scattering fragments far out on the white serene shroud of the frozen Yukon. The miners did their work well, and the fire lagged, for on that side it had nothing more to eat.

"Meanwhile I stood at my warehouse door. My horses were ready harnessed. I had three double teams, and could have had 500 dollars for the night's work. But I preferred to offer them to my friends. The warehouse was filling with merchandise, hurried thither on wagons, sleighs, horses' backs, dogs' backs, men's backs. The large door was quickly opened, the stuff pitched inside, and the door again closed without delay. . . .

"All this time the fire was roaring nearer, leaping towards us with eager strides, and striving enviously to bridge the few feet of ice and frost

between it and my refuge. But the distance was enough, and it gradually died out from starvation, leaving sputtering jets here and there on the wide desolation of blocks and streets. I opened my stores and gave wine and whisky to whosoever came—and they were many—for I felt relieved and grateful. . . .

"The next day everything in the burnt district lay prone, except a number of huge piles composed of square blocks of ice. Within the previous weeks the larger institutions had cut and transported from the river-bed these blocks of ice for summer use. They had been saturated with sawdust, and a wooden shelter erected. The sawdust, shelter, buildings, all were gone; but the ice remained—the only thing that had passed through the heat with impunity. Extraordinary as it seemed, the piles served in some cases as lines of demarcation to the owner's land. For that very afternoon, before the embers were entirely cold, people began to bring lumber and rebuild. Lumber doubled in value that same day.

"Still the sour-doughs were making comparisons with the fire of 1897. It would seem that Dawson was to have its annual big fire, not to count the little ones. 'Why,' said Jim McNamee, when told that lumber had advanced from 100 dollars to 200 dollars a thousand, 'that's nothing. I remember, after the fire in December, 1897, that nails sold for 25 cents each. Men delved in the ashes, broke up old boards and boxes, dismantled old doors and sluices, for nails. There were only a few kegs in town, and they sold for $250 each keg. A man with a bucket full was like one with a good pan of gold. Talk about lumber at $200! why, you couldn't get any then. The lumbermill was burnt in the fire, and there was none nearer than Circle City, 300 miles away. We just had to whip-saw it. We had to cut the trees near town up there on the mountains,' indicating a bare point, 'make a pit in the ice, and whip-saw for all we was worth. I tell you that was hard. Two men couldn't do no more than 100 feet, and then it'ud be filled with knots, and sometimes split in the cold when you druv a little nail in it. And beans and bacon wuz a dollar, flour 40 dollars a sack, and moccasins!—you just had to make 'em yourself out of old clothes, for they wasn't any to be had. Talk about lumber at $200! Why, you fellows ain't in it; you don't know what hard times is!' And Jim stalked away growling his disgust."

Dawson was not to have another major fire until Big Alex McDonald's hotel went up in November, 1901, but this time the equipment worked and Dawson was spared another instant leveling. Time and the elements have since done what fire was never to do again.

Responding to a fire alarm, the men of Dawson rush toward hoses along the river bank (left). Despite such civic zeal, the Aurora Cafe, Palmer Brothers, the Northern Cafe, and other business establishments visible here were wiped out in the fire of April, 1899. Right above: workmen rock gold dust out of the ashes of the Monte Carlo Saloon, which succumbed to the flames of January 10, 1900. Below: Dawsonites turn out to watch a demonstration of a new fire engine.

OLD YUKON TALES

Of domestic relations, canine discipline, and drinks on the house

CIRCLE CITY AND THE MORAL LAW

A Miners' Meeting rights a wrong
in the case of Doe versus Roe

There have been one or two trials for infraction of the moral law, which resulted in each case in exact justice being meted out. The citation of one case of this kind will furnish a striking illustration of the effectiveness and celerity with which a Circle City miners' meeting could repair a wrong done to a helpless woman. The plaintiff charged the defendant with seduction under promise of marriage. The case was tried with due formality, after the exclusion from the room, on the motion of a considerate miner, of "all children of tender age." At 5 o'clock in the evening of the second day of the trial the jury brought in the following verdict:

"We the undersigned jurors, in the case of Alice Doe, plaintiff, and Richard Roe, defendant, find the defendant guilty as charged, and order that said defendant marry Alice Doe, or, in failure to do this, he be fined $1,500 and imprisoned one year in a prison in Circle City, and, in case of failure to pay the said fine, the term of imprisonment be extended to two years. . ."

The meeting then adjourned for two hours. On the reassembling of the meeting at 7:30 the chairman stated that the marriage contract had been witnessed, and that the jury and all officers connected with the case were honorably discharged, and after the adoption of a motion tendering a vote of thanks to the ladies of Circle City for the support and assistance given the plaintiff during the trial, the meeting adjourned.

When it is considered that at the time of this meeting there was no jail in Circle City, and that if the defendant had chosen the alternative of imprisonment the expense of providing a jail and maintaining the prisoner for two years would have fallen on the miners themselves, not only the Draconian justice of their action, but their self-sacrificing devotion to principle becomes apparent.

A DRINKING MAN'S DOG

Arthur Walden's fable of a boastful
drover and a corruptible malamute

I well remember sledding in to the Grand Central Way-House long after dark one night, and, as I was taking off my load of dog-food to carry it into the house, I met a man in the corral who was cooling his. The air outside the corral seemed to be swarming with hungry dogs, drawn by the smell of food. Inquiring about one very obstreperous dog, I was told he was Chris Sohnikson's leader, and that if I wanted to play a joke on Chris I could do so if I followed instructions.

Now Chris was extremely fond of his dog and proud because he would do a certain trick if he was given a piece of salmon. We prepared by filling the dog chock full of salmon. After we had done so I let him into the road-house, shut the door, and inquired in a loud voice whose dog it was. Chris claimed the dog, and, as he came over to let him out, I started a discussion on the merits of the beast, and Chris, as we thought he would, boasted about this trick.

I offered to bet him drinks for the house that the dog would not do it. At this, men who had already gone to bed began to swing out and march to the bar, knowing that it was a drink either way for them. The dog, being full of salmon, turned his head away in disgust, and Chris set up the house. Afterwards, when we told him the joke, he was so pleased because the dog hadn't actually gone back on him that he set up the house again, and, as there were some twenty-five or thirty men and it cost fifty cents a drink, the trick proved to be something of a luxury.

THE OLD MAN

Philanthropy triumphs over business sense
in an exemplary tale by Judge James Wickersham

Every western mining camp has its quota of derelicts. They are generally chair warmers, or swampers in saloons. Almost always one of these men will be known familiarly as "the old man" and be allowed, along with better customers, to have a regular dram of liquor on first appearing in the morning. Of course, he is expected to be on hand when some tipsy miner is throwing his poke on the bar with a loud "come on boys and have a drink on me," and in these ways he does not often lack for drinks, though he may sometimes want bread.

An "outside" barkeeper, who had been employed in one of the numerous Dawson saloons, had brought with him some new ideas about running such a resort, and when "the old man" came for his regular morning's morning, he was ordered to clear out. The old man determined upon a speedy and public revenge. That night when the saloon was crowded the old man furtively entered and took up a position at the end of the bar near the door. Suddenly he stood on the bar rail, waved a stick of dynamite with a burning fuse, and shouted at the barkeeper, "I will blow you to hell, damn you."

In a minute the room was empty, the barkeeper being the first to go through the front door into the 60-below-zero weather outside, with only his linen coat to shield him from the wintry blasts. The crowd fled in terror from the front of the saloon expecting momentarily to see it crash into the street, shouting for the police, and quickly a red-coat policeman appeared. The policeman either had more courage or less sense than the scared barkeeper, for he ran to the front window and quickly raising himself by an iron bar placed there to shield the glass, he stood on the window base and peered above the lower painted glass into the room. He stood there for a minute or two, then dropped to the sidewalk, and entered the saloon.

The old man was behind the bar with a bottle in his hand pouring out his third drink of the best liquor in the house. As the officer entered the old man shouted: "Come on, sergeant, and take a drink on the house with me." What had appeared to be a stick of dynamite was a ten-inch cut of bologna sausage, into the end of which the old man had forced a six-inch fuse which had performed its duty and expired. The whole town laughed, the new barkeeper was discharged, and the old man had his regular morning dram thereafter.

Gentility Moves North

By the time the summer of 1898 arrived, Dawson was not only a rip-roaring town with all the flavor of traditional frontier mining settlements (save the gunplay), but culture and refinement had set in. Theatrical companies, orchestras, and club life competed with gambling, drinking, and wenching, although there surely must have been some overlap in the two life styles. Above, members of the cast of the Lillian M. Hall Stock Company production of *Camille* in the first-act supper scene. Visible above are ads on the curtain for the *Klondike Nugget*, Old Crow, and the Dawson Dental Parlors. Below, a close-up of the orchestra and part of the crowd at the St. Andrew's Ball at the Palace Grand (which has been completely restored). In the Gold Rush days, the Union Jack and Old Glory were often displayed together.

Two of 1898's distinguished social occasions: Left, the first masquerade ball for the benefit of the volunteer fire department, held by the ladies of Dawson. The great fire of April 26, 1899, proved that more than a benefit was necessary to protect the town from fire, but no one could fault them for trying. Center, New Year's Eve fancy-dress ball at Pioneer Hall. Winter was long and dark, and any diversion of this sort was avidly sought. Both pictures were taken with newly developed flash-lighting apparatus.

Professor Freimuth's solemn group performed at the Palace Grand. The imperious Professor sits in the middle of the front row. To his right is the pianist, Mr. Rothschild, of the English banking family. Señor Lopez, far right, was once a trumpeter with the New Orleans Opera Company.

Above, an elaborate Victorian play (Oscar Wilde?) at the Standard Theater. Right, the finale of *The Island of Kokomolo*, presented by the A.B. Dramatic Club.

CHAPTER XIII

THE PLEASURE DOMES OF DAWSON

"You could pay your money and take your choice . . ."

Of all the lingering recollections of those who had made their way to the Klondike diggings and the storied Yukon capital, none will ever match those of the nights and days spent in the pleasure domes designed, built, staffed, and run by men who knew how hot the dust and nuggets burned in the pockets of men who had never known luxury before.

"We strolled around that evening taking in the stores on the beach, the different saloons, watching the gambling games, but it was all Greek to us. We saw the big pokes of gold dust and watched the cashier selling chips by the thousands of dollars or $500 worth. Our hearts beat against our shirts.

"Then the girls began to gather. They had painted cheeks and lips that would give any man painter's colic. Both Jap and I had full beards and looked too pitiful to them so not many bothered us. However, many a man was grabbed and led onto the floor for a waltz that lasted sometimes as much as three or five minutes, then was led to the bar where they had a drink and the dame was handed a pasteboard chip that went into her stocking.

"This dancehall had about seventy-five girls known as dancehall girls and not all of them were by any means degenerate. All of them had nicknames such as The Virgin, Cheechako Lil, Buntie, the Oregon Mare, the Utah Filly, Bunch Grass, the Black Bear and her sister, the Cub, a light-colored Negress known as The African Queen, another called Wiggles, and so on down the line. You could pay your money and take your choice. If you didn't watch out, they would help themselves to your money. Can you imagine four Hoosiers with full beards, mouths agape, listening to the music coming from every place any time of the day or night. . . .

"Do you wonder that we were anxious to get away from that place where everything cost dollars and everything was going out of our pockets and nothing coming in. Painted-cheeked ladies tempted us on every turn. . . ."

So wrote Lynn Smith on his arrival at Dawson in 1898.

If ever a mining camp existed without the presence of saloons, gambling, a lively demimonde, and song, I haven't been able to find it, and Dawson was no exception. The only thing that town lacked was gunplay, which, however exaggerated it may have become by TV and the movies, was in fact always a real part of American frontier life. But the Canadian Mounties simply would not tolerate it. Gambling was enjoyed until it was shut down by edict in 1901, but the ladies of the evening continued to sell their charms until there were not enough buyers to support home industry.

Dawson City's main street on Christmas Day, 1899, offered theatricals, saloons, and gambling casinos—but also such decorous alternatives as a circulating library. Although Col. Sam Steele and his 12-man force of North West Mounted Police allowed low resorts to operate day and night (except on the Sabbath, when all business closed up tight), they would not tolerate rigged games, gunplay, or unpatriotic language.

Tents and shacks sprinkled the banks of the Yukon, and not all of them sheltered miners. Like all gold rush towns, Dawson attracted more than its fair share of murderers, train robbers, con men, and whores. A reporter for the New York *Times* noted, however, that "Dawson has never been what these people would consider an ideal town."

In early June, 1900, the riverboat *Yukoner* loads passengers hoping for easier pickings downriver. Many who left that summer were members of what the New York *Times* correspondent called "the sporting fraternity—saloon men, dance hall magnates, gamblers, pugilists, and . . . women of the adventuress order." Despite the exodus, Dawson continued to offer plenty of wicked recreation to miners who stayed around for the summer cleanup. Below: Crouched by the empty river, surrounded by vacant wilderness, Dawson appears almost as isolated in midsummer as in midwinter. The great land scar above the town is called Moosehide.

The people of Dawson, of whatever persuasion, displayed most of the class and caste discriminations North American society generally exercised, but there were differences. For instance, gamblers were not relegated to a social level below the rest who made their way in mining or business. In like fashion, the most sparkling of the ladies of the evening were part of Dawson's informal social life until the wives and sweethearts, the working girls and husband-seekers swarmed into town to change it at the turn of the century.

From the beginning there were two classes of women: respectable and otherwise. The good were divided between virtuous wives, including the Indian women that most of the pioneers had taken, and independent single, widowed, and occasionally divorced women who pursued their own enterprises but played no part in the frenetic nightlife of the town. The others either filled the cribs or dancehalls or were the courtesans of Klondike aristocracy. In the early years the latter predominated.

Jeremiah Lynch, a former state senator from San Francisco and San Mateo counties, a man of conspicuous perspicacity and by his own admission one with an eye for the ladies and a taste for fine wine, ruminated on the subject in his book *Three Years in the Klondike*:

"I ate a good dinner at the only decent restaurant, and squandered the evening in the dancing houses, where I ordered several bottles of champagne, at 15 dollars a pint, for the gaudy and slightly dressed houris who favored me with a dance and a tête-à-tête in the private boxes. They were numerous, young, and beautiful. From over the whole globe they had flocked to Dawson, for the fame of the Klondike treasures had overspread the world. All classes of beauties from all nations, but beauties all.

"Some had a history and some not before they came, but all had a history after arrival. There was no honest occupation for women. Many went professedly as housekeepers to miners who were rich enough to employ one; but it was only another name. A very few found precarious and unremunerative employment in the stores, and the others drifted into

Front Street, Dawson's raw and treeless esplanade along the river, was ugly to the eye but enticing to lonely men who had spent months in cabins on the creeks, eating sourdough bread and beans, reading, playing cards, and dreaming of the lights of home.

A grizzled miner and a cheerful young woman in a tartan skirt and high-buttoned shoes entrust their fate to a hand-operated tramline spanning the Klondike River just south of Dawson City. The Klondike, which flows into the Yukon at Dawson, separated the rich mine fields along Bonanza and Eldorado Creeks from the attractive nuisances of urban night life.

houses kept for dancing, with gambling at faro and roulette as a principal adjunct. . . .

"Those who have lived and are not altogether lost make excellent exemplars of virtue. Of good women there were few; of bad women plenty. So your lucky miner with cans of gold in his dilapidated cabin, pining in the cold winter days for women's society, dropped down to Dawson, into the music halls, and engaged—a housekeeper. The housekeeper soon became a wife if she handled the gentleman rightly.

"Of course, most of these men, while loyal good fellows of character and rectitude, would scarcely be taken for college graduates. They had led a desultory wandering existence in the North and Northwest for years, and when the Klondike granted them sudden and abounding wealth, it was a Fortunatus's purse. They were amazed, if not abashed. So, from riding on horseback into Dawson saloons, smashing the mirrors and glasses and furniture, and paying thousands of dollars damages therefore without a

The brass-topped roulette tables of Dawson were neither as large nor as elegant as those in a modern Las Vegas casino, but a determined loser could drop a fortune all the same. Edgar Mizner, the unpopular general manager of the Alaska Commercial Company, lost $15,000 in the Opera House saloon one night and, to top it off, was fired for gambling. In the Northern Saloon, a neatly dressed stranger sank $10,000 in ten spins, muttered to the bartender, "I went broke," walked outside and shot himself.

The California Market, staffed (left to right) by Julius Wurtz, Peter Buchbolz, and "Champagne Bill" Knight, catered to the epicures of Dawson with partridge and ptarmigan, goose and moose.

murmur, to marrying ladies of questionable type and career, it was only a natural step."

Sad, but the glitter, like glitter everywhere, was only that. While it's true that some of the girls married and settled into domestic life, only one of the dancehall crowd was to make a lifelong career of the Klondike experience, and that was Kate Rockwell, later to be forever tagged "Klondike Kate" by newspaper reporters. She had the good looks and figure, and she must have had the personality to make it anywhere, as she did. Somehow the tarnish never tarnished her, despite her long and publicly acknowledged liaison with Alexander Pantages, who began his storied career as a theater owner in Dawson.

Nevill Armstrong was a regular guest at Belinda Mulrooney's Fairview Hotel, which was one of Dawson's two best, although even it left a few things to be desired, as his following tale reveals. Armstrong was one of the few writers who witnessed the wondrous years of Dawson's beginnings willing to be something less than ambiguous about what went on in those glittering years.

Of the Fairview and the adventures of one evening he wrote:

". . . The hotel was a wooden structure of two floors. The walls of the bedroom were made of canvas nailed on wooden framework and ordinary wallpaper was pasted over this. Needless to say there was, practically speaking, no privacy whatever; except that the occupants of the rooms were unable to see each other, one might have been in the same room.

"One night I returned to my room at the Fairview and, as I closed my door, I immediately heard a voice I knew quite well. It belonged to an Inspector of the R.N.W.M. Police—an immensely powerful man, about 6 feet 2 inches and weighing some 16 stone [225 pounds]. The friend he was with evidently told him that I was in the next room, because I had no sooner got undressed than he called out to me to join them in a drink. But I was not having any; I knew the hours he kept. So I called out that I was tired and was going to sleep, but he wouldn't leave me alone.

"'Come on in, Army,' he boomed. 'I am celebrating the birth of a son, cabled today from Medicine Hat.'

"'No,' I replied. 'I am going to sleep and I'll have a drink with you tomorrow.'

Paying with gold dust (in this case, a staged scene at the supermarket checkout,) created a side industry in Dawson—panning spilled dust out of shavings from the floors of saloons. Bartenders learned how to catch a few grains under a long fingernail while weighing out the price of a drink; waiters sopped up dust with hands moistened in beer; and one resourceful cashier bragged that he slicked down his hair with syrup to hold unattached morsels of gold that strayed his way.

At a birthday banquet for Sweet Marie, one of Dawson's prima dancehall hostesses, everyone blinked when the flash powder went off, giving an unpleasantly bleary look to this sentimental occasion.

" 'You won't,' he retorted. 'If you don't come in by yourself, I'll come and fetch you.'

" 'I am not coming,' I insisted.

" 'Very well, I'm coming after you.'

"It was no use locking my door, even had it possessed a key, because he would have pulled it off its hinges without the slightest compunction. In he came and chucked me across his shoulder, though I wasn't exactly a featherweight, being 6 feet 1 inch in height and weighing about 11 stone 4 lbs. [158 lbs.]. He arrived with his prize and dropped me on the bed, where I was greeted by 'The Oregon Mare,' a nickname applied to a very handsome woman who was a well-known Dawson demimondaine. 'The Oregon' was wearing a pink silk nightdress over which she had on the scarlet tunic of my friend, his Stetson hat, gauntlet gloves and she had his riding-whip in her hand. She was standing up in the middle of the bed, and I must say presented a very striking figure!"

The Doves of Dance Hall Row

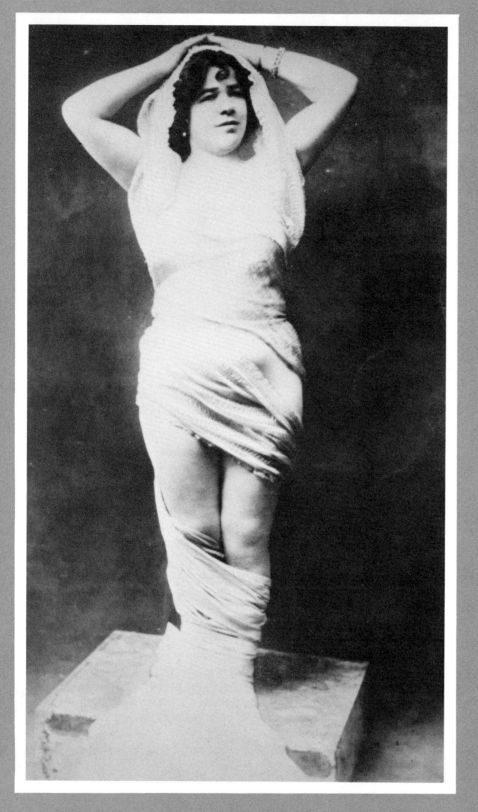

Diamond Tooth Lil, born Honora Ornstein, may well have been the last surviving Dawson dancehall sweetheart. Some may find her a bit gross in this pose, but she was catnip to the lonely miners of Dawson's first years. She made a fortune and squandered it, inherited another and did the same. She died in 1975 after spending most of the last 40 years of her life in mental institutions in the State of Washington.

The dancehall girls of Dawson were a breed apart. They knew it and the men of Dawson knew it. All understood that the game was to separate as much gold as possible from those who had it with all the wiles and charms the ladies had at their disposal. And while they gave their favors with discrimination, they didn't give without a generous *quid pro quo*. Many of the girls were seriously involved with their male counterparts—gamblers, barkeepers, dancehall owners, and the like. They were the playgirls of the great North, but they were not necessarily a happier lot than their unfortunate sisters on Paradise Alley. There were too many tumultuous scenes and even suicides among their number to draw any other conclusion. Many of them posed in the photographers' studios to be immortalized, and these are some of the treasures to come down to us. Only two can be identified by name, but they still hold a fascination that will endure, perhaps forever. The star of them all, Kate Rockwell, *right*, traded on her notoriety until her death in 1957.

MORNIN'

Their names were many—The Oregon Mare, The Pig, Spanish Marie, Passionate Annie, Snow Ball, Kitty the Bitch, Mollie Fewclothes, Three-way Annie, and other delightful sobriquets that were given some of the rougher of the lot.

The more discreet of the dancehall favorites carried their given or adopted names—Gussie Lamore, Myrtle Brocee (who killed herself in despondency over a love affair), Blanche Lamonte, and the fetching Mabel La Rose, who in the winter of 1896–1897 auctioned herself to live as wife to the highest bidder until the spring breakup. It was only $5000, but once again remember that the dollar had ten times the purchasing power of today's dollars.

There were the beguiling Oatley sisters, Lottie and Polly, who sang like angels, and I'd like to think they are the little dolls in the upper-left corner of the facing page. Two more sisters, whose surname has been lost, were known as Jacqueline and Rosalinde. Between the two of them, they ran the dollar-a-dance and the house cut on the drinks into a fortune. As names will be corrupted, they became known popularly as Vaseline and Glycerine.

The girl above left was known as the Belgian Queen and the one lower right on the opposite page is French Marie. The others are consigned to anonymity, but they did have their day.

Miners gather on Front Street, Dawson City, in summer, 1898, to demand "better government." The complaint: scandalous irregularities in registering claims.

William Ogilvie, who had surveyed the frontiers of Alaska and the Yukon Territory for the Canadian government, became virtually the first governor of the Yukon. His predecessor, a former Mountie major and frontier hero named J. M. Walsh (shown at right with his Indian and Caucasian staff at a tent headquarters in Dawson), lasted only two months, then was recalled amid charges that he had profited by manipulating the award of mining claims. Placed in command of a vast and inaccessible wilderness, without postal service or telegraph, roads or bridges, and overrun by a sudden influx of aliens in search of gold, Ogilvie recruited a government, set up courts and schools, maintained order—and even succeeded in having the mail delivered, albeit slowly.

176

From the very beginning, when Captain Charles Constantine brought the first 20 men with him to Fortymile in 1895, the Mounties had formed the cornerstone of Yukon law and the code of conduct that was expected of every man. The miner's law which had prevailed so successfully in the years before had been eroded with the swelling population of the mid-1890s. Miner's law can operate only where dependence of one man upon another is absolute and where recourse to formal tribunal or other outside authority is impossible. Constantine's arrival didn't destroy miner's law; his presence merely filled a growing vacuum that would have led to uncontrollable anarchy.

The Mounties, with perhaps a couple of exceptions, were true to their own proud code and ruled Dawson with as calm and firm a hand as ever was witnessed in North America. But the Mounties, most of them youngsters, were also human, and the attractions of the night were not beyond their ken.

T. Morris Longstreth, in his history of the Mounties, *The Silent Force*, wrote in touching style:

"The men, of course, were not conscious of growing shiny laurels for the future wreath, and the good times that they managed would have given them little prestige with a synod. One evening the sergeant-major told Steele [then in charge of the Dawson detachment] that some of the boys were breaking barracks and asked him if he should 'check rounds.'

"'No,' said Steele. 'They're young and they'll never see a mining camp like this again. So long as they do their duty it won't hurt them to go a bit large.'

"And a bit large was the way they went. An Arabian Nights Entertainment would fail in doing justice to their story, for the nights in Arabia are not that long. That their wild and humorous and extravagant recreations did not hinder a unique and matchless piece of work is history. And it can be left to the magisterial to exclaim as the pious Dr. Arnold exclaimed at the sight of his frivolous boys at Rugby:

"'It is very startling to see so much of sin combined with so little of sorrow.'"

While the Mounties were deeply and almost universally respected, others in the Canadian governmental apparatus were reviled. Gold Commissioner Thomas Fawcett and his underlings were corrupt. Under them a man, for a consideration, could register a claim that another had legally staked but which Fawcett's men refused to record. The staking of Dominion Creek in the summer of 1898 was rigged to serve friends of Fawcett, and the scandals finally became so blatant that he was drummed out of the country. The newly appointed Territorial Commissioner (Governor), Major J.M. Walsh, formerly of the Mounted police and until his Klondike days a respected man, could not withstand the temptations his job offered, and his

greed led to his dismissal two months after he had assumed office.

The splendid old surveyor, William Ogilvie, was named in Walsh's place and he quickly restored confidence by his performance. He was cut of the same stripe as Constantine, Starnes and Steele of the Mounties, and his strength of character brought luster to the office.

During the summer, scandals or not, the streets were jammed with crowds that gathered for celebrations and other events, such as the public reading of the first account of Admiral Dewey's crushing defeat of the Spanish fleet in Manila Bay. The big holidays—Queen Victoria's birthday, Dominion Day, and the Fourth of July—were all observed in great style: 21-gun salutes, orations, races and field events, parades and floats and all the other elements of traditional civic exuberance.

By the time another year had passed, Dawson was to change forever. Of all the special happenings that brought throngs to the streets, none was to be remembered better than that day in July of 1899 when a steamboat arrived from St. Michael with the news of a great new gold discovery far to the west in Alaska on the bleak shores of the Bering Sea. Although Dawson was to continue to thrive and prosper for many years, the news spelled the end of the Klondike rush.

Within a month, more than 2000 men and women had crammed into the only available riverboat space and were on their way to Nome, which in that one summer was to start from nothing and become the largest city in Alaska.

A patrol of Mounties in high-collared tunics and fur caps lines up outside a North West Mounted Police barracks near Dawson. In evidence of their imperturbable valor, eight of the nine wear mustaches, although facial hair had been known to freeze solid in this climate, clamping shut a man's lips.

Klondikers who stuck it out in Dawson enjoyed another crisp winter. It was 50 below zero on January 24, 1900, when the proprietors of the Crown Grocery (above) stepped outside to pose for this picture. The great river was frozen from bank to bank as Mounties marched along Front Street in an impressive funeral cortege. Fortunes would continue to be dug from the creeks southeast of Dawson, but the city's historic role as the capital of the Northern gold rush was over: It had lasted from midsummer, 1898, to midsummer, 1899—just twelve months.

177

The Doxies of Paradise Alley

A stone's throw from Dance Hall Row lived the cribhouse women of Paradise Alley, a ghetto created on the orders of Mountie Sam Steele. In Dawson's early history, the girls advertised so blatantly and indiscriminately, pitching their tents wherever their fancies struck, that Steele decided some controls were required. Unlike the dancehall queens, who could pick and choose, these poor things lived in virtual bondage, and the miners' gold they took soon passed to other hands. Many of the earliest to arrive were the dregs of nearby settlements—Wrangell, for instance. It was not a classy bunch. With the Rush, however, recruiters brought in girls from the States and Europe, primarily from France and Belgium. As a result, if the general tone was not elevated, at least Dawson could boast an international flavor previously unknown in the North.

CHAPTER XIV

THE GOLDEN SANDS OF NOME

"Not another beach in the whole of Alaska, or in the world, was giving the squatter the opportunity to make a living at the throw of a hat . . ."

There was no place called Nome until 1898, when coarse gold was found in the sands of the Snake River. It may be possible to imagine a more unlikely setting for a frontier mining town—or, for that matter, a town of any kind—but I can't think where, except perhaps it be in Antarctica.

Perched at the edge of the ruler-straight southwest coast of the Seward Peninsula, on the treeless, frozen tundra that characterizes that bleak arm of America, Nome is a city unique. There is no harbor at Nome; indeed, the Bering Sea along this stretch is frozen solid for seven months of the year. In the long winter the only way to get to Nome is by plane or dogsled. Poor transportation, little food production, no timber, no oil, no waterpower, no recreational potential—this is Nome today, cold and remote.

Yet an aura of romance is linked with the name: Nome was a great American gold-rush town and was the last of its kind.

It was in July of 1898 that the first promise of wealth was panned from placers near Nome. Summer had brought the first sizable numbers of prospectors into the region, some of them disappointed stampeders from the Klondike. Before, perhaps 2400 Eskimos and a handful of whites were the only people living on the whole Seward Peninsula.

In September the first major strikes were made by three Scandinavian prospectors who staked claims on Anvil and Glacier creeks, tributaries of the Snake upstream from the future site of Nome, and in Snow Gulch, a branch of Glacier Creek. These claims were to make millionaires of the discoverers, Eric Lindblom, John Brinteson, and Jafet Lindeberg.

The news spread through the region and the rush was on. In the first weeks, early arrivals not only staked claims for themselves but, in a flagrant abuse of mining tradition, used the power of attorney to stake claims for family and friends. Some men staked as many as 30 claims, and according to the U.S. Geological Survey report on the Nome fields, 40 men had tied up 7000 acres of the richest land in the region before winter came. Thousands of Americans who arrived later raised hell, but nothing could be done about it.

Winter, which comes to Nome in October, closed in before much gold was washed from the claims. The $1800 taken from Anvil Creek and Snow Gulch was but a tantalizing hint of what the next year would bring. When winter ended in June of 1899, thousands were on the scene or on their way. But it wasn't until the chance finding of gold in the sands of the beach in late July that the Nome rush became full-blown. When word of the beach

By late June, 1900, the Nome waterfront resembled a construction camp, piled high with lumber, drain pipes, boiler tanks, and gunny bags. A few of the canvas tents were restaurants; others were breezy little bordellos. As Judge Wickersham observed: "The first boat and the second dog team to reach a new gold strike always carried a woman of the bright lights, for these women struggled as valiantly as the men to be the earliest in a new camp, where they were classed as 'warm storage' and deemed quite necessary to the comfort and permanence of the place." Right: At the mouth of the Snake River gold hunters were greeted by signs offering parcels of land for sale or rent.

Dumped onto the gravelly beach in a welter of trunks and boxes, wicker baskets and duffel bags, newcomers wandered inland, searching for a few square feet of unoccupied tundra on which to build a shack or pitch a tent.

For a herd of sheep from the States, the journey to Nome inevitably was a one-way trip. Although the sea abounded in fish and mammals, familiar kinds of red meat were rare—and popular. Right: A flat-keeled sternwheeler butts up to the shore to unload crates of canned corn, evaporated milk, and other foodstuffs at Dodwell & Company's landing, designated by a flag.

discovery reached Dawson, it marked the end of the Klondike rush. In one month 2000 men and women left Dawson for the new strike.

The beach at Nome and beyond, a dozen miles or so to the west, proved to be the richest tidewater diggings ever known. And the wonder of it all was that anyone with a shovel and a rocker could work the sands to his heart's content. The commandant in charge of the small detachment of troops dispatched to Nome ruled that under federal law no claims could be staked on the beach beyond a point 60 feet above the high-tide mark. Good feelings abounded, and there was little friction or trouble.

Carrie McLain wrote in her *Gold Rush Nome:* "Ground could not be staked on the beach, but a prospector had the privilege of pitching his tent and mining the ground ahead of it to the water's edge, or for the length of a shovel, one commonly called a 'No. 2.' The first beach gold was mined in 1899 from bedrock six to ten feet below the surface and washed out with sluice boxes. In 1900 fine 'flour gold' was extracted from black sand by long toms, surf washers, and rockers. About 8000 men used these brightly colored rockers, and from offshore they looked like butter and cheese machines at an old-fashioned county fair. A popular expression was that everybody had a squatter's right, and once his bit of ground was worked

Passengers, like bulk cargo, were lightered to the beach in barges while steamers and sailing vessels anchored as far as two miles offshore in the roadstead.

The earliest photograph of the site of Nome (below) shows a handful of prospectors who set up tents on the beach near the mouth of the Snake River in the spring of 1899. Painfully familiar to those who had followed the trail of gold over the Chilcoot and down the Yukon was the crude tent kitchen at the right, with its hand-painted sign: "Stampeders Home Restaurant."

out, he could move on and find another spot on this thirty miles of beach extending from Cape Nome, thirteen miles east of Nome to Cape Rodney, sixteen miles west of Nome. But the heaviest concentration of tents was on the richest ground, which was in the area behind town, and on the stretch from the Sandspit on the Snake River to Jessie Creek and Cripple Creek, ten miles west of town. It was this long beach of miners that lent romance to the word, 'Nome,' since not another beach in the whole of Alaska or in the world was giving the squatter the opportunity to make a living off the beach at the 'throw of a hat,' as was said . . ."

Before the summer of 1899 ended, the population had grown to about 7000 and another 3000 men were blazing trails across the Seward Peninsula in search of new bonanzas. Predictions were made that the next year would bring 30,000. In a short article in the February, 1900, issue of *Scientific American,* an excited reporter predicted that ". . . the summer of 1900 will witness the most gigantic flight of myriads of people that the world has ever known toward these mines."

On a given day that year until winter closed in, in October, anywhere from 1000 to 2500 could be found working the beach sands. The process was simple. Each man—or woman for that matter—took a small plot—perhaps

Nome's downtown commercial district (named, naturally, "Front Street") consisted in the summer of '99 of typical gold rush enterprises: a boot-and-shoe tent and a female-operated grocery tent in the foreground, the scaffolding of an impressive casino-saloon rising down the street.

As Nome's Front Street developed from a straggling line of tents into a row of substantial frame houses, E.A. Hegg, the Yukon photographer, materialized with an assortment of souvenir photographs, many of which appear in this book. Hegg's studio (above) boldly advertised "We Buy and Sell Everything." The City Morgue was right next door. Most of the establishments on Front Street (right) were clothiers, restaurants, or real estate and law offices.

When a shipment of mail arrived from San Francisco or Seattle, crowds stood in line all day outside the Nome post office. From the look of the two women in the foreground, the news from home was disappointing—but almost any message was better than none. A new arrival from Illinois wrote to his wife: "Write me as often as you can for you cannot imagine what a letter is to a man in this country. Everybody I have met is wild to hear from the States."

10 by 15 feet—and dug down two to five feet to the color-bearing streaks. The gold in the beach diggings was exceedingly fine and mixed with ruby sands just above the heavily compacted clays which the miners called bedrock. The pay-streak sands were then shoveled or ladled into the rockers and washed through with water dipped from the bottom of the hole, from the surf, or from rivulets that poured at intervals off the tundra bordering the beach. The fine gold was trapped at the base of the rocker either on a piece of blanket or on copper sheets coated with mercury. Since copper was in short supply in 1899, some of the rocker bottoms were lined with silver dollars to hold the mercury. If the miner used the first method, he merely had to wash the blanket in a tub of water to collect the trapped gold. If he used mercury, which formed an amalgam with the gold, he first squeezed the amalgam through a piece of chamois skin to recover as much mercury as possible, then roasted what was left, generally in an ordinary frying pan, to drive off the remaining mercury.

As thousands worked the beach, other thousands were busy building Nome and consolidating the rich inland claims so that large-scale placer techniques could be used. The beach diggings remained a "poor man's proposition" as long as the gold lasted, but it took capital, and lots of it, to tear the gold from the gravels of the tundra.

Winter in the Arctic is long and harsh. From late October to early April temperatures rarely rise above freezing. The lashing blizzards begin arriving in November, and readings close to 50° below are not unknown.

By midsummer, 1900, more than 18,000 adventurers had arrived at Nome, turning the harsh sandspit into a lively, expensive, unsanitary town. To a prospector from the inland creeks, hankering for a bath, a haircut, a drink, a hot meal of walrus steak and blueberry pie, Nome was an earthly paradise.

Front Street soon took on an air of respectability: plank paving, false-front stores, flagpoles, telegraph wires. But the beaches remained as the Reverend Royal L. Wirt, a Congregational missionary, had found them on his arrival in August of 1899: "The water is deadly, and there is no attempt whatever at sanitation. The tents are three and four deep on the beach for miles. We are only a little way back from the beach, and the men are rocking gold at our very doorstep. I at first thought they were digging to lay a pipe or something—it never occurred to me that there was gold in our front yard . . ."

About 2500 stayed in the new city through the winter of 1899–1900, and when the shore finally became ice-free in June, the expected avalanche of gold-seekers from the "outside" began arriving.

Here is how Judge James Wickersham later described it: "They gathered in great confusion, landing from a fleet of vessels anchored two miles off the shallow roadstead, in front of the hoped-for El Dorado. They climbed from the gravelly beach upon low and soggy tundra meadows, dripping from the summer thaw of winter snow and ice, to sink knee-deep into beds of soft peat, but now made beautiful on the surface by the expanding blossoms of strange Arctic flowers.

"The first thought . . . was to get a small spot on this wet tundra, as near to the center of the town as possible, upon which to erect a cabin or a tent for shelter against Arctic storms and underfoot dampness which threatened them with sickness. Crowding and pushing against one another, with no place to pile their luggage or to lay a bed, they unavoidably trespassed upon claims located by those preceding them; and here the ordinances of the consent government compelled a recognition of the prior rights of those in possession. The municipal court heard all these cases, and

Prices at the 500 Grocery and other retail stores struck new arrivals as extortionate: Bread at three loaves for 25 cents, eggs 30 cents a dozen, and bacon 16 cents a pound! But it was comforting to find familiar products on the shore of the Bering Sea—Postum, Royal Baking Powder, Libby's vegetables, Arm & Hammer Soda, Grape Nuts, and Cracker Jack.

they were many; the court applied the evidence; the titles by prior possession were settled summarily, whereby peace was maintained . . ."

But the "gigantic flight of myriads of people" never materialized. At the height of the 1900 season, the population reached about 18,000. And many of these were soured to learn that the beach sands, which had drawn them there in the first place, had been rather well worked over by the pioneers of 1899.

Even so, there was plenty of work. A carpenter could command $1.50 or more an hour, a teamster $2, and a man with team and wagon $10. Prices were high, perhaps twice San Francisco prices for staples, but wages too were much higher than those that prevailed in the States.

As in all gold-rush boomtowns, there were plenty of ways to part with your money. Gambling, saloons, and dancehalls were as much a fixture as they were in Dawson, but Nome was no Dawson in the eyes of those who knew them both. Arthur Walden said that Nome ". . . never compared in my estimation with Dawson in its palmy days."

Nome was full of toughs, and in the absence of any force like Dawson's North West Mounted Police, crime was rampant. Walden wrote of the town

The embankment of the Snake, rapidly stripped of fine gold, became River Street, a good place to sun oneself on the boardwalk. The Riverside Saloon had begun to show marks of refinement by 1900. It had a separate Ladies' Entrance.

The first log cabin built in Nome was notable not only as a mark of municipal progress but also for the exotic taste of its builders. There were no trees within hundreds of miles of Nome, and even willow wands were treasured by the Eskimos. The absence of windows and the accumulation of several cast-iron stoves indicate the occupants planned to stay the winter.

as he saw it in 1900:

"Robbery of every description was in full swing at Nome, from the highest officials down to the lowest scum. . . . The men down here seemed to be more quarrelsome than they were in Dawson, in fact almost as bad as they were in Skagway when it was controlled by the infamous Soapy Smith, and robbing and stealing were so prevalent that nothing was safe. At one time it was proved here that all the sheriffs and deputy sheriffs had done time in the penitentiary. One of them made his living by robbing the drunks he arrested.

"One day two men and I were given a dose of knockout drops. The three of us had been doped together, and as we had had a drink in three different saloons, it was impossible to tell which one had done the trick. Two of us were already busted and lost nothing, but the other man was robbed of six hundred dollars."

Surrounded by all he possessed of value—his tiny house, his tools, his bedroll, his dogs—this prospector sat for an eloquent portrait by F.H. Nowell. The hardship of his existence is etched in a face that is old beyond the man's years. Note the gravel rocker and gold pan at left, the fur jacket and hat hanging on the wall of the house—all of them undoubtedly so arranged by the portraitist.

Rocking on the Beach

Nome was well under construction in the summer of 1899 when one of the most delightful gold discoveries in American history was made. It was in July of that year that fine gold was found by chance in the sands of the beach at Nome. The shoreline there proved to be the richest tidewater diggings ever known.

The magic of it all was that anyone with a rocker and a shovel could work the sands to his heart's content. That summer, several thousand men and women each took ten or twenty, occasionally as much as a hundred, dollars a day from the sands. It was, in the language of the day, a "true poor man's proposition." When the take had all been counted, it was found that the beach had yielded more than a million dollars that year.

Perhaps nowhere in the history of gold-mining were more odd machines put together than on the beach at Nome. The man in the upper right-hand corner of the facing page built a dredge of corned beef tins. The object of each of the outfits was to lift the very fine gold lying in ruby sand which rested about five feet below the beach level on a hardpan bedrock. Rockers and long toms were used to separate gold from the sands.

191

The lure of free gold at Nome brought thousands pouring down from Dawson and the Klondike creeks, and from West Coast ports to the south. The beaches were open to all, and although they were eventually to be worked to the point of no return, a man, or for that matter a woman, could make wages shoveling sand years after the original discovery.

Following paystreak from the beach inland, some of the more ambitious miners tunneled under Nome itself.

There was no limit to the ingenuity men applied to take gold from the beach. This contraption didn't work.

Photographer E. A. Hegg captioned this picture "Girl rocking out pin money on the beach," but she could have been rocking out a good living as well. Her outfit was as simple as they come: a standard rocker and a tin can with handle attached to pour through the water necessary to wash the gold-bearing sands.

CHAPTER XV

PEOPLE OF THE NORTH

"The Front Street of Nome has more character than the thoroughfare of any other American mining camp. This it owes to the Eskimo . . . Nome is the spot where the people of the Arctic mingle with the invaders from the Temperate Zone . . ."

For thousands of years prior to the Nome gold strike, the Eskimos of northwestern Alaska had gone their old ways and managed to wrench a life, in many respects a rich life, from the cold and forbidding land and sea.

While Norsemen had first made contact with the Eskimos of southern Greenland as far back as the Eleventh Century, it wasn't until the first half of the Nineteenth Century, when Russian traders and American whalers sailed north, that Eskimos of the Bering Straits were exposed to "civilization." Earlier fur trade with Siberia had brought some Western goods (principally tobacco) to northern Alaska, but not until the traders arrived did Western material culture have measurable impact on Eskimo life—and that was only in the way of a few comforts and staples: flour, tea, sugar, cotton yardage, and hardware, which were traded principally for furs.

Essentially, the old ways remained. Virtually all of the things the Eskimos needed—food, shelter, clothing, light and heat, transportation, weapons (except for rifles), and most tools and implements—were still taken from nature. This is, of course, true of all hunting societies, but nowhere else in the world had a people developed a culture so superbly geared to survival.

In 1898 Eskimos of the region were to see 25 or 30 times as many people as they had ever seen gathered in one place in all their lives. Miners from the Klondike and Yukon set out by the thousands for the new fields, and many more thousands embarked for the new Eldorado from the States, urged on by the propaganda of West Coast shipping companies and other commercial boomers.

The Nome adventure was enriched, in small part at least, by the presence of the Bering Straits Eskimos. It is not recorded what the natives thought of their uninvited guests. Although there must have been some friction, at least in isolated incidents, between white and native, accounts in books and periodicals do not reflect it. Certainly there was no open hostility.

Nome itself was built on the site of a small, temporary Eskimo fishing camp, and it became a magnet of Eskimos of King Island, Little Diomede

Launching an oomiak on the beach at Nome, a group of Eskimos sets out for Cape Prince of Wales, a 120-mile journey north, on an August day in 1905. Oomiaks were widely used for travel and for hunting large marine animals during the relatively placid Arctic summer. Built of walrus hide stretched over a wooden frame, the craft could be paddled or sailed. Upended, it made a delightful summerhouse.

Hunters cutting up a great whale (probably a bowhead) conformed to traditional customs in butchering and dividing meat and blubber. Members of the hunting party took preferred parts of the animal, according to the tasks they had performed. The entire community shared not only in the bounty but also in religious ceremonies before the chase and feasting afterward.

Eskimo culture was shaped by sea animals—whales, seals, sea lions, walruses, and beluga that supplied meat, oil, skins, and ivory. These were the basics of survival in a harsh environment.

Island, and other adjacent mainland communities during the summers. Years passed before the Eskimos became any significant part of the labor force, but their ivory work, skin clothing, meat, furs, and basketry all found a ready place in the American market.

With the miners, capitalists, sharpers, thugs, tradesmen, artisans, gamblers, and camp followers who flocked to Nome, there came also photographers. They left a record that a wall of books could not match. From a historical standpoint, one of the great values of these pictures, aside from what they recorded of Eskimo cultural elements now passed and of the bustle of early Nome and the mines, is what the white man saw and felt was worth photographing—for much of what he put on film was governed by what he thought the American print-buying market would want to see. The commercial photographic legacy is, then, as much a reflection of the American culture as it is of the Eskimo.

The animals provided meat for human beings and their dogs; oil for heating, lighting, and nourishment; hides for clothing, shelter, tie-lines, and containers; ivory for harpoon points and decorative carvings; and bones for the framework of igloos. Even walrus intestines found use in rainproof parkas. Relatively easy to capture, walruses in their seasonal abundance supported large populations at King Island, Cape Prince of Wales, and Saint Lawrence Island.

196

The peculiarities of Eskimo culture fascinated and sometimes repelled Caucasians. The diet, housing, clothing, and sexual practices of these tenacious and resourceful people were the subject of thousands of articles, books, and letters home to the States. Commercial portraits by F. H. Nowell, Nome's leading photographer, and scenic views by the Lomen Brothers and E.A. Hegg, the brilliant chronicler of the Klondike rush, sold briskly in all parts of the Northwest. "The Front Street of Nome has more character than the thoroughfare of any other American mining camp," T.A. Rickard wrote in 1909. "This it owes to the Eskimo. As Cairo is the meeting place of the Eastern and Western civilizations, so Nome is the spot where the people of the Arctic mingle with the invaders from the Temperate zone." Below, a family of Eskimos from King Island pose in their summer cabana, an upturned oomiak on the beach at Nome. Left: Eskimos trading with passengers aboard the steamer *Roanoke* in the Bering Sea.

Captioned "Eskimo Automobile Transfer Co., Nome, Alaska," this incongruous display of Bering Straits residents in a late-model touring car was a fast-selling item in the souvenir shops of Nome in 1905. Other popular subjects: Eskimo children, malamute sled dogs, girls in fur parkas, reindeer. The latter, although closely related to the native caribou, were an imported species, some from Siberia, a few from Scandinavia.

Worn and weathered by the hardships of an elemental life, these men were plying their handwork in the comfort of the summer sun when F.H. Nowell, the town portraitist, captured them with his plate camera (undoubtedly paying a small model's fee). The man at center is scrubbing clothes on a wooden washboard while the pipe-smoking ivory carver shapes a walrus tusk with a hand axe. Gold rush photographers considered such activities picturesque circa 1905, and outsiders snapped up the pictures.

"Art has always been a pervading and special part of Eskimo life," anthropologist Dorothy Jean Ray wrote in *Graphic Art of the Alaskan Eskimo,* "though there are no words in the language for 'art' or 'artist.'" The prosperous-looking young couple above are making objects for sale. While the man uses a bow drill to hollow ivory, his wife is making a pair of soft leather mukluks. Presumably, these handcrafts will find their way into a curio store like the one at the right, where furs and baskets, dolls and jewelry are displayed along the boardwalk.

Eskimo children with chubby cheeks and shoebutton eyes were irresistible to the photographers of Nome, although there was a pervasive belief among white settlers that the natives and their habits were peculiar and inferior. The children above are posed among Eskimo-made baskets of a high order of workmanship—patternless, symmetrical, sturdy, embellished here and there with bits of colored yarn or beads. The snake-like object is a woman's belt. Hundreds of caribou teeth were sewn to leather to produce the striped pattern. At left and below are Nowell portraits of Eskimo children bathing in the Bering Sea, showing off mulamute puppies, and helping with the laundry.

Beauty, strength, dignity, and joy shine in these portraits of an Eskimo bride, Wy-Ung-Ena, of Cape Douglas, Alaska, and her husband, A-Pa-Look. At right, Wy-Ung-Ena smokes a pipe among her household chattels; below, the couple's wedding portrait, taken at Teller, Alaska, April 10, 1905.

An Eskimo matron, Mrs. Jim Allen, poses with her young son in a curious setting of tundra grass, a whipsaw, and sled runners (left). Nome portraitists photographed many Eskimo women who had married Caucasian men, as if by these pictures to document a social phenomenon likely to create excitement and disapproval back in the States. Although American photographers pandered to prejudice and morbid curiosity (as in the picture, below, of an Eskimo grave), the best examples of their work reflect the underlying sentiment of white newcomers toward the people they found in the North—kinship, affection, and respect.

The Raging Bering Sea

Nome was built on the shorefront tundra no more than a dozen feet above the mean high-tide mark—in some places, not even that. It was inevitable that the town was going to get battered by the heavy seas and winds that roared ashore, particularly in September and sometimes in October before the freeze. But the only ones who could have predicted it were the natives, who must have wondered what the crazy newcomers thought they were doing. Nome was flooded and smashed year after year—some worse than others—but each time it patched up its wounds and carried on. Nowhere in the North was life ever easy.

Above, when the ice pack broke up in late June, floating ice driven by strong winds would inflict much damage on the barges, boats, and piers near the waterline. Left, the barge *Nome City* bashing in the wharf of one of the trading companies. Wharf also appears in photo above.

The wreck of the schooner *Harriet* on September 7, 1900. Another unidentified schooner has been driven ashore farther down the beach. Note the lines that were attached to the *Harriet* in the attempt to save or salvage her.

Waves break against the Pacific Packing and Navigation Company's offices during an October storm. Below, houses being swept off the sandspit at the mouth of Nome's Snake River.

Of the wreck of the barge *Skookum*, above, the largest in service to Nome, Carrie McLain wrote: "Many boats were tossed about and the barge, *Skookum*, was torn and shattered of all her loose timbers. She had brought up thousands of board feet of lumber, hundreds of tons of coal, and several hundred head of livestock and sheep." Left, the remains of the *Catherine Suddon*, which broke in half three days before the *Skookum*. Picture was taken during the terrible September storm of 1900.

The waterfront as the big October storm of 1902 drove the sea before it and into the streets of Nome.

When the going gets so rough that men are moved to tie ropes to their houses to save them, you know that you have been in a storm. River Street, right; the Snake River Bridge, below.

Although the August, 1900, storm was but a presage of the mighty one that arrived in September, it still managed to wreck, among other things, the schooner *Teaser* and the launch *Siesta*. Left, the September 13, 1900, edition of the *Nome Chronicle*, published almost a week after the big storm first hit. Below, virtually every building in the picture was flooded or lifted from its foundations by the storm.

The Nome Daily Chronicle

Vol. I, No. 79.   NOME, ALASKA, THURSDAY, SEPTEMBER 13, 1900.   Price 25 Cents.

DEVASTATION FOLLOWS IN THE WAKE OF BEHRING'S RAGING STORM

Thousands of Dollars Worth of Property Destroyed and Hundreds of People Rendered Homeless by The Fury of The Elements. Lower Front Street is Wiped Out of Existence as a Thoroughfare and Becomes a Rushing, Turbulent, Debris-Strewn Stream. Many Lives Reported to Have Been Lost. Barge Skookum Drifts Ashore and is Pounded to Pieces Amid the Breakers. Full Account of Nome's First Great Catastrophe.

DESCRIPTION OF A NIGHT OF FURIOUS HORROR.

WHAT WAS ONCE RIVER STREET

ASSISTANCE OFFERED.

SKOOKUM COMES ASHORE.

After Battling the Season's Elements the Mammoth Barge Succumbs at Last.

River Street Wiped Out.

Furniture ✱ ✱ ✱

Oak Bed Room Suites, Chiffoniers, Side Boards, Separate Commodes, Enamel Beds, Springs and Mattresses.

WE HAVE THEM AND THE PRICES ARE RIGHT

AMES MERCANTILE COMPANY

River street: Wiped out.

CHAPTER XVI

BAD GUYS AND BAD SEASONS

*"The high-handed and grossly illegal procedings initiated al-
most as soon as Judge Noyes and McKenzie had set foot in
Alaskan territory . . . may be safely said to have no parallel in
the jurisprudence of this country . . ."*

Aside from the establishment of a few scattered military posts and
customs stations and a handful of often corrupt officials sent from the
States, Alaska was largely left to govern itself until enactment of the Alaska
Act of 1900, which, among other things, created three judicial districts, one
to be based in Nome. It was hoped that law and order, perhaps even justice,
would follow, but this was not to be the case. When Judge Arthur H. Noyes
arrived on July 19, 1900, his mind was on personal enrichment, not on the
fate of the five accused murderers who had been held for his arrival. Noyes
was a thief, as was his traveling companion, Alexander McKenzie.

Both were originally from North Dakota, where McKenzie had flourished as a political boss. Rex Beach said of McKenzie that he was ". . . not
the common municipal vote getter, the manipulator of primaries, but the
man of riches, respectability and standing, who plays the game for gold not
glory." And Beach described Noyes as a "plastic tool" of McKenzie.

The "general sordidness" of Nome, as Walden characterized it, grew
under the reign of the corrupt Judge Noyes. As soon as he and McKenzie
stepped off the boat, they set about stealing the richest mines in the region.
The scheme was as simple as it was audacious: McKenzie had formed the
Alaskan Gold Mining Company, capitalized it at 15 million and gave shares
liberally to his politically influential acquaintances, including a number of
United States senators. The latter, smelling gold, had induced President
William McKinley to appoint McKenzie's crooked pal Noyes to the north-
west Alaskan judicial district.

Soon after their arrival in Nome, McKenzie drew up the papers
necessary to have the Alaskan Gold Mining Company named receiver of a
number of rich claims on Anvil Creek, most of which had been purchased
by the Wild Goose and Pioneer mining companies from the original
stakers. With Judge Noyes's signature on the documents, McKenzie set
forth with a band of hired bullies and physically ejected the legal owners of
five of the claims—*all in less than 24 hours* from the time he first stepped
ashore.

Claim-jumping is part of the history of American mining, but the
McKenzie-Noyes conspiracy must be considered the ultimate incident in
the annals of this crime.

When the miners protested bitterly that they hadn't been notified in
advance of the seizures, nor given a chance to be heard at the time of
McKenzie's appointment as receiver, Noyes refused to hear their appeals. It
didn't take the miners long to realize that redress would have to come from
the outside, if it were to come at all, so they dispatched representatives to

The Arctic winter begins in October,
lasts until June. Snow had fallen on the
beached boats and iron roofs of the Nome
waterfront when the picture above was
taken on October 10, 1904, and ice was
forming along the shallow shores as passengers boarded a barge lightering cargo
out to a departing steamer (right). By the
nineteenth or twentieth of the month,
the "last boat" would have gone. Soon
the Bering Sea would be frozen solid for
miles offshore, and the only contact between Nome and "Outside" would be by
dog team, overland to St. Michael at the
mouth of the Yukon, thence by way of
Fairbanks to Valdez, where there was
steamship service to Seattle. The arrival
of the "first boat" in Nome in early June
was, understandably, an occasion of civic
celebration.

Steamer *Corwin,* surrounded by ice (right), unloads supplies onto dog sleds. Ships making early spring runs to Nome often were trapped by ice, had to spend weeks off St. Lawrence Island, sometimes with hundreds of passengers aboard. Below: A cozy bar attempted to ameliorate the rigors of the climate with drinks and cigars at two for 25 cents.

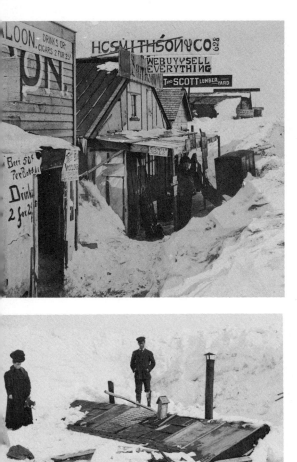

San Francisco by steamer with copies of the court records.

The U.S. Circuit Court of Appeals, Ninth District, reviewed the matter and quickly issued a writ directing McKenzie to cease operations and return the properties to the rightful owners. When the writ arrived in Nome on September 19, McKenzie flatly refused to obey the orders. Noyes as flatly refused to order him to, although it was clearly his duty. Indeed, Noyes even commanded the federal troops under his authority to fend off any attempts the miners might make to take back their claims.

The miners once again sent men to San Francisco. This time they returned with two deputies of the court, bearing orders to bring McKenzie back to San Francisco to stand trial for contempt.

Even before the deputies could reach the scene, things began to go badly for the thieves. The Wild Goose Company managed to retake its claims; and when McKenzie, sensing that time was short, tried to withdraw the dust and nuggets he had deposited in the vaults of the Alaska Banking and Safe Deposit Company, a sullen crowd gathered and made it clear that any attempt to make off with the gold would be mighty unhealthy for him. He left the bank empty handed.

When the court's deputies arrived, they quickly served McKenzie with the summons and hustled him aboard a steamer bound for San Francisco. The gold he had stolen remained behind in Nome, to be returned eventually to the mine owners.

McKenzie was tried in the court of appeals that winter, and upon his conviction on February 11, 1901, Judge Ross had this to say before sentence was passed: ". . . the high-handed and grossly illegal proceedings initiated almost as soon as Judge Noyes and McKenzie had set foot in Alaskan territory . . . may be safely said to have no parallel in the jurisprudence of this country."

The judge sentenced McKenzie to spend a year in prison, but the convict's political friends persuaded President McKinley to pardon him, on the grounds of ill health, after he had served only three months of his term.

Noyes was later tried, removed from the bench, and fined $1000—a curiously light sentence in view of his outrageous betrayal of office.

April was, if not the cruelest month, thoroughly unpleasant for residents of the tar-papered cabin above. Nome City was built like most frontier boom towns with little regard for geography or climate. Front Street (right) was passable only to pedestrians and dog teams—and then only at the cost of constant burrowing. In mid-September the town water supply would be cut off for the winter to prevent pipes from bursting. For the next eight months, Nome dwellers would have to chop holes through the surface of frozen rivers and cart water in barrels.

The long winter, grim in most respects, was "a sociable time," according to Nome's official historian, Carrie McLain. "—The Miners' Home Club was organized for weekly card parties. Dances were annual affairs of the big organizations. ... Surprise parties were given at the drop of a hat (and) women met at various homes to make paper flowers for all occasions, including funerals. Roses, lilies, carnations, and chrysanthemums were favorites."

F.H. Nowell, Nome's leading resident photographer, posed a group of his friends on the boardwalk in front of his studio on a July day in 1905. Among the souvenir pictures on display are several Eskimo portraits that appear in the preceding chapter. Below: These bright little faces at the Nome School were photographed in 1902, after Judge Noyes had departed town, Theodore Roosevelt had become President, and the chaotic days of beach-rocking and claim-jumping were past. Further evidence of civilization has been reported on the blackboard in the best penmanship of one Erwin Wright: "I go to dancing school every Saturday afternoon."

With the departure of McKenzie and Noyes, development of the district's large mines accelerated. The Miocene Ditch Company constructed a channel more than 15 miles up the valley of the Nome River to bring the great volumes of water necessary to wash the placers of its extensive holdings on Glacier Creek. In 1902 Charles D. Lane, a '49er, shipowner and capitalist, built a pumping plant on the Snake River to carry water to the top of Anvil Mountain, which rises above Anvil Creek about five miles inland from Nome. The system supplied 250 miner's inches of water (a miner's inch is a flow of 1.5 cubic feet per minute) and cost $350,000 to build. That's a lot of money in any day, but it paid for itself in the first year of operation.

These are but two examples of what men with capital could do. Men without money or a profession did not fare so well. Once the beach diggings were worked out and every inch of land in the district long since staked, they had to choose either to return to the States, to work for wages, or to set out into the back country of the Seward Peninsula and points beyond to search for new gold fields. Thousands chose to roam the vast countryside. Many went on to uncover the new bonanzas they sought. The names of Candle, Dahl, and Taylor creeks and the Inmachuk, Niukluk, and Kougarok rivers were to become famous in Nome and in the mining exchanges of the world.

In time, trails were blazed up and back across the landscape. The Nome and Arctic Railroad, which extended more than 50 miles into the heart of the peninsula, carried its first passengers in 1905. And the Council City and Solomon River Railroad stretched 30-odd miles from Council City, on the Niukluk River, to Dickson, on the coast south of Nome. Where the railroads didn't go, the trails became well marked, and roadhouses sprang up along the most heavily traveled routes to feed and shelter men and their dogs during their wanderings.

But throughout those early years following the Nome discovery, travel in winter was at each man's peril. Dogpuncher Arthur Walden illustrated this with the story of an incident on a trip he took from Nome with several other men to the northeast corner of the peninsula in mid-winter.

Members of Nome's Radiator Club lift a beerful toast, dutifully recorded by photographer Nowell at the third annual "Footwarming," Christmas, 1908. Several are sporting lapel ribbons that advertise Pabst beer, and one man, for no apparent reason, is thumbing his nose.

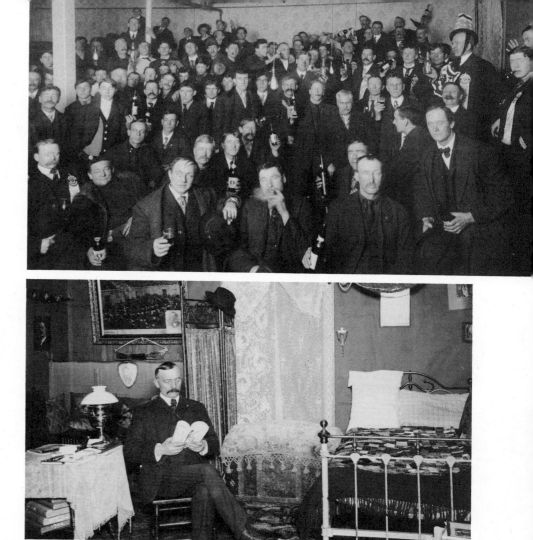

At home in Nome, a gentleman of the merchant class (right) is reading an up-to-date (1904) *Munsey's Magazine*.

King Island Eskimos, lured into the Congregationl Church Mission by the good white ladies of the Nome Society, doze through divine services on a warmish Sunday in late July, 1906 (below). Nome early acquired one Roman Catholic church and separate Protestant churches for whites and Eskimos.

A holiday crowd poses outside a Front Street tavern that was snobbish about class and about serving Western beer. Destroyed in the big fire of September, 1905, the Second Class Saloon reopened in a modest structure of rough boards, now calling itself "The Old Reliable."

"At the mouth of Eschscholtz Bay we found an Eskimo and his family, wintering in their igloo. From there we crossed over to Elephant Point, where three of us were again overtaken by a blizzard, which blew so hard that we couldn't even get our tent up. We lay for three days in the snow, covered up in our robes, and lived on raw bacon and hard-tack.

"It was impossible to feed the dogs properly. All we could do was to throw them pieces of bacon and hope that the right ones would get it. It was impossible to tell day from night, as the raging blizzard made even the lightest part of the day seem dark. We came through all right, but each man owned up that he thought the other men had left him when he was asleep. It is funny how these thoughts will creep up on you."

The change in communications, however, demonstrates more clearly than any other example how quickly Nome was wrenched into the 20th Century. George Edward Adams had written in *Harper's Weekly* in the spring of 1900:

"On March 22 [1900] the writer had the pleasure of reading a letter received on that day from Nome City, bearing the date of December 30, 1899. The letter was but two months and 24 days in traversing 3,000 miles through a land that three years ago was considered practically uninhabitable by white men. Such a feat seems almost miraculous. The reader, sitting near the cozy fireside, can scarce picture the mail carrier, with his trusty team of dogs, gliding along week after week over fields of ice and snow, with the thermometer ranging from 40 to 60 degrees below zero."

By the end of summer 1905 a powerful United States wireless telegraph station was in full operation at Port Safety, 19 miles south of Nome.

The gold camp on the frozen sea had become a cosmopolitan little city, rejoicing in many of the comforts of the temperate zone.

"Come and dine with me at the Royal Cafe," T.A. Rickard wrote in 1909. "It is not the Café Royal, and yet if previously you have walked over the tundra or ridden on horseback along the firm sands of the Bering Sea, you will pronounce it a good restaurant, however you may pronounce the name it bears. The place is crowded but clean; the well-intended efforts of a piano and a violin give a touch of gaiety, and the crowd that passes along the main street can be watched with interest while the reindeer stew or the roast ptarmigan is being prepared. The Eskimo give color to the scene; the women in their pink and yellow parkas and wolverine hoods look like ladies on their way to a party; the men in fur ruffles and light drill parkas wear visored caps or else go bare-headed with masses of long dark hair trimmed with a Dutch cut. Two Eskimos carry the skin of a polar bear on a long pole. Others have carved whalebone for sale. Dogs are numerous. The bright tints of the native costume produce a chromatic liveliness unusual in a mining camp. The huskies and the malamutes accompany the Eskimo and suggest Arctic life.

"An occasional Saxon of fresh complexion looks very pink amid these black and oily denizens of the North. Stalwart miners in high laced boots and stiff, broad-brimmed hats recall Colorado and Nevada. Women dressed conventionally indicate that Nome has homes as well as mines. The superintendent of a mine rides past on a handsome black horse that clatters over the boarded street and scatters the Eskimo children with the dogs.

"And all this time the musicians in the background have been doing their best, as well as the cook. Silver salmon, reindeer steak, and ptarmigan, followed by blueberry pie, represent adequate nourishment of a kind suited to the picturesque environment. A demi-tasse and a Havana cigar emphasize the fact that Nome is no jumping-off place, but on the highway of civilization from New York to Paris, via Bering strait . . ."

Fourth of July in Nome

Time was when the Fourth of July was the most important holiday in the land; and Nome, our last great Wild-West town, celebrated it with all the energy it could muster.

The entire town was decked out in flags and bunting in the early years, and everyone within a day's journey made his way to the celebration. Above, a couple of regulars at the bar of the Commerce Saloon for eye-openers. A drink cost a "bit" —12½ cents. Left, the crowd begins to gather.

213

Above, in front of the milling crowd, several do their best for the photographer's sake. The legal shingles on the right are a hint of the fertile ground Nome became for the barristers from the States. Left, a thoughtful crowd waiting for the parade to begin.

Above and at right, the parade forms and proceeds before the view of a heavily clad audience. Below, a few idlers in one of the many gambling halls of early Nome. The floor was sprinkled to keep the dust down.

Left, the town begins to gather for the ritual endings to the annual outpouring of patriotic expression. Below, Judge R. N. Stevens reads the Declaration of Independence, and the children of Nome Public School sing "My Country, 'tis of Thee" in their sweet and small voices.

216

And then, when all the ceremonies were done, it was off to the country on the Wild Goose Railroad for the traditional Fourth of July picnic—and blueberry-picking on the tundra.

CHAPTER XVII

CAPITAL AND BRAINS

"The output of gold from the Seward Peninsula will increase with each year so long as you and I are on this old earth to watch the hydraulic giants tearing away the gravel . . ."

The last chapter of every gold rush story begins with more or less the same words: Soon the easy gold was gone. The important word is "easy," for it both defines a gold rush and distinguishes that singular outburst of mass self-improvement from the tedious and unromantic business of gold mining, which goes on year after year in remote and generally uncomfortable corners of the earth.

In the Far North the "easy" years were few: two or three along the Klondike creeks, the fingers of one hand at Nome, and then a series of successful strikes—several of them richer than the Klondike and Nome together—in the Tanana Valley, at Iditarod, at Ruby, Marshall, and Livengood. Each new discovery set off another horde of independent prospectors, inflamed with the same unquenchable optimism as the adventurers of '98; and each new stampede followed the same predictable cycle of inflation, exploitation, and collapse.

When T. A. Rickard, a writer who had reported on mining in many countries, visited the Yukon a decade after the Klondike Rush, he found Dawson City a ghostly derelict, wearing a shabby air of "respectability compelled by impoverishment, of the temperance that succeeds dissipation, of the bust after the boom." In 1898 the population of the district had been 50,000. Ten years later it was only 2000.

"Dawson looks like a stout man who has grown very thin and yet wears the cloths made for him in his adipose days," Rickard wrote. "Although it has been difficult for Dawson to accommodate itself to straitened circumstances, the adaptation has been effected heroically. The boom has gone, but business remains."

What had happened, of course, was that the surface gold, the easy stuff, had run out. With it had disappeared the outfitters and freight handlers, the whores and gamblers, and the thousands of ordinary adventurers who had failed to strike it rich. Innumerable small claims that prospectors had staked along the creeks southeast of Dawson were picked off, one by one, by corporations with the capacity to bring in dredges, mills, and other heavy equipment to get at the gold that remained. South of the Klondike watershed individual miners continued their labors with pick and shovel; but along the creeks to the north—the celebrated Eldorado, Hunker, and Bonanza—the gravel now belonged to the Yukon Gold Company, controlled by the Guggenheim family. As a Scottish mining engineer at Dawson put it, the extraction of Klondike gold now required "capital and brains," neither of which had been abundant in the days of the three-month climb over Chilcoot Pass, both of which were adequately present among the Guggenheims.

During the stampede, miners had worked their Klondike claims by

A steam boiler fired with precious bits of wood heats water to thaw the eternally frozen tundra at Golden Feather Bench, a claim owned by a grizzled prospector named Ike Halliday near the Inmachuk River on the Seward Peninsula (1903).

digging holes with hand tools and building wood fires to thaw the frozen ground.

"If you had gone up the narrow valleys of Bonanza and Hunker during the long twilight of the Arctic winter," Rickard wrote, "you would have seen a picture worthy of Gustave Doré. There was no noise, for there was no machinery; there were no whistles to announce the noon hour or the evening rest; there was no drilling in hard rock or cheerful hammering. A weird silence brooded over the waste of snow. The gloom was thickened by a pall of smoke escaping from holes in the ground, whence an occasional figure issued. Not many men were visible, for they were below in the rabbit warren of their diggings. At the top of a shaft, here and there, a weary gnome might be espied turning a windlass and emptying buckets loaded with dirt that came from a small pit beneath. The flare of red fires parting the twilight marked the beginning of the work of shaft-sinking. The snow, the moss, and the fog muffled every foot-fall, deadened every sound. It looked like Hell—but it was freezing."

Before long the old method of softening the ground with fires was superseded by a technique of driving sharp pointed pipes several feet into the frozen muck, then injecting steam from a boiler for several hours until

The ravaging efficiency of high-pressure water came to the outlands of Nome with the construction of the 15-mile Miocene Ditch. The miner above demonstrates the joys of hydraulicking at one of Miocene's mines on Glacier Creek in July, 1906. Below: a family of handsomely moustached entrepreneurs displays evidence of God's rewards to those who applied brains, capital, and 16-inch nozzles to the gravelly banks of the Inmachuk.

Pyramids of paydirt, dug by hand from the carefully thawed benches of Nome's Third Beach Line, await washing to separate gold from gravel during the summer cleanup, 1906.

Grinning in triumph, the young wife of a small-scale miner on the Upper Kougarok River shows off the spoils of a scrounging expedition in July, 1907. Where she found branches in the treeless tundra is a professional secret, for firewood was almost as valuable as gold to prospectors who relied on hot-water thawers to soften the frozen muck.

the ice melted and the gravel could be shoveled out and hauled to the surface in buckets. By this primitive drift mining, the production of gold in the Yukon had reached a peak of $22 million in 1900.

At the same time, however, an Englishman with the appropriately Dickensian name of A. N. C. Treadgold had been gathering options on Klondike claims to form the nucleus of a major company. It was Treadgold's interest that the Guggenheims bought, with the assistance of J. P. Morgan, in 1906. Within two years seven dredges were at work, nosing their way up and down the valleys, plowing up great ridges of stones and gravel.

A 70-mile conduit was under construction to deliver water at 400 feet of pressure. The ditch, like the dredges, would revolutionize the Yukon. Bright young engineers from Stanford, Harvard, and Columbia went north to work on it. With a price of more than $3 million, it was the marvel of the mining industry, the spinning jenny of Klondike gold. Having dredged the valley bottoms to bed rock, the hydraulickers could now turn giant hoses onto the white gravel on the slopes above, washing down whole mountainsides in oozing avalanches that radiated out like fans across the lowlands, drowning and obliterating the mounds and ridges left by drifting and dredging. In a few hours a handful of men could ravage an area that had withstood millennia of natural erosion, while a dredge with a crew of ten could wash more gravel in a day than hundreds of men could shovel in a week. The brief and giddy moment of free gold and self-reliance had ended.

In Nome, too, hydraulic nozzles and $500,000 dredges quickly replaced the primitive one-man rockers that had cluttered the beach during the incredible summer of 1900. Thousands of men worked at $5 a day, chopping 18-foot ditches in the tundra. The ditches ran for hundreds of miles across the Seward Peninsula, bringing water down to the diggings at 400 to 500 feet of head pressure. At this pressure, a 16-inch stream of water had more power than dynamite to tear apart the gravel benches, to swirl the muck into a thick gray slurry that could be run across a riffle to winnow out the precious metal that was worth far more, it seemed, than the land itself.

C. L. Morris, a master ditch-builder, commented with evident glee (the year was 1907): "It's amusing to hear people say that the Seward Peninsula is 'worked out.' The output of gold from the Seward Peninsula will increase each year so long as you and I are on this old earth to watch the hydraulic giants tearing away the gravel."

Morris was more enthusiastic than prophetic; but it is true that the years of gold mining in the Far North had only begun. A federally sponsored guide book to Alaska noted in the early 1940s: "All over Alaska monstrous dredges are pushing their snouts forward, leaving behind mile upon mile of tailings: on the flats of Nome, at Circle, at Flat, at Deadwood, at Ruby, near Fairbanks, where students from the University of Alaska watch beside the hydraulickers for the bones of prehistoric creatures . . . Mining today is an affair of finance, of the latest in engineering skill. Cautious men behind polished desks in San Francisco figure out in advance the amount of metal to a cubic yard, the number of yards washed a day, the cost of each operation."

David B. Wharton theorizes in *The Alaska Gold Rush* that the advent of company-controlled mining, which tended to stifle the enterprise of free-lance miners in Alaska and the Yukon, actually helped preserve the frontier individualism of the Far North. Working on huge barges or in ore beds a hundred feet underground, men who had come north to escape industrial bondage found themselves again enslaved. By hundreds, then thousands, they drifted away to more appealing fields, while the confirmed sourdoughs turned to trapping, fishing, and prospecting the streams of the untracked wilderness.

"Like a lost continent," Wharton writes, "Alaska and the Yukon drifted backward in time. Thus, the principal threat to the free life of the North, the big mining companies, in the end made it possible for that life to continue. It forced back into wilderness what it had torn from wilderness. It re-created frontier conditions after frontier conditions ended."

A more commonly held view—and a less comforting one—is that corporate mining, employing few persons and controlled by financial interests thousands of miles away, turned Alaska and the Yukon into economic vassaldoms and prevented for decades the development of agriculture, commerce, or manufacturing. Dominated by extractive industries, the Far North has, until recently, been like an exploited colony of the United States and Canada.

A miner named Dashley holds a length of copper tubing that carries steam from his wood-fired thawer down the shaft of a mine on the Inmachuk River, 1903. Individual prospectors continued to mine the inland creeks of the Nome district for some years after dredging had all but eliminated small mining in the Klondike. Below: Company miners rake the watery tailings of Glacier Mine #2 in a flume owned by the Miocene Ditch Co. This is the last cleanup of the season, date: September 27, 1905.

Steam Dinkies of the Seward Peninsula

As more and more strikes were made inland, the need for railroads was clear, and those who knew their business made the most of it. C. D. Lane, the old '49er and capitalist who consolidated a healthy collection of claims, built the first dinkie—an almost-five-mile line he named the Wild Goose Railroad. Tracks were laid on the ground without a proper bed and the ride was a careening one. Lida Rose McCabe wrote in the August 5, 1906, issue of *The New York Times* a brief and colorful impression of her experience: "A ride on the Nome–Arctic [the line had been renamed] is a novelty without parallel in steam transportation. It was mid-June when I boarded the train, which consisted of a logging engine, a Pullman, and two roofless freight cars. To be accurate, the whole thing was observation. The Pullman had a canvas roof. Kitchen benches held up the sides. As every bench was occupied, I climbed on to a freighter to find a seat on a miner's oil cloth pack. . . . The cars were piled high with supplies for the camps along the route, and

sandwiched in were miners in various garb, with a sprinkling of women, some modishly white-shirted and veiled, with Kodaks and baskets for wildflower gathering. The engine, not unlike a homely Dutch teakettle, swayed back and forth, to and fro, now picking its way gingerly where a snow thaw had sunk ties or rail, now assured of a clean sweep, it grew 'chesty,' with funny toots from its caricature of a whistle it puffed and snorted up grade, while not infrequently passengers got off to give the whole a lift. . . . Three dollars is the price of a round-trip ticket. The stations are wooden sheds or canvas tents. They are sign posts to mining centers, as the names indicate—Little Creek, Discovery, Banner, Dexter, etc."

Above left, the terminus of the Wild Goose Railroad at Anvil Creek; below left, the first passenger train over the Nome River bridge; above, "The Paystreak Cannonball" on the Seward Peninsula Railway—successor to the Nome–Arctic line; below, Nome–Arctic train at Little Creek Roadhouse.

A passenger train on the never-to-be-completed Council City and Solomon River RR at Dickson.

As summer approached—these two pictures were taken on the 24th of June in 1907—a crew was busy clearing the right-of-way of the Seward Peninsula RR in preparation for the working season.

A Sunday excursion on the Nome–Arctic on the Little Creek bridge near Brownsville.

The photographer captioned this picture "Seward Peninsula RR the end of railroad transportation in the world." The place: Lane's Landing. Today, there is not a foot of working track on the peninsula.

Roped together like mountain climbers, construction workers on the White Pass & Yukon route chipped away at a wall of granite under the clouded dome of Saw Tooth Mountain during the summer of 1898. Two years later, the completed trestle (below) was carrying tourists over the route of the notorious Dead Horse Trail.

The stampede to the Far North, unlike the gold rush to California in 1849 or to the Dakotas in 1877, did not lead to immigration, agricultural development, and statehood for the territory of the big bonanza. Nor did the gold of Alaska and the Yukon create a new generation of capitalists as did the silver of Nevada or the oil of Pennsylvania, Texas, and Oklahoma.

Yet, it would be wrong to say that the last grand adventure had no lasting effects. Gold opened Alaska and the Yukon physically and economically and brought them into the consciousness of the North American people. Older towns of the Alaskan panhandle—Wrangel, Ketchikan, and Juneau—vibrated with renewed life. New towns, such as Seward, sprang up in the wilderness; and the sites of later gold discoveries became permanent settlements, the most notable of which was Fairbanks, a boom town on the banks of the Tanana River, deep in the heartland of Alaska.

One of the visible results of the Klondike Rush was a transportation system between the Canadian interior and the Pacific Ocean—the White Pass and Yukon Railroad, a 110-mile narrow-gauge line from the shore of the panhandle over the Coast Mountains to Whitehorse, at the head of steamer navigation on the Yukon. Built while the stampede was in full heat, the WP&Y was a difficult and costly piece of engineering that might never have been undertaken—or undertaken decades later—had it not been for the momentary impetus to hasten men and supplies to Dawson City.

The railroad was at first a Canadian enterprise; but the three Victoria businessmen who obtained a government charter to build the line in 1897 sold their franchise to Close Brothers, a British company. This resourceful firm, with considerable bravado and virtually no planning, immediately bought out Brackett's toll road from Skagway to Lake Bennett and dispatched a team of construction engineers to southeastern Alaska to start laying tracks. The engineers had no construction equipment, no rolling stock, no subcontractors to feed and house laborers, no foodstuffs except what could be brought from Puget Sound, and only the sketchiest of preliminary surveys of the countryside. The only easy aspect of their job was to choose between the Dyea–Chilcoot Pass and the Skagway–White Pass routes. White Pass, at 2887 feet, is 1000 feet lower than Chilcoot.

In late May, 1898, a few months before Skagway rid itself of Soapy Smith, the WP&Y broke ground. For the next four months, until the first snows of autumn curtailed work on the mountain slopes, there were 1000 to 1900 men on the White Pass payroll. Shifts worked round-the-clock, drawing 30 cents an hour for an 11-hour work day. After paying $1 a day for board and lodgings, a man netted $2.30 a day. Understandably, any gold strike in the neighborhood distracted the work force. A discovery at Lake Atlin, just over the divide, almost put the railroad out of business.

Every inch of track, every tie, stringer, and bridge timber had to be imported. So did 450 tons of explosives to blast out the right-of-way. To further complicate the logistics, the United States had gone to war with Spain and chartered most of the seaworthy vessels in North America. The WP&Y rounded up a fleet of wrecked ships, patched the largest holes, and had the whole leaky flotilla towed, fully loaded, up the Inland Passage from Vancouver to Skagway. While thousands of stampeders were struggling up the Brackett road by wagon or on foot, the railroad slowly thrust its pair of tracks along the slope above. Each time a crew would blast rocks from a mountainside, they would have to descend to the valley below and clear the rubble off the Brackett road. Thirty-five workmen were killed in the course of construction, most of them buried under tons of sliding granite.

In little over a year the road was open from Skagway to Lake Bennett. By the following July it had reached Whitehorse. The "ugly dream of crossing the Pass," as Chief Engineer E. C. Hawkins called it, was ended.

So, too, were alternate routes to the Yukon. Within a few weeks after the first trains ran to Lake Bennett, the wire rope tramways from The Scales to the crest of Chilcoot Pass shut down forever. The terrible "Golden Stairs," where thousands of men had toiled upward with heavy burdens on their backs, became a hikers' trail. A traveler crossing the Chilcoot in the last week of April, 1899, saw only two men coming down and one ascending the Pass. The town of Lindeman, by then, had been deserted and was falling into ruins. Alders and wild gooseberries grew through the floorboards of the dancehalls, and flocks of ptarmigan flew among the crumbling timbers of the overnight hotels. Forest reclaimed the camps along the trails: Sheep Camp, Canyon, White Pass City, Bennett.

Dyea held on for a year or two, literally shrinking day by day as its buildings were dismantled and moved away to be reassembled in Skagway. In ten years the population had dwindled to one—a farmer, peacefully employed amid the foundation stones of a vanished town. Even Skagway, as the stampede ended, went into a long decline. Having counted a population of 10,000 in 1899, it shriveled to 600 by 1910. The railroad guaranteed a trickle of life, not a current of destiny.

Dawson City survived, a frail ghost, at the center of corporate mining in the Yukon Territory. Virtually every rivulet of the Yukon watershed was mined in the four decades between 1926 and 1966 by the dredges of Yukon Consolidated. Then, the last major mining operation closed, and Dawson was left with 750 diehards, living out the bitter winters and the brief, blazing summers in log cabins by the river. It took the rising gold prices of the 1970s to bring back prospectors and miners. With them have come tourists, curious about the isolated land and charmed by images of the last grand adventure.

Images and memories have always been in good supply along the Yukon. The sourdough came early into the pantheon of North American

Tunnels and trestles made it possible for trains to cross the formidable range that had exhausted and destroyed thousands of pack animals, but construction of the 110-mile, narrow-gauge road cost up to $125,000 a mile. The decision to locate the terminus at Skagway (below) assured continued life to that rough and raucous town but condemned its rival, Dyea, to instant death.

Excursionists on the WP&Y in 1900 found the trip scenic, scary, and gratifying, inasmuch as they were not slogging the trail in company with hundreds of dying animals.

227

Urbanization on Dexter Creek (right), 7 miles from Nome, consisted in 1904 of Shel Wettach's grandly named roadhouse, overlooking acres of tundra stripped of turf, vegetation, gravel, gold, and virtually everything else.

Downtown Ketchikan (above), infused with new wealth and promise by the great stampede, had planked roads, electric streetlights, and an atmosphere of sober prosperity in the first decade of this century.

Wrangel, like other established Alaskan towns, profited merely by being in the vicinity of a gold rush. Jack London estimated that the stampeders of '97-'98 spent $75 million getting themselves and their gear to the Klondike. A lot of it rubbed off along the way.

folk heroes, brought to eternal life by the hundreds of young writers who went over the Passes in '98. Jack London's first story about the Rush, "A Klondike Christmas," was published in San Francisco's *Overland Monthly* in January, 1899. Tappan Adney's dispatches to *Harper's Weekly* began appearing when the creeks were still lively with bearded boys from Seattle. A bit later, Robert Service, who had worked in Dawson in the inglorious capacity of a bank clerk, began reconstructing an imaginary boom town of the immediate past, peopled with good-hearted dance hall doxies, sourdoughs, and gambling men, all rendered in Kiplingesque verse that is maddeningly easy to remember—and persistently popular. As for Kipling, himself, he used Alaska as a locale for two short stories and a poem. The

prolific Rex Beach found inspiration even in the sordid dealings of Noyes and McKenzie at Nome: They form the basis of his novel *The Spoilers*.

Back in the States a strong market developed for sourdoughs, or pseudo-sourdoughs, and their recollections. When a gold commotion started in the Tonopah district of southwestern Nevada, "Tex" Rickard, who had run The Northern Saloon and Casino in Nome, reopened that beloved institution in the town of Goldfield. It was like an imprimature of historic authenticity upon the last gold rush of all. Drifters and grifters came in to get out of the desert heat and retail their reminiscences of storms along the Bering Sea.

The true sourdoughs stayed up north, of course, and domesticated, after their fashion. One Henry Davis, a veteran of the early days at Circle and Fortymile, recalled in the 1930s: "Forgot to say that Helen died. Later on I married another native woman who only lived a few years. They were fine pardners, good workers, good fish cutters and I got used to the fish smell and loved them both very much. I busted up when they went to another happy hunting ground."

Falling into a sentimental mood, Davis went on: "There are only a few of the old boys alive. . . . We will all soon make our last trip over the last divide. . . ."

All of them are gone now, growing larger every year.

High on a hill in southeastern Alaska this neatly engineered log cabin is last camp for two prospectors who decided to settle down.

At home in Nome (below), the Frank Waskey family of Flat Creek posed for the town portraitist on an April day in 1906. With a snug cabin of milled boards, a brand-new galvanized washtub, a healthy baby, a painted wooden sleigh, and an extra female (the mother-in-law?) to pitch in doing the dishes, the Waskeys could look forward to a life of abundance, fulfillment, and joy.

232

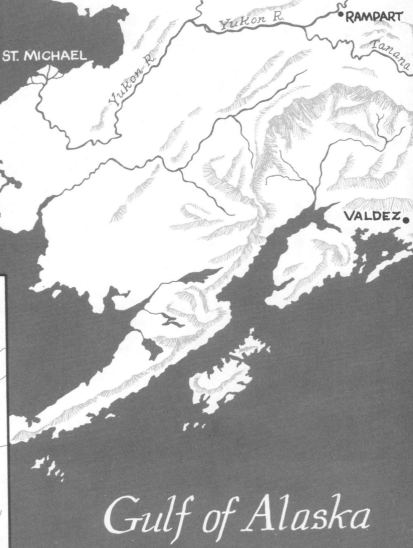

Bering
Sea

NOME

ST. MICHAEL

Ft. YUKON

RAMPART

Yukon R.

Yukon R.

Tanana R.

VALDEZ

Gulf of Alaska

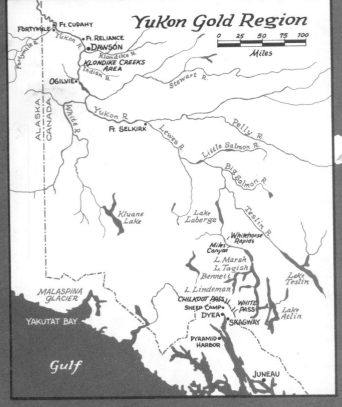

Yukon Gold Region

0 25 50 75 100
Miles

FORTYMILE
Ft. CUDAHY
Ft. RELIANCE
DAWSON
Klondike R.
KLONDIKE CREEKS AREA
Indian R.
Stewart R.
OGILVIE
Fortymile R.
Yukon R.
ALASKA
CANADA
White R.
Yukon R.
Ft. SELKIRK
Lewes R.
Pelly R.
Little Salmon R.
Big Salmon R.
Kluane Lake
Lake Laberge
Teslin R.
Whitehorse Rapids
Miles Canyon
L. Marsh
L. Tagish
Bennett
Lake Teslin
L. Lindeman
MALASPINA GLACIER
CHILKOOT PASS
SHEEP CAMP
DYEA
WHITE PASS
SKAGWAY
Lake Atlin
YAKUTAT BAY
PYRAMID HARBOR
Gulf
JUNEAU